PrimeFaces Cookbook

Over 90 practical recipes to learn PrimeFaces – the rapidly evolving, leading JSF component suite

Mert Çalışkan

Oleg Varaksin

BIRMINGHAM - MUMBAI

PrimeFaces Cookbook

First published: January 2013

Production Reference: 1100113

Published by Packt Publishing Ltd.
Livery Place
35 Livery Street
Birmingham B3 2PB, UK.

ISBN 978-1-84951-928-1

www.packtpub.com

Cover Image by John M. Quick (john.m.quick@gmail.com)

Credits

Authors
Mert Çalışkan
Oleg Varaksin

Reviewers
Andy Bailey
Hebert Coelho de Oliveira

Acquisition Editor
Usha Iyer

Lead Technical Editor
Azharuddin Sheikh

Technical Editors
Prasad Dalvi
Pooja Pande

Copy Editors
Aditya Nair
Alfida Paiva

Project Coordinator
Abhishek Kori

Proofreader
Chris Smith

Indexer
Tejal Soni

Production Coordinator
Manu Joseph

Cover Work
Manu Joseph

About the Authors

Mert Çalışkan is a Principle Software Architect living in Ankara, Turkey. He has over 10 years of expertise in Software Development and he has mainly worked on architectural design of Enterprise Web Applications with specialty in Java. He is also an open source advocate for software projects such as PrimeFaces, and has also been a committer and founder to various others. He shares his knowledge and ideas at local and international conferences such as JSFDays 2008, JDC 2010, CeTURK 2010, and Gelecex 2012. He is also a member of OpenLogic Expert Community and Apache Software Foundation.

I would like to thank my family, my beloved, our advisers at Packt Publishing, Usha Iyer and Abhishek Kori, my good old friend Çağatay Çivici, and our reviewers Andy Bailey and Hebert Coelho de Oliveira. These people accompanied us during the entire writing process and made the book publication possible with their support, suggestions, and reviews.

Oleg Varaksin is a Senior Software Engineer living in the Black Forest, Germany. He is a graduate computer scientist who studied Informatics at Russian and German universities. His main occupation and "daily bread" in the last 6 to 7 years has consisted of building web applications based on Struts, JSP, JSF, Spring, and jQuery—mostly document management systems. He is an experienced JSF expert and has been working with the component library PrimeFaces since its beginning in 2009. He is also a well-known member of the PrimeFaces community and co-creator of the PrimeFaces Extensions project—additional JSF 2 components for PrimeFaces. Besides these mentioned technologies, he has worked as a Frontend Developer with many other web and JS frameworks—GWT, Prototype, YUI Library, and so on—and implemented his own AJAX framework before all the hype about AJAX began.

Oleg normally shares the knowledge he has acquired on his blog `http://ovaraksin.blogspot.com`.

I would like to thank my family, especially my wife Veronika, our advisers from Packt Publishing, Usha Iyer and Abhishek Kori, and our reviewer Andy Bailey and the PrimeFaces project lead Çağatay Çivici. These people accompanied us during the entire writing process and made the book publication possible with their support, suggestions, and reviews.

About the Reviewers

Andy Bailey was born in the United Kingdom in 1964 and after several years' hiatus doing various jobs and conducting various training courses, he finally completed his degree in Computer Science and Artificial Intelligence at the University of Sussex in 1996.

He emigrated from the UK to Germany after completing his degree and has been working on various projects both as a freelancer and a normal employee in a variety of fields. Andy has been involved with Java since 1995 and has worked on desktop, backend, and web applications since then. He has also dabbled in ASP.NET and SharePoint.

He is married, has two children, a cat, a varying population of African Giant Snails, and a Jaguar.

He is currently employed by a world leader in potato harvesting equipment, to develop web applications using the J2EE platform with PrimeFaces as the primary component library and SharePoint-based applications in C#.

This is the first time he has been involved in the publication of a book.

A lot of thanks should go to the PrimeFaces development team for producing what has become a leading component library for JSF-based applications. Far from resting on their laurels, they are very diligent about making the library run stably and are always looking for ways to expand and improve the things that PrimeFaces is capable of doing.

I was very pleased and happy to collaborate on this book, all the more so because the authors and the publisher trusted me on what is my first book as a reviewer.

Last but not least, thanks should go to my wife and kids for giving me the time and the peace to work.

Hebert Coelho de Oliveira has been developing systems for more than 10 years, and is working as Java Senior / Team Leader at Credilink, Rio de Janeiro, Brazil. He has a Postgraduate Degree in Software Engineering from MIT, has completed four Java certifications (SCJP, SCWCD, OCBCD, and OCJPAD), and is studying to get the Web Services certification.

He is the creator of the blog `http://uaihebert.com`, which has been visited by people from more than 155 different countries and has had more than 300,000 page views in two years.

He has worked on mini books such as *JSF Tips* and *JPA for beginners*, posted in the blog.

I would like to thank God for my knowledge and health. To my wife, who has the most beautiful smile on Earth, to my mom and dad for supporting me, and I cannot forget my sister who is always mad at me.

---

www.PacktPub.com

Support files, eBooks, discount offers and more

You might want to visit www.PacktPub.com for support files and downloads related to your book.

Did you know that Packt offers eBook versions of every book published, with PDF and ePub files available? You can upgrade to the eBook version at www.PacktPub.com and as a print book customer, you are entitled to a discount on the eBook copy. Get in touch with us at service@packtpub.com for more details.

At www.PacktPub.com, you can also read a collection of free technical articles, sign up for a range of free newsletters and receive exclusive discounts and offers on Packt books and eBooks.

http://PacktLib.PacktPub.com

Do you need instant solutions to your IT questions? PacktLib is Packt's online digital book library. Here, you can access, read and search across Packt's entire library of books.

Why Subscribe?

- Fully searchable across every book published by Packt
- Copy and paste, print and bookmark content
- On demand and accessible via web browser

Free Access for Packt account holders

If you have an account with Packt at www.PacktPub.com, you can use this to access PacktLib today and view nine entirely free books. Simply use your login credentials for immediate access.

Table of Contents

Preface

PrimeFaces Cookbook is the first PrimeFaces book that provides a head start to its readers by covering all the knowledge needed for working with the PrimeFaces components in the real world. It's a quick, practical guide to learn PrimeFaces—the rapidly evolving, leading JSF component suite. It is written in a clear, comprehensible style and addresses a wide audience interested in modern, trend-setting Java or JEE web development.

What this book covers

Chapter 1, Getting Started with PrimeFaces, provides details on the setup and configuration of PrimeFaces along with the basics of the PrimeFaces AJAX mechanism and the integration with other JSF component libraries. The goal of this chapter is to provide a sneak preview on some of the features of PrimeFaces, such as the AJAX processing mechanism and resource handling with internationalization and localization, along with the necessary steps to go through for implementing a simple web application powered by PrimeFaces, which will give a head start to the user.

Chapter 2, Theming Concept, introduces the PrimeFaces themes and the concepts involved. Readers will learn about the theming of PrimeFaces components. The difference between structural and skinning CSS, installing and customizing of PrimeFaces themes, along with creating new themes, will be detailed. Readers will also see how to adjust font family and font size throughout PrimeFaces components to provide a consistent look and feel. Discussion about two variants of the theme switcher—stateless versus stateful—finish this chapter.

Chapter 3, Enhanced Inputs and Selects, explains how to work with the input and select components available in PrimeFaces. Such components are the main parts of every web application. PrimeFaces provides nearly 25 components for data input, which extend standard corresponding JSF components with skinning capabilities and useful features such as user-friendly interfaces, AJAX interactions, and validation.

Chapter 4, Grouping Content with Panels, covers various container components such as `Panel`, `Accordion`, `ScrollPanel`, and `TabView`, which allow grouping of the JSF components. Various settings to configure panel components are detailed in this chapter.

Chapter 5, Data Iteration Components, covers the basic and advanced features to visualize data with data iteration components provided by PrimeFaces. Such data iteration components are, for instance, `DataTable`, `Tree`, and `TreeTable`. The discussed features include sorting, pagination, filtering, lazy loading, and single and multiple selections.

Chapter 6, Endless Menu Variations, explains about several menu variations. PrimeFaces' menus fulfill all major requirements. They come with various facets—static, dynamic, tiered, iPod-styled, and so on—and leave nothing to be desired. Readers will face a lot of recipes that discuss the menus' structure, configuration options, customizations, and integration with other components. At the end of this chapter, readers will know what kind of menu to choose and how to put it on a page for this or that use case.

Chapter 7, Working with Files and Images, provides ways of managing operations on files such as uploading and downloading, and image operations such as capturing, cropping, and comparing. Readers will learn basic as well as advanced configuration of components and use cases.

Chapter 8, Drag Me, Drop Me, explains how the drag-and-drop utilities in PrimeFaces allow you to create draggable and droppable user interfaces efficiently. They abstract developers from dealing with implementation details on the browser level. In this chapter, readers will learn about PrimeFaces' drag-and-drop utilities—`Draggable` and `Droppable`. AJAX-enhanced drag-and-drop and a special integration with data iteration components will be explained as well.

Chapter 9, Creating Charts and Maps, covers the ways to create visual charts with PrimeFaces' extensive charting features, and create maps based on Google Maps. PrimeFaces offers basic and advanced charting with its easy-to-use and user-friendly charting infrastructure. Throughout the chapter, mapping abilities such as drawing polylines, polygons, handling markers, and events are also covered.

Chapter 10, Miscellaneous, Advanced Use Cases, introduces more interesting features of the PrimeFaces library. You will learn about `RequestContext`—a helpful utility that allows marking components as updatable targets at runtime, adding AJAX callback parameters, and more. In this chapter, a number of real-world samples will also be developed—blocking UI during AJAX calls, periodic polling, focus handling, controlling form submission, and targetable messages, to name a few. Furthermore, after reading this chapter, readers will be aware of pitfalls of menus within layout units and nested panels.

Chapter 11, Writing Custom Components, explains the complete process of building reusable PrimeFaces components. First of all, readers will learn the component's structure and constituent parts. After that, a custom Layout component as an alternative implementation to the PrimeFaces one, will be developed. At the end of this chapter, readers will be equipped with necessary knowledge to be able to create different custom components for the next few JSF or web applications.

You can download this chapter from `http://www.packtpub.com/sites/default/files/downloads/92810S_Chapter_11_Writing_Custom_Components`.

Chapter 12, PrimeFaces Extensions in Action, introduces PrimeFaces Extensions, a community-driven, open source project. The aim of this chapter is the presentation of some additional components, such as `InputNumber`, `CodeMirror`, `DynaForm`, and `Timeline`. This young project can spark interest in developing rich web applications.

You can download this chapter from `http://www.packtpub.com/sites/default/files/downloads/92810S_Chapter_12 PrimeFaces Extensions_in_Action`.

What you need for this book

PrimeFaces only requires Java 5+ runtime. With the help of the Maven tool, you can easily get the artifact for PrimeFaces library (for more information on installing Maven, visit `http://maven.apache.org`). Please note that Maven demands readers Java Development Kit is installed on your local environment instead of the Java Runtime Environment.

To get the Cookbook showcase up and running, you need to pull the source code with a Git client. The details on how to run the showcase web application in your local environment can be found on GitHub (`https://github.com/ova2/primefaces-cookbook`).

Who this book is for

This book is for everybody who would like to learn modern Java web development based on PrimeFaces and is looking for a quick introduction to this matter. Prerequisites for this book are basic JSF, jQuery, and CSS skills.

Conventions

In this book, you will find a number of styles of text that distinguish between different kinds of information. Here are some examples of these styles, and an explanation of their meaning.

Code words in text are shown as follows: "For the first page, we also needed to provide the `contentType` parameter for `f:view`."

A block of code is set as follows:

```
<repository>
  <id>prime-repo</id>
  <name>PrimeFaces Maven Repository</name>
  <url>http://repository.primefaces.org</url>
</repository>
```

When we wish to draw your attention to a particular part of a code block, the relevant lines or items are set in bold:

```
<p:contextMenu for="..." nodeType="...">
    <p:menuitem value="..." update="..."
        icon="..." oncomple="..."/>
</p:contextMenu>
```

Any command-line input or output is written as follows:

```
-rw-r--r--   1 primeuser staff    834 May 21 16:45 log.roo
-rw-r--r--   1 primeuser staff  17650 May 21 16:45 pom.xml
drwxr-xr-x   3 primeuser staff    102 May 21 16:45 src
```

New terms and **important words** are shown in bold. Words that you see on the screen, in menus or dialog boxes for example, appear in the text like this: "The add-on can be opened after its installation by navigating to **Tools** | **Web Developer** | **Firebug**."

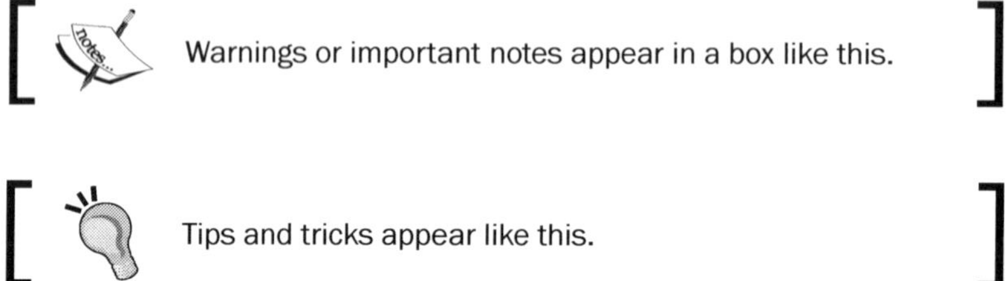

Warnings or important notes appear in a box like this.

Tips and tricks appear like this.

Reader feedback

Feedback from our readers is always welcome. Let us know what you think about this book—what you liked or may have disliked. Reader feedback is important for us to develop titles that you really get the most out of.

To send us general feedback, simply send an e-mail to `feedback@packtpub.com`, and mention the book title via the subject of your message.

If there is a book that you need and would like to see us publish, please send us a note in the **SUGGEST A TITLE** form on `www.packtpub.com` or e-mail `suggest@packtpub.com`.

If there is a topic that you have expertise in and you are interested in either writing or contributing to a book, see our author guide on www.packtpub.com/authors.

Customer support

Now that you are the proud owner of a Packt book, we have a number of things to help you to get the most from your purchase.

Downloading the example code

You can download the example code files for all Packt books you have purchased from your account at http://www.PacktPub.com. If you purchased this book elsewhere, you can visit http://www.PacktPub.com/support and register to have the files e-mailed directly to you.

Errata

Although we have taken every care to ensure the accuracy of our content, mistakes do happen. If you find a mistake in one of our books—maybe a mistake in the text or the code—we would be grateful if you would report this to us. By doing so, you can save other readers from frustration and help us improve subsequent versions of this book. If you find any errata, please report them by visiting http://www.packtpub.com/support, selecting your book, clicking on the **errata submission form** link, and entering the details of your errata. Once your errata are verified, your submission will be accepted and the errata will be uploaded on our website, or added to any list of existing errata, under the Errata section of that title. Any existing errata can be viewed by selecting your title from http://www.packtpub.com/support.

Piracy

Piracy of copyright material on the Internet is an ongoing problem across all media. At Packt, we take the protection of our copyright and licenses very seriously. If you come across any illegal copies of our works, in any form, on the Internet, please provide us with the location address or website name immediately so that we can pursue a remedy.

Please contact us at copyright@packtpub.com with a link to the suspected pirated material.

We appreciate your help in protecting our authors, and our ability to bring you valuable content.

Questions

You can contact us at questions@packtpub.com if you are having a problem with any aspect of the book, and we will do our best to address it.

1

Getting Started with PrimeFaces

In this chapter we will cover:

- Setting up and configuring the PrimeFaces library
- AJAX basics with Process and Update
- Internationalization (i18n) and Localization (L10n)
- Improved resource ordering
- PrimeFaces scaffolding with Spring Roo

Introduction

This chapter will provide details on the setup and configuration of PrimeFaces along with the basics of the PrimeFaces AJAX mechanism. The goal of this chapter is to provide a sneak preview on some of the features of PrimeFaces, such as the AJAX processing mechanism and resource handling with Internationalization and Localization, along with the necessary steps to go through for implementing a simple web application powered by PrimeFaces, which will give a head start to the user.

Setting up and configuring the PrimeFaces library

PrimeFaces is a lightweight JSF component library with one JAR file, which needs no configuration and does not contain any required external dependencies. To start with the development of the library, all we need is to get the artifact for the library.

Getting ready

You can download the PrimeFaces library from `http://primefaces.org/downloads.html`, and you need to add the `primefaces-{version}.jar` file to your classpath. After that, all you need to do is import the namespace of the library, which is necessary to add the PrimeFaces components to your pages, to get started.

If you are using Maven (for more information on installing Maven, please visit `http://maven.apache.org/guides/getting-started/maven-in-five-minutes.html`), you can retrieve the PrimeFaces library by defining the Maven repository in your **Project Object Model** (**POM**) file as follows:

> **Downloading the example code**
>
> You can download the example code files for all Packt books you have purchased from your account at `http://www.PacktPub.com`. If you purchased this book elsewhere, you can visit `http://www.PacktPub.com/support` and register to have the files e-mailed directly to you.

```
<repository>
  <id>prime-repo</id>
  <name>PrimeFaces Maven Repository</name>
  <url>http://repository.primefaces.org</url>
</repository>
```

Add the dependency configuration as follows:

```
<dependency>
  <groupId>org.primefaces</groupId>
  <artifactId>primefaces</artifactId>
  <version>3.4</version>
</dependency>
```

At the time of writing this book, the latest and most stable version of PrimeFaces was 3.4. To check out whether this is the latest available or not, please visit `http://primefaces.org/downloads.html`. The code in this book will work properly with PrimeFaces 3.4. In prior versions or the future versions, some methods, attributes, or components' behaviors may change.

How to do it...

In order to use PrimeFaces components, we need to add the namespace declarations into our pages. The namespace for PrimeFaces components is as follows:

```
xmlns:p="http://primefaces.org/ui"
```

For PrimeFaces Mobile, the namespace is as follows:

```
xmlns:p="http://primefaces.org/mobile"
```

That is all there is to it. Note that the `p` prefix is just a symbolic link and any other character can be used to define the PrimeFaces components. Now you can create your first page with a PrimeFaces component as shown in the following code snippet:

```
<html xmlns="http://www.w3.org/1999/xhtml"
      xmlns:h="http://java.sun.com/jsf/html"
      xmlns:f="http://java.sun.com/jsf/core"
      xmlns:p="http://primefaces.org/ui">
    <f:view contentType="text/html">
        <h:head />
        <h:body>
            <h:form>
                <p:spinner />
            </h:form>
        </h:body>
    </f:view>
</html>
```

This will render a spinner component with an empty value as shown in the following screenshot:

A link to the working example for the given page is given at the end of this recipe.

How it works...

When the page is requested, the `p:spinner` component is rendered with the renderer implemented by the PrimeFaces library. Since the spinner component is a UI input component, the request-processing lifecycle will get executed when the user inputs data and performs a post back on the page.

For the first page, we also needed to provide the `contentType` parameter for `f:view`, since the WebKit-based browsers, such as Google Chrome and Apple Safari, request the content type `application/xhtml+xml` by default. This would overcome unexpected layout and styling issues that might occur.

There's more...

PrimeFaces only requires Java 5+ runtime and a JSF 2.x implementation as mandatory dependencies. There are some optional libraries for certain features.

Dependency	Version	Type	Description
JSF runtime	2.0 or 2.1	Required	Apache MyFaces or Oracle Mojarra
iText	2.1.7	Optional	`DataExporter` (PDF)
Apache POI	3.7	Optional	`DataExporter` (Excel)
Rome	1.0	Optional	`FeedReader`
commons-fileupload	1.2.1	Optional	`FileUpload`
commons-io	1.4	Optional	`FileUpload`

Please ensure that you have only one JAR file of PrimeFaces or specific PrimeFaces Theme in your classpath in order to avoid any issues regarding resource rendering.

Currently PrimeFaces supports the web browsers IE 7, 8, or 9, Safari, Firefox, Chrome, and Opera.

PrimeFaces Cookbook Showcase application

This recipe is available in the PrimeFaces Cookbook Showcase application on GitHub at `https://github.com/ova2/primefaces-cookbook`. You can find the details there for running the project. When the server is running, the showcase for the recipe is available at `http://localhost:8080/primefaces-cookbook/views/chapter1/yourFirstPage.jsf`.

AJAX basics with Process and Update

PrimeFaces provides a **partial page rendering** (**PPR**) and view-processing feature based on standard JSF 2 APIs to enable choosing what to process in the JSF lifecycle and what to render in the end with AJAX. PrimeFaces AJAX Framework is based on standard server-side APIs of JSF 2. On the client side, rather than using the client-side API implementations of JSF implementations, such as Mojarra and MyFaces, PrimeFaces scripts are based on the jQuery JavaScript library.

How to do it...

We can create a simple page with a command button to update a string property with the current time in milliseconds on the server side and an output text to show the value of that string property, as follows:

```
<p:commandButton update="display" action="#{basicPPRController.
updateValue}" value="Update" />
<h:outputText id="display" value="#{basicPPRController.value}"/>
```

If we would like to update multiple components with the same trigger mechanism, we can provide the IDs of the components to the `update` attribute by providing them a space, comma, or both, as follows:

```
<p:commandButton update="display1,display2" />
<p:commandButton update="display1 display2" />
<p:commandButton update="display1,display2 display3" />
```

In addition, there are reserved keywords that are used for a partial update. We can also make use of these keywords along with the IDs of the components, as described in the following table:

Keyword	Description
`@this`	The component that triggers the PPR is updated
`@parent`	The parent of the PPR trigger is updated
`@form`	The encapsulating form of the PPR trigger is updated
`@none`	PPR does not change the DOM with AJAX response
`@all`	The whole document is updated as in non-AJAX requests

We can also update a component that resides in a different naming container from the component that triggers the update. In order to achieve this, we need to specify the absolute component identifier of the component that needs to be updated. An example for this could be the following:

```
<h:form id="form1">
  <p:commandButton update=":form2:display"
action="#{basicPPRController.updateValue}" value="Update" />
</h:form>

<h:form id="form2">
  <h:outputText id="display" value="#{basicPPRController.value}"/>
</h:form>

public String updateValue() {
  value = String.valueOf(System.currentTimeMillis());
  return null;
}
```

PrimeFaces also provides partial processing, which executes the JSF lifecycle phases—Apply Request Values, Process Validations, Update Model, and Invoke Application—for determined components with the `process` attribute. This provides the ability to do group validation on the JSF pages easily. Mostly group-validation needs arise in situations where different values need to be validated in the same form, depending on an action that gets executed. By grouping components for validation, errors that would arise from other components when the page has been submitted can be overcome easily. Components like `commandButton`, `commandLink`, `autoComplete`, `fileUpload`, and many others provide this attribute to process partially instead of the whole view.

Partial processing could become very handy in cases when a drop-down list needs to be populated upon a selection on another drop down and when there is an input field on the page with the `required` attribute set to `true`. This approach also makes immediate subforms and regions obsolete. It will also prevent submission of the whole page, thus this will result in lightweight requests. Without partially processing the view for the drop downs, a selection on one of the drop downs will result in a validation error on the required field. An example for this is shown in the following code snippet:

```
<h:outputText value="Country: " />
<h:selectOneMenu id="countries" value="#{partialProcessingController.
country}">
<f:selectItems value="#{partialProcessingController.countries}" />
  <p:ajax listener=
  "#{partialProcessingController.handleCountryChange}"
    event="change" update="cities" process="@this"/>
</h:selectOneMenu>
```

```
<h:outputText value="City: " />
<h:selectOneMenu id="cities" value="#{partialProcessingController.
city}">
  <f:selectItems value="#{partialProcessingController.cities}" />
</h:selectOneMenu>

<h:outputText value="Email: " />
<h:inputText value="#{partialProcessingController.email}"
required="true" />
```

With this partial processing mechanism, when a user changes the country, the cities of that country will be populated in the drop down regardless of whether any input exists for the `email` field.

How it works...

As seen in partial processing example for updating a component in a different naming container, <p:commandButton> is updating the <h:outputText> component that has the ID `display`, and absolute client ID `:form2:display`, which is the search expression for the `findComponent` method. An absolute client ID starts with the separator character of the naming container, which is `:` by default.

The <h:form>, <h:dataTable>, composite JSF components along with <p:tabView>, <p:accordionPanel>, <p:dataTable>, <p:dataGrid>, <p:dataList>, <p:carousel>, <p:galleria>, <p:ring>, <p:sheet>, and <p:subTable> are the components that implement the `NamingContainer` interface. The `findComponent` method, which is described at `http://docs.oracle.com/javaee/6/api/javax/faces/component/UIComponent.html`, is used by both JSF core implementation and PrimeFaces

There's more...

JSF uses `:` (a colon) as the separator for the `NamingContainer` interface. The client IDs that will be rendered in the source page will be like `:id1:id2:id3`. If needed, the configuration of the separator can be changed for the web application to something other than the colon with a `context` parameter in the `web.xml` file of the web application, as follows:

```
<context-param>
  <param-name>javax.faces.SEPARATOR_CHAR</param-name>
  <param-value>_</param-value>
</context-param>
```

It's also possible to escape the `:` character, if needed, in the CSS files with the \ character, as `\:`. The problem that might occur with the colon is that it's a reserved keyword for the CSS and JavaScript frameworks, like jQuery, so it might need to be escaped.

PrimeFaces Cookbook Showcase application

This recipe is available in the PrimeFaces Cookbook Showcase application on GitHub at `https://github.com/ova2/primefaces-cookbook`. You can find the details there for running the project. For the demos of the showcase, refer to the following:

- *Basic Partial Page Rendering* is available at `http://localhost:8080/primefaces-cookbook/views/chapter1/basicPPR.jsf`
- *Updating Component in Different Naming Container* is available at `http://localhost:8080/primefaces-cookbook/views/chapter1/componentInDifferentNamingContainer.jsf`
- A Partial Processing example at `http://localhost:8080/primefaces-cookbook/views/chapter1/partialProcessing.jsf`

Internationalization (i18n) and Localization (L10n)

Internationalization (i18n) and Localization (L10n) are two important features that should be provided in the web application's world to make it accessible globally.

With Internationalization, we are emphasizing that the web application should support multiple languages; and with Localization, we are stating that the texts, dates, or any other fields should be presented in the form specific to a region.

PrimeFaces only provides the English translations. Translations for the other languages should be provided explicitly. In the following sections, you will find the details on how to achieve this.

Getting ready

For Internationalization, first we need to specify the resource bundle definition under the `application` tag in `faces-config.xml`, as follows:

```
<application>
    <locale-config>
        <default-locale>en</default-locale>
        <supported-locale>tr_TR</supported-locale>
    </locale-config>
    <resource-bundle>
        <base-name>messages</base-name>
        <var>msg</var>
    </resource-bundle>
</application>
```

A resource bundle would be a text file with the `.properties` suffix that would contain the locale-specific messages. So, the preceding definition states that the resource bundle `messages_{localekey}.properties` file will reside under classpath and the default value of `localekey` is `en`, which is English, and the supported locale is `tr_TR`, which is Turkish. For projects structured by Maven, the `messages_{localekey}.properties` file can be created under the `src/main/resources` project path.

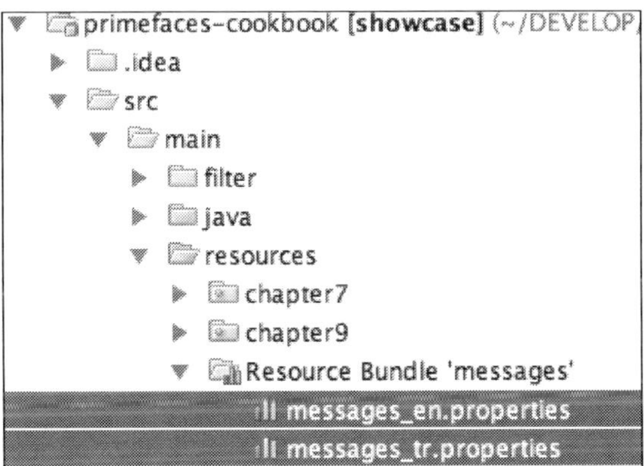

How to do it...

For showcasing Internationalization, we will broadcast an information message via FacesMessage mechanism that will be displayed in the PrimeFaces growl component. We need two components, the growl itself and a command button, to broadcast the message.

```
<p:growl id="growl" />
<p:commandButton action="#{localizationController.addMessage}"
value="Display Message" update="growl" />
```

The `addMessage` method of `localizationController` is as follows:

```
public String addMessage() {
    addInfoMessage("broadcast.message");
    return null;
}
```

That uses the `addInfoMessage` method, which is defined in the static `MessageUtil` class as follows:

```
public static void addInfoMessage(String str) {
FacesContext context = FacesContext.getCurrentInstance();
    ResourceBundle bundle = context.getApplication().
getResourceBundle(context, "msg");
    String message = bundle.getString(str);
```

```
        FacesContext.getCurrentInstance().addMessage(null, new
    FacesMessage(FacesMessage.SEVERITY_INFO, message, ""));
    }
```

Localization of components, such as `calendar` and `schedule`, can be achieved by providing the `locale` attribute. By default, locale information is retrieved from the view's locale and it can be overridden by a string locale key or the `java.util.Locale` instance.

Components such as `calendar` and `schedule` use a shared `PrimeFaces.locales` property to display labels. PrimeFaces only provides English translations, so in order to localize the calendar we need to put corresponding locales into a JavaScript file and include the scripting file to the page.

The content for the German locale of the `Primefaces.locales` property for calendar would be as shown in the following code snippet. For the sake of the recipe, only the German locale definition is given and the Turkish locale definition is omitted.

```
PrimeFaces.locales['de'] = {
    closeText: 'Schließen',
    prevText: 'Zurück',
    nextText: 'Weiter',
    monthNames: ['Januar', 'Februar', 'März', 'April', 'Mai',
    'Juni', 'Juli', 'August', 'September', 'Oktober', 'November',
    'Dezember'],
    monthNamesShort: ['Jan', 'Feb', 'Mär', 'Apr', 'Mai', 'Jun',
    'Jul', 'Aug', 'Sep', 'Okt', 'Nov', 'Dez'],
    dayNames: ['Sonntag', 'Montag', 'Dienstag', 'Mittwoch',
    'Donnerstag', 'Freitag', 'Samstag'],
    dayNamesShort: ['Son', 'Mon', 'Die', 'Mit', 'Don', 'Fre',
    'Sam'],
    dayNamesMin: ['S', 'M', 'D', 'M ', 'D', 'F ', 'S'],
    weekHeader: 'Woche',
    FirstDay: 1,
    isRTL: false,
    showMonthAfterYear: false,
    yearSuffix: '',
    timeOnlyTitle: 'Nur Zeit',
    timeText: 'Zeit',
    hourText: 'Stunde',
    minuteText: 'Minute',
    secondText: 'Sekunde',
    currentText: 'Aktuelles Datum',
```

```
        ampm: false,
        month: 'Monat',
        week: 'Woche',
        day: 'Tag',
        allDayText: 'Ganzer Tag'
    };
```

Definition of the calendar components with the `locale` attribute would be as follows:

```
<p:calendar showButtonPanel="true" navigator="true" mode="inline"
id="enCal"/>

<p:calendar locale="tr" showButtonPanel="true" navigator="true"
mode="inline" id="trCal"/>

<p:calendar locale="de" showButtonPanel="true" navigator="true"
mode="inline" id="deCal"/>
```

They will be rendered as follows:

How it works...

For Internationalization of the Faces message, the `addInfoMessage` method retrieves the message bundle via the defined variable `msg`. It then gets the string from the bundle with the given key by invoking the `bundle.getString(str)` method. Finally, the message is added by creating a new Faces message with severity level `FacesMessage.SEVERITY_INFO`.

There's more...

For some components, Localization could be accomplished by providing labels to the components via attributes, such as with `p:selectBooleanButton`.

```
<p:selectBooleanButton
      value="#{localizationController.selectedValue}"
      onLabel="#{msg['booleanButton.onLabel']}"
      offLabel="#{msg['booleanButton.offLabel']}" />
```

The `msg` variable is the resource bundle variable that is defined in the resource bundle definition in Faces configuration file. The English version of the bundle key definitions in the `messages_en.properties` file that resides under classpath would be as follows:

```
booleanButton.onLabel=Yes
booleanButton.offLabel=No
```

PrimeFaces Cookbook Showcase application

This recipe is available in the PrimeFaces Cookbook Showcase application on GitHub at `https://github.com/ova2/primefaces-cookbook`. You can find the details there for running the project. For the demos of the showcase, refer to the following:

- Internationalization is available at `http://localhost:8080/primefaces-cookbook/views/chapter1/internationalization.jsf`
- Localization of the calendar component is available at `http://localhost:8080/primefaces-cookbook/views/chapter1/localization.jsf`
- Localization with resources is available at `http://localhost:8080/primefaces-cookbook/views/chapter1/localizationWithResources.jsf`

For already translated locales of the calendar, see `http://code.google.com/p/primefaces/wiki/PrimeFacesLocales`.

Improved resource ordering

PrimeFaces 3.x provides improved resource ordering to support customization. This ability could be used when Internet Explorer demands special meta tags that are expected to be placed at first or for scenarios where styling for PrimeFaces components needs to be overridden by custom styling.

Getting ready

Make sure you have at least the 3.x version of PrimeFaces in your classpath.

How to do it...

Just define `<h:head>` by using facet definitions where necessary.

```
<h:head title="PrimeFaces Cookbook - ShowCase">
<f:facet name="first">
</f:facet>
...
<f:facet name="middle">
</f:facet>
...
<f:facet name="last">
</f:facet>
...
</h:head>
```

The `<h:head>` tag is used by the JSF components for adding their resources into pages, thus it's a must-have tag throughout your JSF-based applications. One of the commonly made mistakes among developers is to forget putting in the `head` tag.

For instance, if a stylesheet gets declared in multiple CSS files, which would be linked in the middle and last facet respectively, the stylesheet definition referred to in the `middle` facet will be overridden by the one defined in the `last` facet.

How it works...

With PrimeFaces' own `HeadRenderer` implementation, the resources are handled in the following order:

1. First facet, if defined
2. PF-JSF registered CSS
3. Theme CSS
4. Middle facet, if defined
5. PF-JSF registered JS
6. Head content
7. Last facet, if defined

There's more...

Internet Explorer introduced a special tag named `meta`, which can be used as `<meta http-equiv="X-UA-Compatible" content="..." />`. The content of the X-UA-Compatible `<meta>` tag helps to control document compatibility such as specifying the rendering engine. For example, inserting the following statement into the head of a document would force IE 8 to render the page using the new standards mode:

```
<meta http-equiv="X-UA-Compatible" content="IE=8" />
```

X-UA-Compatible must be the first child of the `head` component. Internet Explorer won't accept this `<meta>` tag if it's placed after the `<link>` or `<script>` tag. Therefore, it needs to be placed within the `first` facet. This is a good demonstration of the resource ordering with the usage of the `first` facet.

PrimeFaces Cookbook Showcase application

This recipe is available in the PrimeFaces Cookbook Showcase application on GitHub at `https://github.com/ova2/primefaces-cookbook`. You can find the details there for running the project. When the server is running, the showcase for the improved resource ordering is available at `http://localhost:8080/primefaces-cookbook/views/chapter1/resourceOrdering.jsf`.

PrimeFaces scaffolding with Spring Roo

Spring Roo is a next-generation rapid application development tool that uses *Convention over Configuration* principles. It is a text-based open source tool that can be used for creating and managing Spring-based applications. It uses mature libraries such as Spring framework, Java Persistence API, Java Server Pages (JSP), Spring Security, Spring Web Flow, Log4J, and Maven. Spring Roo also provides scaffolding for web-based applications that are powered by PrimeFaces.

Getting ready

At the time of writing this book, the latest version of Spring Roo was version 1.2.2. It can be downloaded at `http://www.springsource.com/download/community?project=Spring%20Roo`. More information on Spring Roo, along with the list of commands, can be found at `http://www.springsource.org/spring-roo`.

Also, Maven—the Apache build manager for Java projects—needs to be installed as a prerequisite. At the time of writing this book, Maven v3.0.4 was used. For more information on this, please visit `http://maven.apache.org/guides/getting-started/maven-in-five-minutes.html`.

How to do it...

For PrimeFaces scaffolding with Spring Roo, follow these steps:

1. We will create the folder where the project will reside and then change directory to it.

   ```
   mkdir primefaces-cookbook-roo
   cd primefaces-cookbook-roo
   ```

2. Now we can execute the `roo` command within the folder. Linux, Unix, or Mac OS users should execute `roo.sh`, and Windows users should execute the `roo.bat` file. Then, we should see the console output as shown in the following screenshot:

```
Merts-MacBook-Pro-2:bin mertcaliskan$ ./roo.sh

                                 1.2.2.RELEASE [rev 7d75659]

Welcome to Spring Roo. For assistance press TAB or type "hint" then hit ENTER.
roo>
```

3. Then, in the command line, we can create the sample `roo` project by specifying its name and its packaging structure as follows:

   ```
   roo> project --projectName primefaces-cookbook-roo
   --topLevelPackage org.primefaces.cookbook
   ```

4. After that, we can add a persistency layer to the project structure as follows:

   ```
   roo> persistence setup --provider HIBERNATE
   --database HYPERSONIC_IN_MEMORY
   ```

   With the `persistence` command, we are specifying the provider as `HIBERNATE` and stating that an in-memory database will be used for testing purposes.

5. Create `enum` for the type of manufacturer of the car.

   ```
   roo> enum type --class ~.domain.Manufacturer
   roo> enum constant --name Volkswagen
   roo> enum constant --name Mercedes
   roo> enum constant --name BMW
   roo> enum constant --name Audi
   ```

6. Then we can create the class for the car.

```
roo> entity jpa --class ~.domain.Car
```

```
roo> field number --fieldName yearOfManufacture --type java.lang.
Integer --notNull
```

```
roo> field string --fieldName name --notNull
```

```
roo> field enum --fieldName manufacturer --type ~.domain.
Manufacturer --notNull
```

7. After that, we can create the project and package it as a `.war` file:

```
roo> web jsf setup --implementation APACHE_MYFACES --library
PRIMEFACES --theme EGGPLANT
```

```
roo> web jsf all --package org.primefaces.cookbook
```

8. Then, finally exit Spring Roo console with:

```
roo> quit
```

When we list the directory for the files, we have two files and a source directory created as follows in the Linux, Unix, or Mac OS environment:

```
-rw-r--r--   1 primeuser staff    834 May 21 16:45 log.roo
-rw-r--r--   1 primeuser staff  17650 May 21 16:45 pom.xml
drwxr-xr-x   3 primeuser staff    102 May 21 16:45 src
```

Now our project is ready to run. From the command line, we can execute `jetty` to get the web application context up and running.

```
mvn jetty:run
```

Now we can request for the URL on local via browser (`http://localhost:8080/primefaces-cookbook-roo`), which will bring up the scaffold user interface of the web application, as shown in the following screenshot:

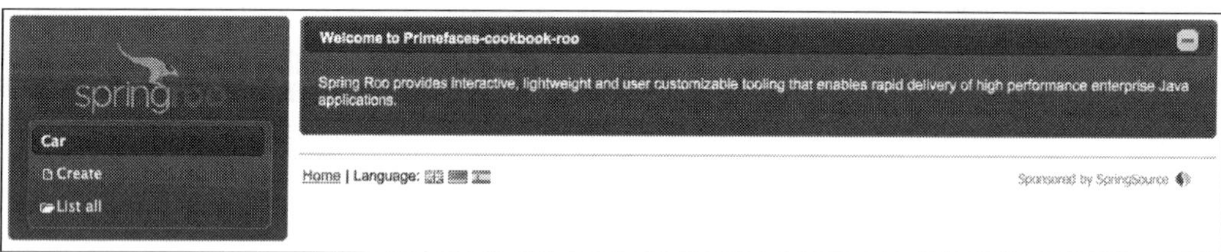

How it works...

With the commands provided, Spring Roo does all the scaffolding to create a web application powered by PrimeFaces. In the end, it will create the `Car` and `Manufacturer` domain classes, the converter for the `Car` class, and the web pages for providing the CRUD operations on the `Car` class.

2
Theming Concept

In this chapter we will cover:

- Understanding structural and skinning CSS
- Installing themes
- Customizing theme styles
- Customizing default styles on input components
- Adjusting the font and size throughout the web application
- Why does the theme look different in Internet Explorer?
- Simple ways to create a new theme
- Default stateless theme switcher
- Alternative stateful theme switchers

Introduction

In this chapter, readers will be introduced to PrimeFaces themes and the concepts involved. Later on, we will build on these concepts to learn the theming of the PrimeFaces components. The theming concept used in PrimeFaces is similar to the jQuery ThemeRoller CSS Framework (`http://jqueryui.com/themeroller`). All PrimeFaces components are designed to allow a developer to integrate them seamlessly into the look and feel of an entire web application. At the time of writing, there are 35 plus ready-to-use themes, which you can preview and download from the PrimeFaces theme gallery (`http://primefaces.org/themes.html`).

Powered by ThemeRoller, PrimeFaces separates structural CSS from skinning CSS. The difference between the two CSS concepts is the topic of the first recipe. Installation and customization of PrimeFaces themes along with creation of new themes will be detailed. We will also see how to adjust the font family and font size throughout the PrimeFaces components .Adapted font settings provide a consistent look and feel in a multi-themable web application. Discussion about two variants of theme switcher—stateless versus stateful —will finish this chapter.

Understanding the structural and skinning CSS

Each component is styled with CSS and contains two layers of style information—structural or component-specific and skinning or component-independent styles.

In this recipe, you will understand the difference between these two types of CSS, learn some useful selectors, and see an exemplary styling of the `PickList` component in the generated HTML.

Getting ready

To learn about different layers of style information, you can go to the PrimeFaces ShowCase (`http://primefaces.org/showcase/ui/home.jsf`) and look at it in the Firefox browser with an installed Firebug add-on (`http://getfirebug.com`). Firebug allows live editing, debugging, and monitoring CSS, HTML, and JavaScript in any web page. The add-on can be opened after its installation by navigating to **Tools** | **Web Developer** | **Firebug** or by pressing the *F12* key. Another useful tool is built-in Developer Tools for the Google Chrome browser, which is similar to the Firebug.

How to do it...

Go to the PrimeFaces ShowCase and choose the menu item **PickList** from the sidebar. Open the Firebug now. It has a toolbar with tabs and a small icon having the tooltip **Click an element in the page to inspect**. Select the **HTML** tab and then click on that small icon. After that, click on the left (source) area in the displayed **Basic PickList** box. You will see the **HTML** code that belongs to the selected area.

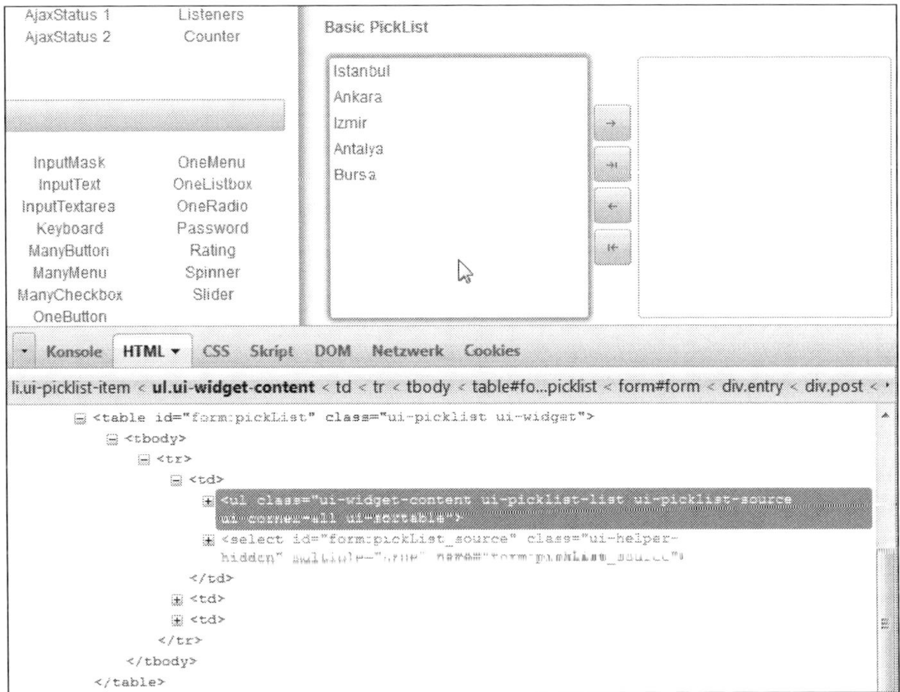

This is exactly the highlighted line in the preceding screenshot. The source area of `PickList` is presented as an HTML `ul` element with style classes:

- `ui-picklist-list`
- `ui-picklist-source`
- `ui-widget-content`
- `ui-corner-all`
- `ui-sortable`

Firebug also shows the corresponding styling with CSS next to the generated HTML code. For **Aristo** theme, it looks like as follows:

```
.ui-picklist .ui-picklist-list {
    height: 200px;
    list-style-type: none;
    margin: 0;
    overflow: auto;
    padding: 0;
    width: 200px;
}
```

```
.ui-widget-content {
    background: none repeat scroll 0 0 #FFFFFF;
    border: 1px solid #A8A8A8;
    color: #4F4F4F;
}

.ui-corner-all {
    border-radius: 3px 3px 3px 3px;
}
```

How it works...

The first two style classes `ui-picklist-list` and `ui-picklist-source` are generated by PrimeFaces and provide a semantic presentation to indicate the role of an element within a component. In this case, it is a list of the `PickList` items in the source area. Other roles could be **table header**, **layout pane**, or **button text**. These are structural style classes. In general, structural style classes define the skeleton of the components and include CSS properties such as margin, padding, display type, overflow behavior, dimensions, and positioning.

As already said, PrimeFaces leverages the jQuery ThemeRoller CSS Framework. The `ui-widget-content` and `ui-corner-all` classes in the preceding listing are defined by ThemeRoller and they affect the look and feel. These are skinning style classes, which define CSS properties such as text colors, border colors, and background images. The most important selectors are listed in the following table:

Selector	Applies
`.ui-widget`	Class applied to all PrimeFaces components. It applies, for example, font family and font size to any component.
`.ui-widget-header`	Class applied to the header section(s) of a component.
`.ui-widget-content`	Class applied to the content section(s) of a component.
`.ui-state-default`	Default class applied to clickable, button-like components or their elements.
`.ui-state-hover`	Class applied on mouseover to clickable, button-like components or their elements.
`.ui-state-active`	Class applied on mousedown to clickable, button-like components or their elements.
`.ui-state-disabled`	Class applied to components or their elements when they are disabled.
`.ui-state-highlight`	Class applied to components or their elements when they are highlighted or selected.
`.ui-state-error`	Class applied to error messaging container elements.

Selector	Applies
`.ui-icon`	Class applied to elements representing an icon. It sets dimensions, hides inner text, background image.
`.ui-corner-all`	Class applies corner-radius to all four corners of a component.
`.ui-corner-top`	Class applies corner-radius to both top corners of a component.
`.ui-corner-bottom`	Class applies corner-radius to both bottom corners of a component.

These styles are applied consistently across all PrimeFaces components, so a clickable button and accordion tab have the same `ui-state-default` class applied to indicate that they are clickable. When a user moves the mouse over one of these elements, this class gets changed to `ui-state-hover`, and then to `ui-state-active` when these elements are selected. This approach makes it easy to ensure that all elements with a similar interaction state will look identical across all components.

The main advantage of the presented PrimeFaces selectors is a great flexibility in theming, because you don't need to know each and every skinning selector to change the styles of all available components in your web application consistently.

There's more...

Some style classes are not generated by PrimeFaces explicitly and not defined by the ThemeRoller. There is, for instance, the structural class `ui-sortable` (listed in the *How to do it...* section of this recipe). This class defines a sortable behavior and tells us that `PickList` items can be sorted by a drag-and-drop action. PrimeFaces library utilizes the jQuery Sortable plugin (`http://jqueryui.com/demos/sortable`) for the underlying JavaScript widget used in `PickList` to enable a group of DOM elements to be sortable. The plugin adds the structural style class `ui-sortable` automatically, on the fly, while the component gets rendered.

It is also important to say that the prefix of both types of style classes is `ui`. Most jQuery-based plugins typically have this prefix too. This fact might lead to a CSS collision when you use a jQuery plugin, which overrides PrimeFaces styles. An example is the jQuery UI (native) and PrimeFaces dialogs. Both use the style class `ui-dialog`. Manage this case properly with a CSS selector weight– applied rules when multiple selectors affect the same element (`http://w3.org/TR/CSS21/cascade.html#specificity`)—to avoid CSS collisions.

More information on the ThemeRoller selectors can be found in the description of the framework classes at `http://jqueryui.com/docs/Theming/API`

Almost every component description in the PrimeFaces User's Guide (`http://primefaces.org/documentation.html`) contains a "Skinning" section with the component's structural style classes.

Installing themes

PrimeFaces themes are bundled as JAR files and available for download at the PrimeFaces repository (`http://repository.primefaces.org/org/primefaces/themes`). Each theme can be quickly previewed before download at PrimeFaces Theme Gallery (`http://primefaces.org/themes.html`) or tested in the PrimeFaces ShowCase with an integrated theme switcher.

In this recipe, we will install and configure themes to use them in an JSF application. The steps to accomplish this task are straightforward.

Getting ready

If you are a Maven (`http://maven.apache.org`) user, ensure that you have Maven installed. Maven is a build and project management tool, which manages installation of all dependencies in an easy way. PrimeFaces is a Maven-based project and offers all artifacts, including themes, as Maven dependencies.

How to do it...

Maven users should define any desired theme artifact in their project's `pom.xml` as follows:

```
<dependency>
  <groupId>org.primefaces.themes</groupId>
  <artifactId>cupertino</artifactId>
  <version>1.0.9</version>
</dependency>
```

`artifactId` is the name of the theme as defined at the Theme Gallery page. Also, make sure that you have the `PrimeFaces` repository in your `pom.xml`.

```
<repository>
  <id>prime-repo</id>
  <name>PrimeFaces Maven Repository</name>
  <url>http://repository.primefaces.org</url>
  <layout>default</layout>
</repository>
```

Non-Maven users should download the theme manually from the `PrimeFaces` repository and place it in the classpath of your application. You can repeat this step for all the themes you need.

Once you have included one or multiple themes, configure PrimeFaces to use them. Set the `primefaces.THEME` context parameter in `web.xml` (deployment descriptor) with its value as the name of the theme that you would like to use as default. Assuming you would like to use **Home** theme, then, the configuration is:

```
<context-param>
    <param-name>primefaces.THEME</param-name>
    <param-value>home</param-value>
</context-param>
```

That's all. You don't need to manually include any CSS files on your pages or anything else; PrimeFaces will handle everything for you. In case you would like to make the theme dynamic, define an EL expression as the `param` value. Assume you have a managed bean `UserSettings` keeping the current theme name in a `theme` variable. A proper configuration is as follows:

```
<context-param>
  <param-name>primefaces.THEME</param-name>
  <param-value>#{userSettings.theme}</param-value>
</context-param>
```

This is a case when you have installed multiple themes and let users switch them as per a theme switcher.

How it works...

The PrimeFaces component library has a special implementation for the JSF standard `Head` component. PrimeFaces provides the `HeadRenderer` class, which is responsible for the rendering of the `<h:head>` tag. `HeadRenderer` automatically detects the current configured theme in `web.xml`—regardless if static or dynamic via managed bean—and renders theme-related resources on the page. After that the page contains a link to `theme.css`:

```
<link type="text/css" rel="stylesheet" href="/showcase/javax.faces.
resource/theme.css.jsf?ln=primefaces-home" />
```

There's more...

Aristo is the built-in default theme of PrimeFaces. There is no separate JAR file for it; the theme is delivered with the core PrimeFaces JAR file itself. Therefore, you don't need to install it via Maven or have it extra in the classpath.

If you are using Apache Trinidad (`http://myfaces.apache.org/trinidad`) or JBoss RichFaces (`http://jboss.org/richfaces`), PrimeFaces Theme Gallery includes Trinidad's **Casablanca** and RichFaces's **BlueSky** themes. You can use them to make the PrimeFaces components look like Trinidad or RichFaces ones during migration.

See also

- You also may want to check the *Themes* section in *PrimeFaces User's Guide* (`http://primefaces.org/documentation.html`)
- See the use of dynamic themes in the *Alternative stateful theme switchers* recipe

Customizing theme styles

How to customize theme styles is one of the most asked questions by the PrimeFaces users. There are simple rules to be followed to overwrite bundled theme styles with custom CSS. There is no need to edit bundled themes and repackage theme JAR files.

In this recipe, we will present two examples for theme customization—one for `SelectOneMenu` and another for the `Tree` component. We will see how to change styles for a particular component or for all components of the same type. Furthermore, we will learn tips for where to place custom CSS in order to overwrite the PrimeFaces styles.

How to do it...

Let's set a fixed width for `p:selectOneMenu` and remove the background and border for `p:tree`. The default width of `p:selectOneMenu` is calculated at runtime. That means, the width of `p:selectOneMenu` is dynamic and depends on its content (select items). Large select items cause large `p:selectOneMenu`. A fixed width would show a better (from visual point of view) `p:selectOneMenu` for items with short text. `p:tree` without background and border could better fit a custom design in certain circumstances. This is demonstrated in the following screenshot:

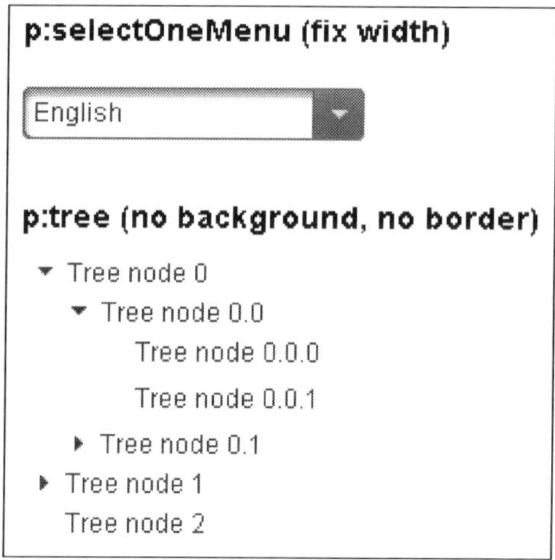

The corresponding XHTML part looks as follows:

```
<h:panelGrid id="customStyles">
    <h3 style="margin-top:0;">p:selectOneMenu (fix width)</h3>

    <p:selectOneMenu value="dummy">
        <f:selectItem itemLabel="English" itemValue="en"/>
        <f:selectItem itemLabel="German" itemValue="de"/>
        <f:selectItem itemLabel="Russian" itemValue="ru"/>
    </p:selectOneMenu>

    <h3 style="margin:20px 0 0 0;">
        p:tree (no background, no border)
    </h3>

    <p:tree value="#{treeController.root}" var="node">
        <p:treeNode>
            <h:outputText value="#{node}"/>
        </p:treeNode>
    </p:tree>
</h:panelGrid>
```

The tree is created in a bean `TreeController`.

```
@ManagedBean
@ViewScoped
public class TreeController implements Serializable {

    private TreeNode root;

    public TreeController() {
        root = new DefaultTreeNode("Root", null);

        TreeNode node0 = new DefaultTreeNode("Tree node 0", root);
        node0.setExpanded(true);

        TreeNode node1 = new DefaultTreeNode("Tree node 1", root);
        new DefaultTreeNode("Tree node 2", root);

        ...
    }

    public TreeNode getRoot() {
        return root;
    }
}
```

The most interesting part is CSS. Our aim is to customize styles for only two particular components, which are placed below a `PanelGrid` (`h:panelGrid`) with ID `customStyles`. Use namespacing to do this. Simply prepend the ID `#customStyles` to the PrimeFaces styles.

PrimeFaces styles can be inspected by the Firefox add-on Firebug or Google Chrome built-in Developer Tools.

```
#customStyles .ui-selectonemenu {
    width: 157px !important;
}

#customStyles .ui-selectonemenu .ui-selectonemenu-label {
    width: 130px !important;
}

#customStyles .ui-tree {
    border: none;
    background: none;
}
```

Any other CSS selector can be used for namespacing too. Namespacing is not needed if you want to change styles for all components of the same type. In this case, `#customStyles` should be omitted.

Appropriate places to put custom CSS files are the <h:head> tag, last facet of <h:head>, or a place before the closed `body` tag. The following code snippet demonstrates all three possibilities:

```
<!DOCTYPE html>
<html xmlns="http://www.w3.org/1999/xhtml"
      xmlns:f="http://java.sun.com/jsf/core"
      xmlns:h="http://java.sun.com/jsf/html"
      xmlns:ui="http://java.sun.com/jsf/facelets"
      xmlns:p="http://primefaces.org/ui">
<f:view contentType="text/html">
  <h:head>
      <h:outputStylesheet .../>

      <f:facet name="last">
          <h:outputStylesheet .../>
      </f:facet>
  </h:head>
    <h:body>
        <h:form>
          ... some component tags ...
        </h:form>
        ...
      <h:outputStylesheet library="css" name="customStyles3.css"/>
    </h:body>
  </f:view>
</html>
```

How it works...

Custom styles will be rendered after the PrimeFaces theme (skinning) and component (structural) styles. The correct output is ensured by the PrimeFaces resource ordering. Therefore, custom styles, being rendered after PrimeFaces ones, overwrite the default settings.

We used the `!important` keyword to set a fixed width for the container and the label of `SelectOneMenu`. This was necessary because `SelectOneMenu` renders the width as an inline style in HTML markup, for example, `style="width:76px"`. Inline styles always have the highest specificity and win against IDs and other CSS selectors. The different weight of selectors is usually the reason why your CSS rules do not apply to some elements, although you think they should have.

To remove the default border and background settings for `Tree`, we applied the `none` keyword on the `border` and `background` properties.

There's more...

Order of resource rendering may be broken when you use dynamic includes (the `ui:include` tag with the dynamic `src` attribite bound to a bean). CSS resources for dynamic included component tags, which were not presented on the page before including, are being added to the head as the last elements. That means, maybe existing custom styles will be rendered before and not after the newly added PrimeFaces styles.

> You can learn about CSS specificity (weight of selectors) at **World Wide Web Consortium** (**W3C**) `http://w3.org/TR/CSS21/cascade.html#specificity`.

PrimeFaces Cookbook Showcase application

This recipe is available in the demo web application on GitHub (`https://github.com/ova2/primefaces-cookbook`). Clone the project if you have not done it yet, explore the project structure, and execute the built-in Jetty Maven plugin to see this recipe in action. Follow instructions in the `README` file if you do not know how to run Jetty.

When the server is running, the showcase for the recipe is available under `http://localhost:8080/primefaces-cookbook/views/chapter2/customThemeStyles.jsf`.

See also

- Refer to the *Improved resource ordering* recipe from *Chapter 1, Getting Started with PrimeFaces* for better understanding of PrimeFaces resource ordering

Customizing default styles on input components

Customizing default styles on input components is a special task often asked about by the PrimeFaces users. They also ask for a recommended method for removing styles on form components. The reason to do that can be a company style guide and corporate identity throughout all applications.

In this recipe, we will find out a way to customize the PrimeFaces styles on input components and see if it is possible at all to disable theming on such components.

How to do it...

We will develop two groups of components having input elements. The first group is styled with the PrimeFaces default styles (here the **Home** theme). The second one has a custom styling. We have removed the border, background, shadow, and round corners on them. Furthermore, we have changed the styling of disabled inputs. Disabled elements get assigned the `ui-state-disabled` style class, so that we can adjust it as we want. Generally, to distinguish between input and non-input elements, there is a style class `ui-inputfield` assigned to every input element. Style classes such as `ui-state-disabled` are additional CSS selectors on those elements and affect the look and feel for various states.

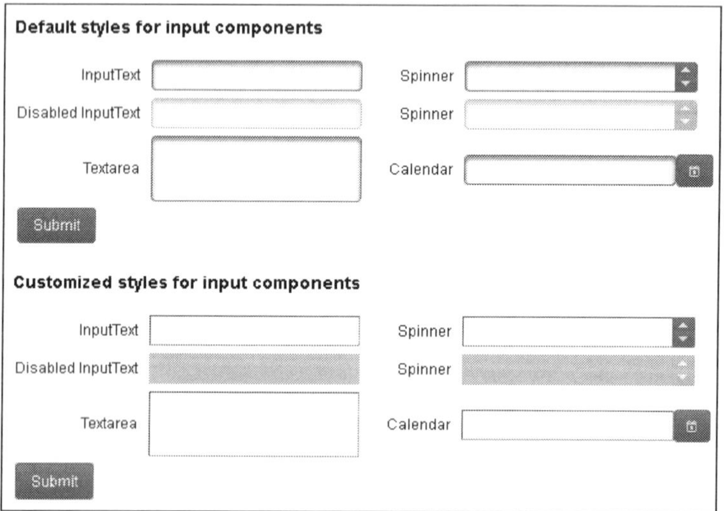

It is also interesting to see how elements look in an error case. When, for example, validation fails, PrimeFaces input components get the `ui-state-error` style class assigned. You see red borders around elements. For custom styled elements, we would like to have a red background in the error case. This is demonstrated in the following screenshot:

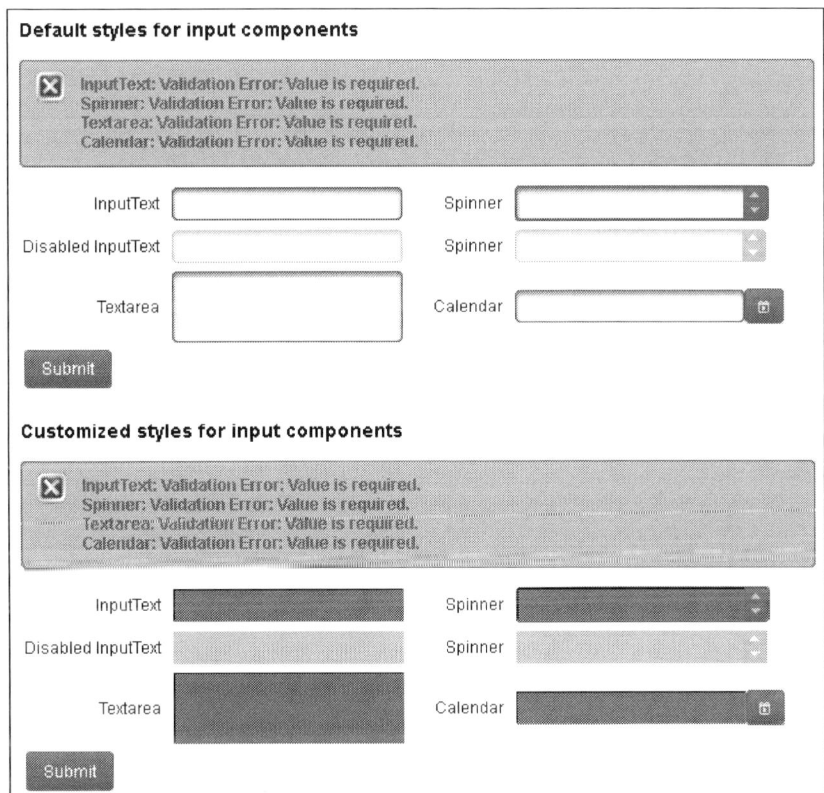

All components are placed within `h:panelGrid` as shown in the following code snippet:

```
<h:panelGrid id="customInputStyles" columns="4">
    <h:outputText value="InputText"/>
    <p:inputText required="true" label="InputText"/>

    <h:outputText value="Spinner"/>
    <p:spinner required="true" label="Spinner"/>

    <h:outputText value="Disabled InputText"/>
    <p:inputText label="Disabled InputText" disabled="true"/>

    <h:outputText value="Spinner"/>
    <p:spinner label="Spinner" disabled="true"/>

    <h:outputText value="Textarea"/>
    <p:inputTextarea required="true" label="Textarea"/>
```

```
        <h:outputText value="Calendar"/>
        <p:calendar required="true" showOn="both" label="Calendar"/>
    </h:panelGrid>
```

How it works...

To modify default styles on input components, we should overwrite the style classes `ui-inputfield`, `ui-state-disabled`, `ui-state-error` together with `ui-state-default`, `ui-state-focus`, and `ui-corner-all`. Prepend `#customInputStyles` for namespacing.

```
#customInputStyles .ui-inputfield {
    background: #ffffff;
    -moz-box-shadow: none;
    -webkit-box-shadow: none;
    box-shadow: none;
    color: #000000;
}

#customInputStyles .ui-inputfield.ui-state-focus {
    -moz-box-shadow: none;
    -webkit-box-shadow: none;
    box-shadow: none;
}

#customInputStyles .ui-inputfield.ui-state-default {
    background: none;
    border: 1px inset;
}

#customInputStyles .ui-inputfield.ui-corner-all {
    border-radius: 0;
}

#customInputStyles .ui-inputfield.ui-state-disabled,
#customInputStyles .ui-state-disabled .ui-inputfield {
    background-color: #8F8F8F;
    border: solid 1px gray;
}

#customInputStyles .ui-inputfield.ui-state-error,
#customInputStyles .ui-state-error .ui-inputfield {
    background-color: #F43939;
}
```

We write `.ui-inputfield` concatenated with `.ui-state-default`, `.ui-state-disabled`, `.ui-state-error`, `.ui-state-focus`, and `.ui-corner-all` because these style classes are defined on the same HTML elements.

There's more...

We cannot disable theming completely with the same look and feel in all browsers. For instance, set `2px` border as shown in the following code snippet

```
#customInputStyles .ui-inputfield.ui-state-default {
    background: none;
    border: 2px inset;
}
```

Can disable `p:inputText` or `p:inputTextarea` in Google Chrome, but not in Firefox. In Firefox, it still looks different.

Previous PrimeFaces versions had a context parameter `primefaces.THEME_FORMS` (`web.xml`) with the `false` value to disable the themable styling. It proved to be inefficient by reason of too much complexity in components and their renderers. Imagine `if-else-`blocks for themable and native HTML elements. For example, themable checkboxes and radio buttons are rendered as `div`, `span`, and not native `input` elements.

The main lesson of this recipe is that we cannot set default browser styles in order to completely overwrite PrimeFaces' ones. However, we can have a different look and feel by playing with style classes mentioned in this recipe.

PrimeFaces Cookbook Showcase application

This recipe is available in the demo web application on GitHub (`https://github.com/ova2/primefaces-cookbook`). Clone the project if you have not done it yet, explore the project structure, and execute the built-in Jetty Maven plugin to see this recipe in action. Follow instructions in the `README` file, if you do not know how to run Jetty.

When the server is running, the showcase for the recipe is available under `http://localhost:8080/primefaces-cookbook/views/chapter2/customInputStyles.jsf`.

Adjusting the font and size throughout the web application

Each PrimeFaces theme has a specific font family and font size, which can be different from theme to theme. This may have a disadvantage in a multi-theme application because switching from one theme to another would cause a broken layout. Furthermore, default font sizes of themes might be bigger than expected. Hence, it is important to know how to change font properties of the PrimeFaces components globally.

In this recipe, we will learn how to adjust the font family and font size throughout the web application.

How to do it...

A simple way to change fonts globally can be accomplished by using the `.ui-widget` style class. An example of smaller font is as follows:

```
.ui-widget, .ui-widget .ui-widget {
    font-size: 90% !important;
}
```

This might not be enough in some cases, especially when you mix PrimeFaces and JSF standard components based on native HTML pendants. In this case, more CSS selectors are required to be listed in order to adjust fonts globally. Assume we have decided to use the font `Arial` with size as 12 pixel. CSS selectors working for all known components would be as in the following listing.

```
body,
input,
select,
textarea,
button,
.ui-widget,
.ui-widget input,
.ui-widget select,
.ui-widget textarea,
.ui-widget button,
.ui-widget-header,
.ui-widget-content,
.ui-widget-header .ui-widget-header,
```

```
.ui-widget-content .ui-widget-content {
    font-family: Arial, Verdana, sans-serif;
    font-size: 12px !important;
}
```

> The universal selector * is much shorter, but it has no CSS specificity. Its specificity is `0,0,0,0`. That means, it can not overwrite, for example, an inline style with a specified font size.

How it works...

All PrimeFaces components are styled by the `ui-widget` style class. It is a skinning style specified by jQuery ThemeRoller and applied to HTML elements rendered by PrimeFaces. An input element has it for instance.

```
<input type="text" class="ui-inputfield ui-inputtext ui-widget ui-
state-default ui-corner-all" name="..." id="..." role="textbox">
```

In rare cases, when some component parts have assigned font properties, but are not styled by `.ui-widget` or you use non PrimeFaces components, more CSS selectors are needed for changing font properties throughout the web application.

See also

- More explanation for CSS selectors in the PrimeFaces-based applications can be found in the recipes *Understanding the structural and skinning CSS* and *Customizing theme styles*

Why does the theme look different in Internet Explorer?

Themable components look different in Internet Explorer 7 and 8, and browsers such as Google Chrome, Safari, or Firefox. There is a reason for that, which will be explained in this recipe. The main question is, do we need to take care of that? An update to Internet Explorer 9 or higher would be enough, but it is not always possible by reason of supporting web applications running in "old" browsers or due to some company-wide restrictions.

In this recipe, we will see if there are any ways to overcome this issue.

How to do it...

PrimeFaces does not officially support Internet Explorer 6. Internet Explorer 7 and 8 do not implement rounded corners, gradients, and advanced CSS3 effects. They do not follow CSS standards the same way as modern browsers or do not implement the latest CSS specifications. As a result, pages with themes like "Aristo", "Afterdark", or "Afternoon" look different in Internet Explorer 7 and 8—no round corners, no CSS3 shadow on input elements, no gradients, and so on. Furthermore, these browsers do not conform to the CSS specification in some parts. A well-known bug in earlier versions of Internet Explorer (also in Opera browser) was, for example, the Internet Explorer box model bug. Therefore, users are dependent on special CSS hacks to control CSS properties, which are only evaluated by these old browsers. For instance, universal selector with a plus character will only be interpreted by Internet Explorer 7. For example, `* + html div {width: 20em;}`.

JSF components in Internet Explorer 9 and higher should look similar to in modern browsers because new Internet Explorer versions support most of the new CSS3 properties and conform more to the CSS specification.

But be aware of missing support for gradients in Internet Explorer 9. It is still necessary to use the Microsoft-specific CSS filters instead of background property, such as this one:

```
filter: progid:DXImageTransform.Microsoft.gradient
(GradientType=0,startColorstr='#ffffff',
endColorstr='#000000');
```

There are two ways to overcome the preceding shortcoming. The first way is to style components in modern browsers without round corners, gradients, shadows, and so on. The *Customizing theme styles* and *Customizing default styles on input components* recipes show an approach on how to accomplish this task. The second way is to make Microsoft Internet Explorer behave like a standards-compliant browser. There are a lot of scripts trying to do this. Two of them are listed here:

- Authors: *Remiz Rahnas* and *Nick Fetchak*

  Resource: `http://fetchak.com/ie-css3`

- Author: *Dean Edwards*

  Resource: `http://code.google.com/p/ie7-js`

The first script provides Internet Explorer with an ability to support new styles available in the CSS3 standard. The second JavaScript library fixes many HTML and CSS issues, and makes transparent PNG work correctly under old IE versions.

We start with the `ie-css3` script. Download the `ie-css3.htc` file and place it in any resource folder. Assume it is `resources/css`. Add a selector, let's say `.box`, to your custom CSS file, let's say `iecss3.css`, with settings for `border-radius` and `box-shadow` you need. Add the following behavior too:

```
behavior: url(/resources/css/ie-css3.htc)
```

Example:

```
.box {
    border-radius: 15px;
    box-shadow: 10px 10px 20px #000;
    behavior: url(/resources/css/ie-css3.htc);
}
```

Now include `iecss3.css` within the `h:head` tag.

```
<link type="text/css" rel="stylesheet" href="#{request.contextPath}/
resources/css/iecss3.css"/>
```

The second script from Dean Edwards is easy to use. To upgrade old IE versions to be compatible with modern ones (IE 9 and higher), download the script from `http://ie7-js.googlecode.com/svn/version/2.1(beta4)/IE9.js` and put it to your page within the IE conditional comments `<!--[if lt IE 9]>` ... `<![endif]-->`.

How it works...

Using the `behavior` property lets IE know when to call the `htc` script on all elements, which get the `box` class. Now, if you are viewing the page in Internet Explorer, some of the elements have been rebuilt by the script in **Vector Markup Language** (**VML**), an IE-specific vector drawing language. VML supports things that are missing from IE's CSS Implementation, such as rounded corners and blur effects.

> You may have to configure the web server to handle the `htc` mime-type properly.

Dean Edwards' script fixes a number of bugs present in old IE versions and can enhance IE 7 or IE 8. Discover enhancements in a test page `http://ie7-js.googlecode.com/svn/test/index.html`. Conditional comments are required to avoid clashing with browsers other than the specified Internet Explorer version.

There's more...

If you are only interested in seeing round corners in Internet Explorer 7 and 8, you can use the beautiful jQuery corner plugin written by Mike Alsup (`http://jquery.malsup.com/corner`). The corner rounding is simple. Call the `corner()` method on any HTML element, for example, tabs of the `TabView` component.

```
$('.ui-tabs .ui-tabs-nav li').corner('top 6px');
```

The script doing this call should be placed at the page's bottom or in a jQuery-ready method specifying a function to be executed when the DOM is fully loaded.

Simple ways to create a new theme

We sometimes need to create our own themes instead of using the pre-defined ones. Web applications should often feature a company-specific look and feel, which is constant and preset by company-wide style guides. Creating new themes is easy with PrimeFaces because it is powered by the ThemeRoller CSS framework (`http://jqueryui.com/themeroller`). ThemeRoller provides a powerful and easy-to-use online visual tool.

In this recipe, we will go on systematically and show all needed steps to create a new theme.

Getting ready

To gain first-hand experience with the ThemeRoller online visual tool, go to the ThemeRoller home page, explore the available theme **Gallery**, and play with the CSS properties to see changes for jQuery widgets embedded on the page. All CSS changes will be applied on the fly.

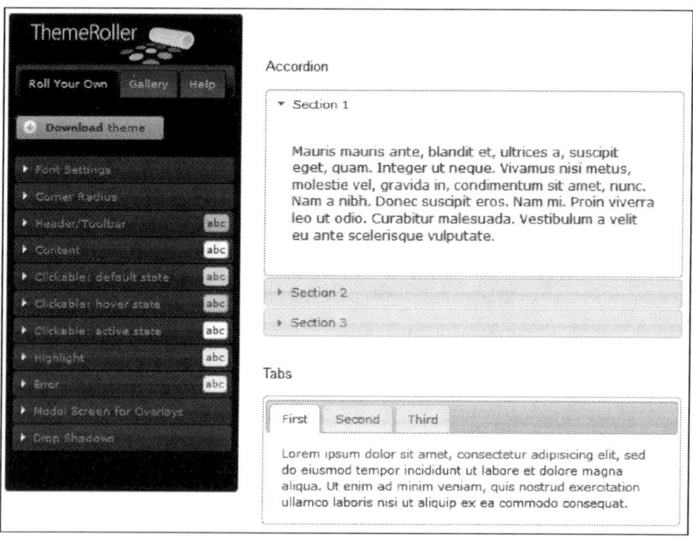

How to do it...

The simplest way to make our own theme is to modify one of the existing PrimeFaces themes. Choose one from the PrimeFaces Theme Gallery (`http://primefaces.org/themes.html`), which is close to your needs. All the themes are downloadable JAR files. The JAR structure is listed here (for example **Home** theme):

```
- jar
    - META-INF
        - resources
            - primefaces-home
                - theme.css
                - images
                    - ...
```

Assume, our new theme has a name `funny`. We can now create the following structure in a web project below the `resources` folder:

```
- war
    - resources
        - primefaces-funny
            - theme.css
            - images
                - ...
```

Or create a quite new JAR project for the new theme.

```
- jar
    - META-INF
        - resources
            - primefaces-funny
                - theme.css
                - images
                    - ...
```

The second way is preferred because it would be conforming to the PrimeFaces theme convention. JAR files can be shared across multiple web applications by adding them to the classpath. The last step consists of modifying `theme.css` according to our needs. Knowledge of CSS selectors is necessary.

If no pre-defined theme matches our requirements, we should use the ThemeRoller online tool. We have to select one of the existing themes (the **Gallery** tab) and edit it (the **Roll Your Own** tab). A click on the **Download theme** button accomplishes the work.

We should choose the **Deselect all components** option on the **Download** page so that our new theme only includes the skinning styles.

Next, we need to migrate the downloaded theme files from ThemeRoller to the PrimeFaces theme infrastructure. The migration steps are straightforward.

1. The theme package that we have downloaded will have a CSS file `jquery-ui-{version}.custom.css` and a folder `images`. Extract the package and rename the CSS file to `theme.css`.
2. Image references in the `theme.css` file must be converted to JSF expressions, which can be understood by the JSF resource loading mechanism. An example for the original CSS file would be as follows:

   ```
   url("images/ui-bg_highlight-hard_100_f9f9f9.png")
   ```

   This should be converted to the following:

   ```
   url("#{resource['primefaces-funny:images/ui-bg_highlight-hard_100_
   f9f9f9.png']}")
   ```

3. Create a JAR theme project with the structure shown in this section.
4. Once the JAR file is in the classpath, we can use it as per the configuration in `web.xml`.

   ```
   <context-param>
           <param-name>primefaces.THEME</param-name>
           <param-value>funny</param-value>
   </context-param>
   ```

How it works...

JSF 2 has a built-in facility for serving resources. The JSF implementation looks for resources in two locations and in the following order:

- `/resources`: This location represents resources in the web application itself
- `/META-INF/resources`: This location represents resources on the classpath

The syntax for image references in CSS files is `#{resource[...]}` and it activates this facility and allows to load resources from JAR files.

PrimeFaces' renderer implementation for the `<h:head>` tag automatically detects the current configured theme in `web.xml` and renders theme-related resources on the page.

Default stateless theme switcher

Multi-themable web applications require a theme switcher component. The default PrimeFaces' theme switcher is a component, which enables switching themes on the fly without a round-trip to the server. We speak about a stateless theme switcher because the current selected theme is only known on the client side.

In this recipe, we will show the usage of such a stateless theme switcher.

How to do it...

The theme switcher usage is very similar to the usage of `p:selectOneMenu`. The component is represented by the `p:themeSwitcher` tag and accepts `f:selectItem` or `f:selectItems`.

```
<p:themeSwitcher style="width:165px" effect="fade">
    <f:selectItem itemLabel="Choose Theme" itemValue=""/>
    <f:selectItems value="#{userSettingsController.themes}"/>
</p:themeSwitcher>
```

Themes are prepared in a managed bean `UserSettingsController`.

```
@ManagedBean
@SessionScoped
public class UserSettingsController implements Serializable {

    public Map<String, String> getThemes() {
        return themes;
    }

    @PostConstruct
    public void init() {
        themes = new TreeMap<String, String>();
        themes.put("Afterdark", "afterdark");
        ... put all other themes ...
        themes.put("Vader", "vader");
    }
}
```

How it works...

The resource URL to `theme.css` contains a current theme name. The default theme switcher changes the theme name in the resource URL by JavaScript. The changed resource link streams down a new `theme.css` to the page dependent on the user selection.

There's more...

Theme switchers in action can also be viewed in the PrimeFaces ShowCase (`http://primefaces.org/showcase/ui/themeswitcher.jsf`).

PrimeFaces Cookbook Showcase application

This recipe is available in the demo web application on GitHub (`https://github.com/ova2/primefaces-cookbook`). Clone the project if you have not done it yet, explore the project structure, and execute the built-in Jetty Maven plugin to see this recipe in action. Follow instructions in the `README` file if you do not know how to run Jetty.

When the server is running, the showcase for the recipe is available under `http://localhost:8080/primefaces-cookbook/views/chapter2/stdThemeSwitcher.jsf`.

See also

- Alternative stateful theme switchers are implemented in the *Alternative stateful theme switchers* recipe of this chapter

Alternative stateful theme switchers

By default, PrimeFaces theme switcher only changes the theme on the fly without sending an AJAX or full-page request. Users often want to get notified when the current theme has been changed in order to be able to update user preferences or settings.

In this recipe, we will implement two stateful theme switchers, which are able to save the current selected theme on the server side.

How to do it...

The next listing demonstrates a stateful theme switcher with attached AJAX behavior.

```
<p:themeSwitcher id="statefulSwitcher1"
                 value="#{userSettingsController.theme}"
                 style="width:165px" effect="fade">
    <f:selectItem itemLabel="Choose Theme" itemValue=""/>
    <f:selectItems value="#{userSettingsController.themes}"/>
    <p:ajax listener="#{userSettingsController.saveTheme}"/>
</p:themeSwitcher>
```

Another advanced theme switcher supports displaying theme previews in the form of small images.

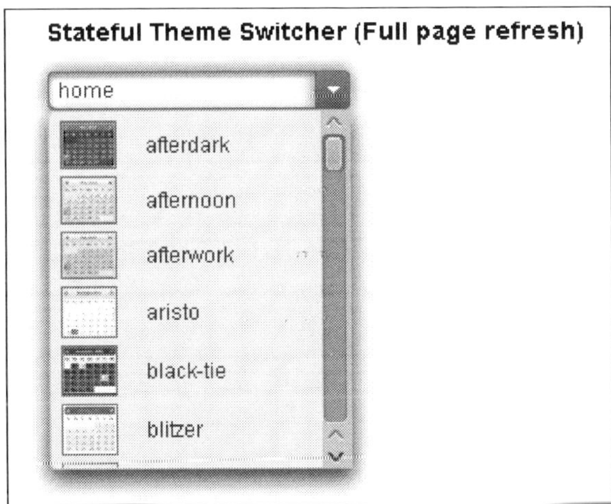

We can develop it either with `p:themeSwitcher` or `p:selectOneMenu`. Both implementations require `p:column`. The following code snippet demonstrates how to develop a stateful theme switcher by using `p:selectOneMenu`. This theme switcher sends full-page requests when the user changes themes.

```
<p:selectOneMenu id="statefulSwitcher2"
                 value="#{userSettingsController.currentTheme}"
                 var="theme" effect="drop"
                 onchange="$('#mainForm').submit()">
    <f:converter converterId="org.primefaces.cookbook.converter.
ThemeConverter"/>
    <f:selectItems var="t"
                   value="#{userSettingsController.availableThemes}"
                   itemLabel="#{t.name}"
                   itemValue="#{t}"/>
    <p:column>
        <p:graphicImage value="#{theme.image}"/>
    </p:column>
    <p:column>
        <h:outputText value="#{theme.name}"/>
    </p:column>
</p:selectOneMenu>
```

UserSettingsController is a bean class providing getter/setter for the current selected theme and a public method List<Theme> getAvailableThemes(). This method returns all available themes as a list of instances of type Theme. The model class Theme consists of two attributes name (theme name) and image (image path).

```
@ManagedBean
@SessionScoped
public class UserSettingsController implements Serializable {

  private List<Theme> availableThemes;
  private Theme currentTheme;

  public UserSettingsController() {
     currentTheme = AvailableThemes.instance().getTheme("home");
     availableThemes = AvailableThemes.instance().getThemes();
     }

  public List<Theme> getAvailableThemes() {
    return availableThemes;
  }

  // more getter / setter
}

public class AvailableThemes implements Serializable {

  private static AvailableThemes INSTANCE = null;

  public static AvailableThemes instance() {
    if (INSTANCE == null) {
      INSTANCE = new AvailableThemes();
    }

    return INSTANCE;
  }

  private final HashMap<String, Theme> themesAsMap;
  private final List<Theme> themes;

  private AvailableThemes() {
    List<String> themeNames = new ArrayList<String>();
    themeNames.add("afterdark");
      ... put all other themes ...
          themeNames.add("vader");
```

```
        themesAsMap = new HashMap<String, Theme>();
        themes = new ArrayList<Theme>();

        for (String themeName : themeNames) {
          Theme theme = new Theme(
          themeName,
          "/resources/images/themeswitcher/" + themeName + ".png");

          themes.add(theme);
          themesAsMap.put(theme.getName(), theme);
        }
    }

    public final List<Theme> getThemes() {
      return themes;
    }

    public Theme getTheme(String name) {
        return themesAsMap.get(name);
    }
}
```

How it works...

In the first example, the current selected theme is being saved by the `onchange` event via the AJAX listener. In the second example, we defined a JavaScript `onchange` callback to submit the closest form with a current selected theme. It results in a regular HTTP request. The `p:column` tag is needed to display table-like custom content.

The `AvailableThemes` class is a singleton instance providing all theme names along with their paths below the web root. The model class `Theme` encapsulates this information for every single theme and is exposed on the page via the `var` attribute.

There's more...

The theme switcher developed on the basis of `p:selectOneMenu` has an attached JSF converter with the ID `org.primefaces.cookbook.converter.ThemeConverter`.

```
@FacesConverter("org.primefaces.cookbook.converter.ThemeConverter")
public class ThemeConverter implements Converter {

    public Object getAsObject(FacesContext context, UIComponent
    component, String value) {
```

```
        return AvailableThemes.instance().getTheme(value);
    }

    public String getAsString(FacesContext context, UIComponent
    component, Object value) {
        return ((Theme) value).getName();
    }
}
```

Theme switchers in action can also be viewed in the PrimeFaces ShowCase (`http://primefaces.org/showcase/ui/themeswitcher.jsf`). You may also want to check the *ThemeSwitcher* chapter in *PrimeFaces User's Guide* (`http://primefaces.org/documentation.html`) and learn how to develop stateful theme switchers with `p:themeSwitcher`.

PrimeFaces Cookbook Showcase application

This recipe is available in the demo web application on GitHub (`https://github.com/ova2/primefaces-cookbook`). Clone the project if you have not done it yet, explore the project structure, and execute the built-in Jetty Maven plugin to see this recipe in action. Follow instructions in the `README` file, if you do not know how to run Jetty.

When the server is running, the showcase for the recipe is available under `http://localhost:8080/primefaces-cookbook/views/chapter2/altThemeSwitcher1.jsf` and `http://localhost:8080/primefaces-cookbook/views/chapter2/altThemeSwitcher2.jsf`.

See also

- A stateless theme switcher is discussed in the *Default stateless theme switcher* recipe of this chapter

3
Enhanced Inputs and Selects

In this chapter we will cover:

- Formatted input with inputMask
- Auto suggestion with autoComplete
- Usable features of inputTextArea
- Discovering selectBooleanCheckbox and selectManyCheckbox
- Basic and advanced calendar scenarios
- Spinner–different ways to provide input
- Slider–different ways to provide input
- Rich text editing with the editor
- Advanced editing with in-place editor
- Enhanced password input
- Star-based rating input

Introduction

In this chapter, we will learn how to work with input and select components available in PrimeFaces. PrimeFaces provides nearly 25 components for data input, which extend standard corresponding JSF components with skinning capabilities and useful features such as user-friendly interface, validation, and so on.

Formatted input with inputMask

`inputMask` minimizes the chances for the user to input incorrect data. It applies client-side validation with the provided masking template.

How to do it...

A basic example of input mask for a phone number input would be as follows:

```
<p:inputMask value="#{maskController.phone}" mask="(999) 999-9999"/>
```

As can be seen with the mask `(999) 999-9999`, it is stated that only numbers can be input along with the parenthesis and dashed structure. The initial visual of the input will be as seen in the following image:

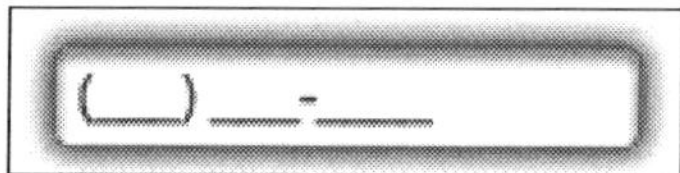

The fields that are filled up with number `9` in the mask will be empty and the rest will be rendered with the initial phase. The numeric character `9` is used to depict only numeric characters that could be input for the field in this example. By providing alphabetic character `a`, input could be restricted only to alphabetic characters. An example would be the input of a product key, as follows:

```
<p:inputMask value="#{maskController.productKey}" mask="a999-a9"/>
```

This will restrict the input of the first characters of the two sections that are separated by the dash, only to the alphabetic characters.

How it works...

The `inputMask` component decorates the input text component with JavaScript to provide the masking feature. With each `keypress` event, the value is checked against the mask provided for the validation on the client side. The component will unmask itself when the `readonly` attribute is set to `true`. PrimeFaces wraps Masked Input Plugin of jQuery for the `inputMask` component.

There's more...

There is also the `placeholder` attribute, which renders the character(s) given in the template. The default placeholder is the _character. For instance, we can change the placeholder value for the phone input, and with the placeholder definition of `X` the component would be defined as follows:

```
<p:inputMask value="#{maskController.phone}" mask="(999) 999-9999"
placeHolder="X" />
```

The component will be rendered as shown in the following screenshot:

Using the asterisk (*) character

With the asterisk character, we can represent an alphanumeric character to be input by the user, which could be `A` to `Z`, `a` to `z`, or `0` to `9`.

```
<p:inputMask value="#{inputMaskController.productKey}" mask="a*-
999-a999" />
```

With the preceding `inputMask` definition, inputs such as `ac-223-a481` or `a2-223-a481` will be validated as `true`.

Making a part of the mask optional

It is also possible to make a part of the mask optional with the usage of a question mark character. Anything listed after `?` within the mask will be considered as an optional user input. A common example for this is a phone number with an optional extension.

```
<p:inputMask value="#{inputMaskController.phoneExt}" mask="(999)
999-9999? x99999" />
```

When the user finishes the input by reaching the `?` character and un-focusing the component, the rest of the validation will be skipped and the input till that section will not be erased. Input values such as `(555) 204-2551` or `(555) 204-2551 x1980` will be valid for this optional input.

PrimeFaces Cookbook Showcase application

This recipe is available in the PrimeFaces Cookbook Showcase application on GitHub at `https://github.com/ova2/primefaces-cookbook`. You can find the details there for running the project. When the server is running, the showcase for the recipe is available at `http://localhost:8080/primefaces-cookbook/views/chapter3/inputMask.jsf`.

Auto suggestion with autoComplete

The `autoComplete` component provides suggestions while you type into the input field. This enables users to quickly find and select from the list of looked-up values as they type, which leverages the searching and filtering abilities.

How to do it...

For simple usage of the `autoComplete` component, all we need is to define the complete method that will be invoked with the user input as follows:

```
<p:autoComplete id="simple" value="#{autoCompleteController.txt1}"
    completeMethod="#{autoCompleteController.complete}" />
```

This will be rendered as shown in the following screenshot:

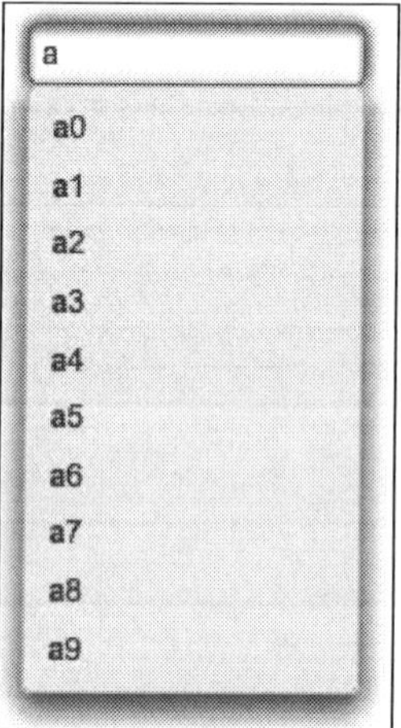

As the user types characters into the input text, as shown in the preceding screenshot, the component will assist 10 selections by appending numbers from 0 to 9. The `completeMethod` implemented for this in the `autoCompleteController` backing bean is shown in the following code snippet. The user input is given as the parameter to the method.

```
public List<String> complete(String input) {
  List<String> result = new ArrayList<String>();

  for (int i = 0; i < 10; i++) {
    result.add(input + i);
  }

  return result;
}
```

There are several attributes that could be used with the `autoComplete` component. With the `minQueryLength` attribute, we can specify the number of characters to be typed before starting to query; its default value is `1`. This minimizes the unnecessary lookups that could be done to the server since the input provided by the user, a couple of characters probably, is not enough for meaningful prediction most of the time.

With the `queryDelay` attribute, we can specify the delay to wait in milliseconds before sending each query to the server; its default value is 300 ms. This minimizes the round trips that are done to the server to reduce the load on the execution of `completeMethod`.

With the `forceSelection` attribute, a component only accepts input from the selection list; so the typed characters will be transient if no selection is made. This forces the user to select the proper content that could be validated properly via the assistance of the component. The user can also leave the component intact with no selection.

When set to `true`, the `dropdown` attribute provides the `autoComplete` component to be used as a drop down by rendering the drop-down icon. This will enable the selection of any of the `autoComplete` items by the user without inputting any character.

There's more...

Instead of working with primitive types, most of the time we would be using the `autoComplete` component with domain objects. The basic definition of the component for listing the cars for a given brand would be as follows:

```
<p:autoComplete id="carPOJO"
    value="#{autoCompleteController.selectedCar}"
    completeMethod="#{autoCompleteController.completeCar}"
    var="car" itemLabel="#{car.name}" itemValue="#{car}"
    forceSelection="true">
  <f:converter
  converterId="org.primefaces.cookbook.converter.CarConverter" />
  <p:column>
    <p:graphicImage value=
    "/resources/images/autocomplete/#{car.name}.png"/>
  </p:column>
  <p:column>#{car.name}</p:column>
</p:autoComplete>
```

Here, the component contains column definitions along with a converter declaration. The converter is responsible for converting the submitted value for each car, and with the help of the columns we render images along with the name of each car. This will enhance the autocompletion for the user, and will ease the selection.

Instant AJAX selection

It's also possible to invoke a server-side method instantly when an item from `autoComplete` is selected. The `autoComplete` component provides the `itemSelect` AJAX behavior event that will be fired instantly when an item is selected.

```
<p:autoComplete value="#{autoCompleteController.txt1}"
completeMethod="#{autoCompleteController.complete}">
  <p:ajax event="itemSelect"
  listener="#{autoCompleteController.handleSelect}"
  update="messages" />
</p:autoComplete>
```

The `itemSelect` method will be invoked with `org.primefaces.event.SelectEvent`. The current value of the selected item can be retrieved with `event.getObject()`, and a Faces message could be added with the current item, as in the following code snippet:

```
public void handleSelect(SelectEvent event) {
  Object selectedObject = event.getObject();
  MessageUtil.addInfoMessage("selected.object", selectedObject);
}
```

Multiple selection

With `autoComplete`, it is also possible to select multiple items by setting the `multiple` attribute to `true`.

```
<p:autoComplete id="multipleSelect" value="#{autoCompleteController.
selectedTexts}" completeMethod="#{autoCompleteController.complete}"
multiple="true" />
```

With the help of multiple select, the selected texts can be retrieved as a list in `autoCompleteController.selectedTexts`, which maps to the property `List<String> selectedTexts`.

PrimeFaces Cookbook Showcase application

This recipe is available in the PrimeFaces Cookbook Showcase application on GitHub at `https://github.com/ova2/primefaces-cookbook`. You can find the details there for running the project. When the server is running, the showcase for the recipe is available at `http://localhost:8080/primefaces-cookbook/views/chapter3/autoComplete.jsf`.

Usable features of inputTextArea

`inputTextArea` is an extension to the HTML `<textarea>` component with special capabilities such as auto-growing, auto-resizing, and remaining-character count.

How to do it...

A basic definition for the input text area would be as follows:

```
<p:inputTextarea value="#{inputTextAreaController.value}" />
```

This will render an input text area with default value `rows='3'` and `cols='20'` as shown in the following screenshot:

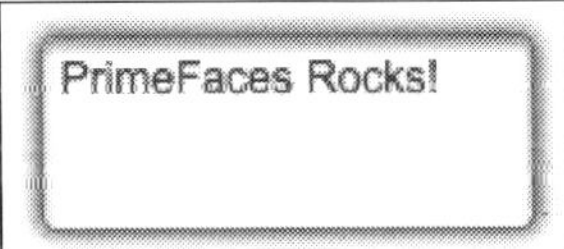

The component also provides auto-resizing with the `autoResize` attribute that allows us to expand the height automatically when the text input overflows. The default value is `false`.

```
<p:inputTextarea value="#{inputTextAreaController.value}"
autoResize="true"/>
```

Like the HTML `<textarea>` component, we can also specify the `rows` and `cols` attributes to specify the size of the text area component in rows and columns.

How it works...

The JavaScript plugin for the `inputTextArea` component is solely implemented by PrimeFaces with jQuery. Auto-resizing is executed on the `keyup`, `focus`, and `blur` JavaScript events and it increases the number of rows that the component owns. Remaining character count is executed on the `keyup` event, and the content gets trimmed if `maxlength` is exceeded.

There's more...

With the `maxlength` attribute, we can limit the maximum allowed characters to be input to the component. There are two more attributes, `counter` and `counterTemplate`, which will dynamically output the number of characters left to be input to the component easily.

```
<p:inputTextarea value="#{bean.propertyName}" counter="display"
         maxlength="20" counterTemplate="{0} characters remaining" />
<h:outputText id="display" />
```

The `counter` attribute should refer to the ID of the `label` component to display the remaining characters and `counterTemplate` will contain the template text to display in `counter`, with default value `{0}`.

PrimeFaces Cookbook Showcase application

This recipe is available in the PrimeFaces Cookbook Showcase application on GitHub at `https://github.com/ova2/primefaces-cookbook`. You can find the details there for running the project. When the server is running, the showcase for the recipe is available at `http://localhost:8080/primefaces-cookbook/views/chapter3/inputTextArea.jsf`.

Discovering selectBooleanCheckbox and selectManyCheckbox

`selectBooleanCheckbox` and `selectManyCheckbox` extend the default JSF components <h:selectBooleanCheckbox> and <h:selectManyCheckbox> respectively to provide skinning.

How to do it...

Basic definitions for `selectBooleanCheckbox` and `selectManyCheckbox` would be as follows:

```
<p:selectBooleanCheckbox value="#{selectCheckboxController.
selectedValue}" />

<p:selectManyCheckbox value="#{selectCheckboxController.
selectedCountries}">
  <f:selectItem itemLabel="Turkey" itemValue="Turkey" />
  <f:selectItem itemLabel="Germany" itemValue="Germany" />
```

```
    <f:selectItem itemLabel="Switzerland" itemValue="Switzerland" />
</p:selectManyCheckbox>
```

Adding labels to the checkbox is easy with the `itemLabel` attribute. `itemLabel` displays a label next to the checkbox.

```
<p:selectBooleanCheckbox value="#{selectCheckboxController.
selectedValue}" itemLabel="#{msg['selectBooleanCheckbox.label']}" />
```

The text that will be rendered right next to the `checkbox` component with the `itemLabel` attribute can also be clicked to select/unselect the checkbox.

The direction of contents of the `selectManyCheckbox` component can be changed from the default horizontal rendering to vertical by setting the `layout` attribute with the `pageDirection` value. The output for both horizontal and vertical rendering for the example given in the basic definition is shown in the following screenshot:

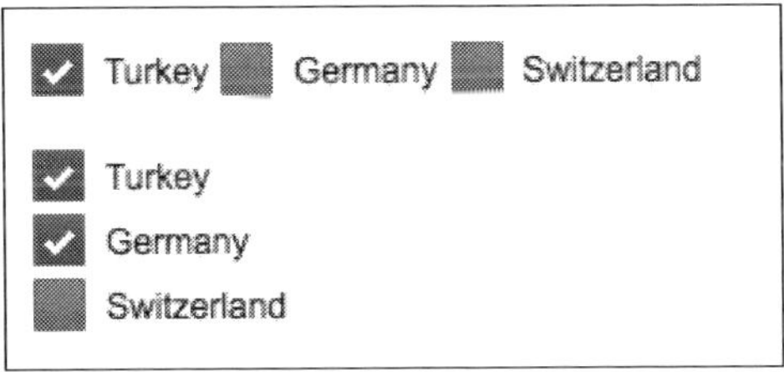

There's more...

It's also possible to get the state of the checkbox at the client side via JavaScript. To achieve this, the `widgetVar` attribute needs to be specified to the component. The `widgetVar` attribute defines the client-side variable, which has various responsibilities such as progressive enhancement of the markup and communication with the server side via AJAX. It can also be used directly from the JavaScript code.

```
<p:selectBooleanCheckbox value="#{selectCheckboxController.
selectedValue}" widgetVar="mySelection" />

<p:commandLink value="Alert Selection" onclick="alert(mySelection.
isChecked());" />
```

Within the `alert` method of the `onclick` event of `commandLink` (a client-side JavaScript call), the state will be retrieved by the `mySelection.isChecked()` code section. The `checkbox` component is being accessed by `mySelection`, which is the name of the client-side widget variable of the checkbox.

Selection with AJAX behavior on selectBooleanCheckbox

We can also invoke server-side code when the checkbox is checked/unchecked. The definition will update the `growl` message component when it's clicked.

```
<p:selectBooleanCheckbox value="#{selectCheckboxController.
selectedValue}">
  <p:ajax update=
  "growl" listener="#{selectCheckboxController.addMessage}" />
</p:selectBooleanCheckbox>
```

The server-side `addMessage` method that is called for adding the actual message is as follows:

```
public void addMessage() {
    String summaryKey =
    selectedValue ? "checkbox.checked" : "checkbox.unchecked";
    MessageUtil.addInfoMessage(summaryKey);
}
```

This will add a Faces message that corresponds to the given key from the defined resource bundle.

PrimeFaces Cookbook Showcase application

This recipe is available in the PrimeFaces Cookbook Showcase application on GitHub at `https://github.com/ova2/primefaces-cookbook`. You can find the details there for running the project. When the server is running, the showcase for the recipe is available at `http://localhost:8080/primefaces-cookbook/views/chapter3/selectBooleanCheckboxSelectManyCheckbox.jsf`.

See also

- For details about the `MessageUtil` class, see the *Internationalization (i18n) and Localization (L10n)* section in *Chapter 1, Getting Started with PrimeFaces*

Basic and advanced calendar scenarios

The `calendar` component is used to provide `date` input with customizable features such as localization, paging of months and restriction mechanisms on the date selection.

How to do it...

The simplest component declaration for a basic date selection would be as follows:

```
<p:calendar value="#{calendarController.date}" />
```

This renders an input text that opens up a pop-up date selection dialog when clicked, as shown in the following screenshot:

The pop-up visual of the calendar can also be configured to render as an inline visual on the page with the `mode` attribute, as follows:

```
<p:calendar value="#{calendarController.date}" mode="inline" />
```

The output of the `calendar` component in the inline mode will be as shown in the following screenshot:

The default value of `mode` is `popup`. It is also possible to render multiple months side by side on the page with the `pages` attribute.

```
<p:calendar id="paging" value="#{calendarController.date}" pages="3"
mode="inline" />
```

Paging will start with the month that the given date exists in, and will continue with the number of months specified by the `pages` attribute. The `inline` attribute can also be used along with the paging to display, for instance, three months in a row, as in the preceding example.

`showOn` is an attribute that defines a client-side event that displays the pop-up calendar. The value `button` can be specified with the attribute to render a button right next to the input text field to show the pop-up calendar when clicked. The default value for the `showOn` attribute is `focus`, which will render the pop up when the input field gets the focus.

The `mindate` and `maxdate` attributes set the calendar's minimum visible and maximum visible dates. With the following example, the calendar will be rendered with three days available for selection, which are yesterday, today, and tomorrow respectively.

```
<p:calendar id="restrictedDates" value="#{calendarController.date}"
mode="inline"
  mindate="#{calendarController.yesterday}"
  maxdate="#{calendarController.tomorrow}" />
```

It's also possible to disable the manual input on the input text of a pop-up calendar by setting the `readonlyInput` attribute to `true`.

There's more...

It's also possible to invoke a server-side method instantly when a date is selected. The `calendar` component provides the `dateSelect` AJAX behavior event that will be fired instantly when a date is selected.

```
<p:calendar id="ajaxCalendar" value="#{calendarController.date}"
mode="inline">
  <p:ajax event="dateSelect"
listener="#{calendarController.onDateSelect}" update="growl" />
</p:calendar>
```

The `onDateSelect` method will be invoked with `org.primefaces.event.DateSelectEvent`. The current value of the calendar can be retrieved with `event.getDate()`, and a Faces message could be added with the current date, as in the following code snippet:

```
public void onDateSelect(DateSelectEvent event) {
  Date date = event.getDate();
  MessageUtil.addInfoMessage("selected.date", date);
}
```

Localization of the calendar

Defining the locale value to the `locale` attribute provides the localization of the calendar. Definition of a calendar in a Turkish locale would be as follows:

```
<p:calendar locale="tr" mode="inline" id="trCal"/>
```

The calendar component uses a shared PrimeFaces.locales property to display the labels. PrimeFaces only provides English translations, so in order to localize the calendar we need to put corresponding locales into a JavaScript file and include the scripting file to the page, as follows:

```
<h:outputScript library="js" name="turkishLocale.js" />
```

For the usage of the outputScript tag, refer to http://www.mkyong.com/jsf2/how-to-include-javascript-file-in-jsf. For already translated locales of the calendar, visit http://code.google.com/p/primefaces/wiki/PrimeFacesLocales.

Effects with the calendar

When the calendar component is in the popup mode, effects can be applied for the hide/unhide mechanism of the pop-up dialog box.

```
<p:calendar value="#{calendarController.date}" effect="bounce"
effectDuration="slow" />
```

The effectDuration attribute can also be set with values slow, normal, and fast to define the duration of the effect. The default value for the duration is normal. The list of all the effects that could be used is as follows:

- blind
- bounce
- clip
- drop
- fadeIn
- fold
- show
- slide
- slideDown

Picking time with the calendar

By providing a time format to the pattern attribute, the timePicker functionality can be enabled.

```
<p:calendar id="timeCalendar" value="#{calendarController.date}"
pattern="dd/MM/yyyy HH:mm:ss"/>
```

The appearance of the calendar with the time-picking ability would be as shown in the following screenshot:

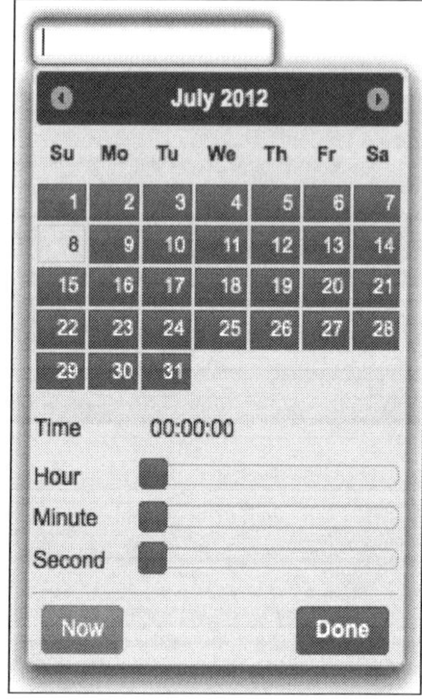

To select only time with the `calendar` component, the `timeOnly` attribute should be set to `true` along with the `pattern` value as `"dd/MM/yyyy HH:mm"`. Sliders of the time input section of the calendar should have the step value `1`. In order to change this, the `calendar` component provides three attributes: `stepHour`, `stepMinute`, and `stepSecond`. We can also define ranges for the hour, minute, and second input, such as to just enable the user to input hours between 3 and 5, minutes between 0 and 30, and seconds between 45 and 55. This is shown in the following code snippet:

```
<p:calendar id="rangeTimeCalendar" value="#{calendarController.date}"
pattern="dd/MM/yyyy HH:mm:ss"
minHour="3" maxHour="5" minMinute="0" maxMinute="30" minSecond="45"
maxSecond="55"/>
```

PrimeFaces Cookbook Showcase application

This recipe is available in the PrimeFaces Cookbook Showcase application on GitHub at `https://github.com/ova2/primefaces-cookbook`. You can find the details there for running the project. When the server is running, the showcase for the recipe is available at `http://localhost:8080/primefaces-cookbook/views/chapter3/calendar.jsf`.

See also

- For details about the localization of the `calendar` component, refer to the *Internationalization (i18n) and Localization (L10n)* recipe in *Chapter 1, Getting Started with PrimeFaces*

Spinner – different ways to provide input

`spinner` is an input component that provides a numerical input via increment and decrement buttons.

How to do it...

A basic definition of the component would be as follows:

```
<p:spinner value="#{spinnerController.intValue}" />
```

This will render an input text box on the page, with controls to increase and decrease the value.

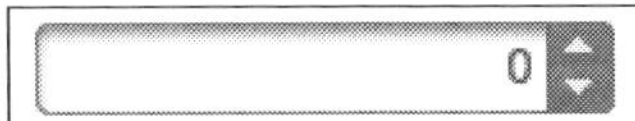

There's more...

The `stepFactor` attribute defines the stepping factor that will be applied for each increment and decrement with the default value `1`. The following definition will increase or decrease the value by 0.5.

```
<p:spinner value="#{spinnerController.doubleValue}" stepFactor="0.5" />
```

Adding prefix and suffix

The `prefix` and `suffix` attributes provide the ability to place fixed strings on the input field as prefix or suffix to the input respectively. The first definition will render the `$` sign as a prefix and second one will render the `%` sign with the value of the input field.

```
<p:spinner value="#{spinnerController.intValue}" prefix="$" />

<p:spinner value="#{spinnerController.intValue}" suffix="%" />
```

Applying boundaries to the input

The spinner component also provides attributes to set boundary values on the input value. The min attribute defines the minimum boundary value with default value of the minimum value of java.lang.Double. The max attribute defines the maximum boundary value with default value of maximum value of java.lang.Double.

The minimum and maximum control on the input field will only get applied on the increment and decrement buttons and not on manual input done by the keyboard. In order to disable manual input, we need to specify onkeydown="return false;" to disable the keystrokes.

```
<p:spinner value="#{spinnerController.intValue}" suffix="%" min="0"
max="100" onkeydown="return false;" />
```

This will result in rendering the spinner component with the restriction from 0 to 100, suffixed with the % sign, and disabled with the keyboard input.

Adjusting the width of the spinner

One misleading approach on setting the width of the spinner component is defining the style attribute with the width value, for example, style="width:50px;", since it'll increase the width of the spinner component by having fixed width for the input part. We can easily resize the field with the size attribute, which defines the number of characters used to determine the width of the input element.

```
<p:spinner value="#{spinnerController.intValue}" size="3" />
```

AJAX update with spinner

It is also possible to update an output field on each click on the spinner, with the <p:ajax> component.

```
<p:spinner id="ajaxSpinner" value="#{spinnerController.intValue2}" >
  <p:ajax update="output" process="@this" />
</p:spinner>
<h:outputText id="output" value="#{spinnerController.intValue2}" />
```

Referring the ID of the output component with the update attribute does the actual update.

PrimeFaces Cookbook Showcase application

This recipe is available in the PrimeFaces Cookbook Showcase application on GitHub at https://github.com/ova2/primefaces-cookbook. You can find the details there for running the project. When the server is running, the showcase for the recipe is available at http://localhost:8080/primefaces-cookbook/views/chapter3/spinner.jsf.

Slider – different ways to provide input

The slider component provides the ability to the user to input a value by using a slider bar. The component requires an input component to work properly.

How to do it...

As mentioned earlier, we first need to define an input component that will be used by the slider component. The for attribute is used to set the ID of the input component whose input will be provided by the slider component. The basic definition of a slider would be as follows:

```
<h:inputText id="basicSlider" value="#{sliderController.intValue}" />
<p:slider for="basicSlider" />
```

This will render an input text along with a horizontal slider bar as follows:

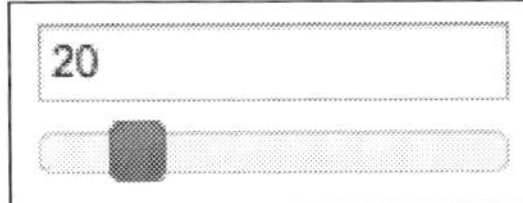

By default, the slider renders a horizontal bar for sliding. With the type attribute, the slider can also be set to render a vertical bar with the value set as vertical. The minValue attribute defines the minimum value of the slider with default value 0. The maxValue attribute defines the maximum value of the slider with default value 100. Also, by default, the slider provides animation when the background of the slider is clicked. This animation can be enabled/disabled with the animation attribute by setting its value as true or false. Its default value is true.

There's more...

The step attribute defines the amount of fixed pixels, which increments the movement of the slider with the default value of 1. The step attribute only supports integer values.

```
<h:inputText id="steppingSlider"
value="#{sliderController.intValue}" />
<p:slider for="steppingSlider" step="10" />
```

Displaying the value of the slider

With the `display` attribute, we can display the output of the slider while getting input from the user by using an `inputHidden` component. The `display` attribute should refer the `output` component while the `for` attribute refers the hidden input field.

```
<h:outputText id="output" value="#{sliderController.intValue}" />
<h:inputHidden id="displaySlider" value="#{sliderController.intValue}"
/>
<p:slider for="displaySlider" display="output"/>
```

Disabling manual input with the slider

By default, the `slider` component does not disable the manual input. To get input only with the slider bar without keyboard input, we need to define the `onfocus` attribute as follows:

```
<h:inputText id="minMaxSlider"
value="#{sliderController.intValue}" onfocus="this.readOnly=true;" />
<p:slider for="minMaxSlider" step="10" minValue="0" maxValue="100"  />
```

This will render an input field and a slider bar for which the user can enter values from `0` to `100` with an increment of 10 only by using the slider bar.

AJAX behavior events on slider

The `slider` component provides the `slideEnd` AJAX behavior event that will be fired when the slide gets completed.

```
<h:inputText id="ajaxSliderInput" value="#{sliderController.intValue}"
/>

<p:slider id="ajaxSlider" for="ajaxSliderInput">
  <p:ajax event="slideEnd" listener=
  "#{sliderController.onSlideEnd}" update="growl" />
</p:slider>
```

The `onSlideEnd` method will be invoked with `org.primefaces.event.SlideEndEvent`. The current value of the slider can be retrieved with `event.getValue()`, and a Faces message could be added with the current value, as in the following code snippet:

```
public void onSlideEnd(SlideEndEvent event) {
    int value = event.getValue();
    MessageUtil.addInfoMessage("selected.value", value);
}
```

PrimeFaces Cookbook Showcase application

This recipe is available in the PrimeFaces Cookbook Showcase application on GitHub at `https://github.com/ova2/primefaces-cookbook`. You can find the details there for running the project. When the server is running, the showcase for the recipe is available at `http://localhost:8080/primefaces-cookbook/views/chapter3/slider.jsf`.

See also

For details about the localization of the calender component, refer to the *Internationalization (i18n) and Localization (L10n)* recipe in *Chapter 1, Getting started with PrimeFaces*

Rich text editing with editor

`editor` is an input component that provides rich text editing features. It contains a toolbar that can also be configured with custom controls to provide more functionality to the user.

How to do it...

The basic component declaration for `editor`, which renders default controls such as indentation and font and color selection would be as follows:

```
<p:editor value="#{editorController.text}" />
```

The component will be rendered on the page with default controls as shown in the following screenshot:

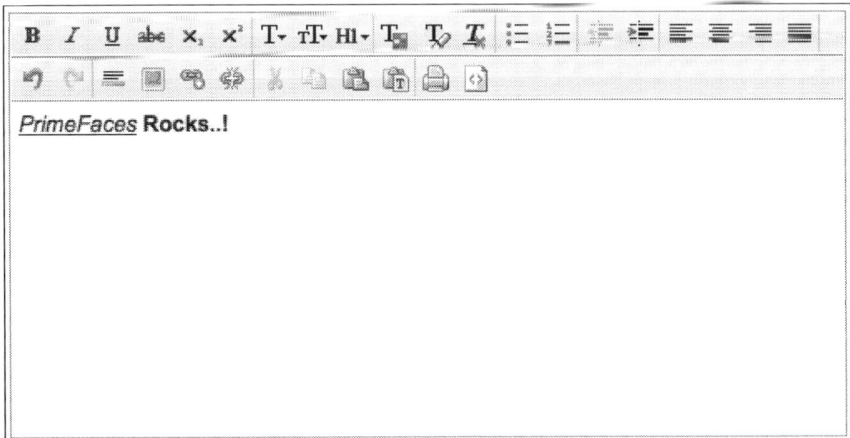

There's more...

The `editor` component offers the `controls` attribute, which can be used to customize the toolbar of the editor. For instance, the following declaration will render only three controls, `bold`, `italic`, and `strikethrough`:

```
<p:editor value="#{editorController.text}" controls="bold italic
strikethrough" />
```

The component will be rendered as shown in the following screenshot:

The list of available controls is as follows:

- `alignleft`
- `alignright`
- `bold`
- `bullets`
- `center`
- `color`
- `copy`
- `cut`
- `font`
- `highlight`
- `image`
- `indent`
- `italic`
- `justify`
- `link`
- `numbering`
- `outdent`

- paste
- pastetext
- print
- redo
- removeFormat
- rule
- size
- source
- strikethrough
- style
- subscript
- superscript
- underline
- undo
- unlink

Clearing the contents of the editor

The editor component also provides a client-side JavaScript API for execution of methods such as clearing the content of the editor. The editor can be reached within JavaScript with the declaration of the widgetVar attribute.

```
<p:editor value="#{editorController.text}" widgetVar="editor" />
<p:commandButton type="button" value="Clear" onclick="editor.clear()"
icon="ui-icon-close" />
```

Embedding the editor inside a dialog box

We can also embed the editor component inside a dialog box to get input from the user in a more user friendly manner.

```
<p:dialog widgetVar="editorDialog" modal="true">
  <p:editor />
</p:dialog>
<p:commandButton value="Show" onclick="editorDialog.show()" />
```

By clicking on the command button, the dialog box that contains the editor component will be rendered on the page as a modal dialog.

> editor is not integrated with ThemeRoller since there is only one icon set for the controls.
>
> At the time of writing this book, Internationalization is not supported by the editor component. All the tool tips for the controls are rendered in English.

PrimeFaces Cookbook Showcase application

This recipe is available in the PrimeFaces Cookbook Showcase application on GitHub at `https://github.com/ova2/primefaces-cookbook`. You can find the details there for running the project. When the server is running, the showcase for the recipe is available at `http://localhost:8080/primefaces-cookbook/views/chapter3/editor.jsf`.

Advanced editing with in-place editor

The `inplace` component provides easy in-place editing and inline content display. `in-place` consists of two members:

- The `display` element that is the initial clickable label
- The `inline` element, which is the hidden content that'll be displayed when the `display` element is toggled

How to do it...

The basic declaration of the component would be as follows:

```
<p:inplace>
  <h:inputText value="Edit Me!" />
</p:inplace>
```

This would render an input text field that could be clicked by the user to go into the edit mode. To go out of the edit mode, the user needs to click on the `enter` button after typing.

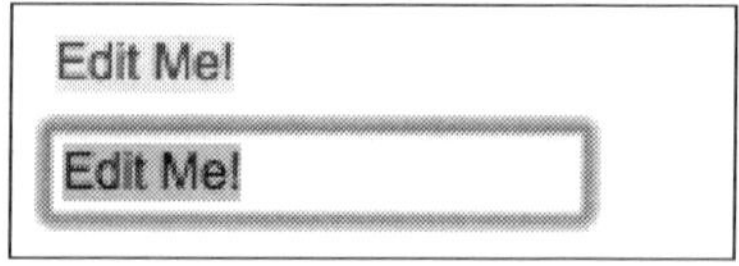

By default, the `inplace` component displays its first child's value as the label; this can also be customized with the `label` attribute. This attribute defines the label that will be shown in the display mode regardless of the text input by the user.

```
<p:inplace label="My Input Field">
  <h:inputText value="Edit Me!" />
</p:inplace>
```

The `emptyLabel` attribute defines the label that will be shown to the user when the value of the input field is empty. The value displayed will change to the provided one if the user, for instance, enters any text into the input field.

```
<p:inplace emptyLabel="My Empty Input Field">
  <h:inputText value="" />
</p:inplace>
```

Besides the input text field, other components such as the drop-down list could also be used with the in-place editor as seen in the following example:

```
<p:inplace label="Countries">
  <h:selectOneMenu>
    <f:selectItem itemLabel="Turkey" itemValue="Turkey" />
    <f:selectItem itemLabel="Germany" itemValue="Germany" />
  </h:selectOneMenu>
</p:inplace>
```

There's more...

The `editor` attribute specifies the mode of the editor with the default value `false`. When set to `true`, the `approve` and `cancel` buttons will be rendered right next to the editor, as shown in the following screenshot:

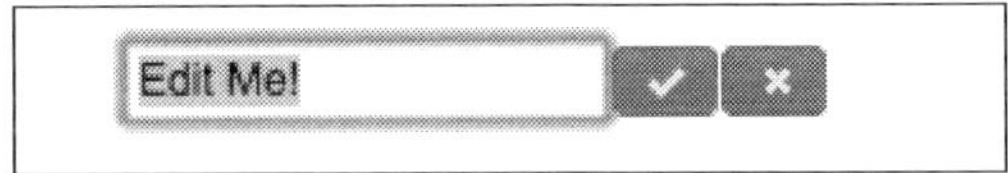

There are two attributes available for introducing i18n to the in-place input when the editor mode is set to `true`. The `saveLabel` attribute sets the tool-tip text of the `save` button with the default value `save`. The `cancelLabel` attribute sets the tool-tip text of the `cancel` button with the default value `Cancel`.

Giving effects to the in-place input

The `inplace` component also provides ways to customize the effects of editing with the attributes `effect` and `effectSpeed`. The `effect` attribute sets the effect to be used when toggling, with the default value `fade`. The other option is `slide`. When set to `slide`, the component will slide its content upside down when it's toggled. The `effectSpeed` attribute sets the speed of the effect with the default value `normal`. The other options for the attribute are `slow` and `fast`.

PrimeFaces Cookbook Showcase application

This recipe is available in the PrimeFaces Cookbook Showcase application on GitHub at `https://github.com/ova2/primefaces-cookbook`. You can find the details there for running the project. When the server is running, the showcase for the recipe is available at `http://localhost:8080/primefaces-cookbook/views/chapter3/inPlaceEditor.jsf`.

Enhanced password input

The `password` component is an extended version of the JSF `<h:inputSecret>` component, which also provides a strength indicator and the match mode.

How to do it...

The basic declaration for the component will provide no feedback on the input password, and will just render a simple input component.

```
<p:password value="#{passwordController.password}" />
```

To enable the strength indicator, the `feedback` attribute should be set to `true`. By default, the indicator will be rendered right next to the component when it is hovered.

When `feedback` is enabled, it's also possible to set the prompt label and the strength label with the `promptLabel`, `weakLabel`, `goodLabel`, and `strongLabel` attributes. This will help to localize the `password` input component `according to need`.

```
<p:password value="#{passwordController.password}"
        promptLabel="#{msg['password.promptLabel']}"
        weakLabel="#{msg['password.weakLabel']}"
        goodLabel="#{msg['password.goodLabel']}"
        strongLabel="#{msg['password.strongLabel']}"/>
```

To render the indicator in the inline mode without hovering, the `inline` attribute should be set to `true`.

How it works...

Strength testing is done by differently weighing the characters in the ranges [0-9], [a-zA-Z], and [!@#$%^&*?_~.,;=].

There's more...

It is also possible to check a password match by providing the match attribute, which identifies another password component with its ID to match the value against. The following panel grid definition contains a message component along with two password components and a command button, to invoke the validation.

```
<h:panelGrid id="passwords" columns="1">
  <p:messages id="messages" showDetail="true" />
  <p:password id="passwordMatch1"
  value="#{passwordController.password}" match="passwordMatch2" />
  <p:password id="passwordMatch2"
  value="#{passwordController.password}" />
  <p:commandButton update="passwords" value="Save" />
</h:panelGrid>
```

When the input password does not match the actual password, the validation error will be thrown as shown in the following screenshot:

PrimeFaces Cookbook Showcase application

This recipe is available in the PrimeFaces Cookbook Showcase application on GitHub at https://github.com/ova2/primefaces-cookbook. You can find the details there for running the project. When the server is running, the showcase for the recipe is available at http://localhost:8080/primefaces-cookbook/views/chapter3/password.jsf.

Star-based rating input

The `rating` component provides star-based rating with the ability to select and cancel.

How to do it...

The basic declaration for the component would be as follows:

```
<p:rating value="#{ratingController.rate}" />
```

Here `rate` is a `java.lang.Integer` definition. The default visual of the component will be as shown in the following screenshot:

The `stars` attribute sets the number of stars to display with a default value `5`.

There's more...

It is also possible to invoke a server-side method instantly when the user rates or cancels the rating. The `rating` component provides two AJAX behavior events for this, `rate` and `cancel`.

A sample definition that updates the `growl` component would be as follows:

```
<p:rating id="instantRating" value="#{ratingController.rate}">
  <p:ajax event="rate"
  listener="#{ratingController.handleRate}" update="growl" />
  <p:ajax event="cancel"
  listener="#{ratingController.cancelRate}" update="growl" />
</p:rating>
```

The `handleRate` method gets `org.primefaces.event.RateEvent`, as shown in the following code snippet, despite the `cancelRate` method that has no arguments. `rateEvent` contains the rating and can be retrieved as an object with the `getRating()` method.

```
public void handleRate(RateEvent rateEvent) {
  Integer rate = (Integer) rateEvent.getRating();
  MessageUtil.addInfoMessage("rating.selected", rate);
}
public void cancelRate() {
  MessageUtil.addInfoMessage("rating.cancelled");
}
```

PrimeFaces Cookbook Showcase application

This recipe is available in the PrimeFaces Cookbook Showcase application on GitHub at `https://github.com/ova2/primefaces-cookbook`. You can find the details there for running the project. When the server is running, the showcase for the recipe is available at `http://localhost:8080/primefaces-cookbook/views/chapter3/rating.jsf`.

See also

For details about the localization of the calender component, refer to the *Internationalization (i18n) and Localization (L10n)* recipe in *Chapter 1, Getting started with PrimeFaces*

4
Grouping Content with Panels

In this chapter we will cover:

- Grouping content with a standard panel
- Panel grid with colspan and rowspan support
- Vertical stacked panels with accordion
- Displaying overflowed content with scrollPanel
- Working with a tabbed panel
- Grouping of buttons and more with toolbar
- Simulating the portal environment with dashboard
- Creating complex layouts

Introduction

In this chapter, we will cover various container components such as panel, accordion, scroll panel, and tabbed panel, which allow grouping of JSF components.

Grouping content with a standard panel

`panel` is a generic grouping component for JSF components, with features such as toggling, closing, a built-in pop-up menu, and AJAX event listeners.

How to do it...

A basic definition for the panel would be as follows:

```
<p:panel id="simple" header="PrimeFaces" footer="The Cookbook">
  <h:outputText value="Open Source Primefaces is the leading JSF
Component Suite in the industry, which is adopted widely and being
used in production ready projects around the globe." />
</p:panel>
```

The preceding panel definition will be rendered as shown in the following screenshot:

PrimeFaces

Open Source Primefaces is the leading JSF Component Suite in the industry, which is adopted widely and being used in production ready projects around the globe.

The Cookbook

How it works...

The `header` and `footer` attributes can be used to render text at the top of the panel as a header and at the bottom of the panel as a footer. In order to make the panel closeable and toggleable, the `closeable` and `toggleable` attributes should be set to `true`. Once the panel gets closed, the page should be refreshed or the panel should be rerendered again to see the panel back. The toggling speed can also be adjusted by using the `toggleSpeed` attribute, which has the default value `1000` milliseconds. The title values for the buttons can be localized with the `closeTitle` and `toggleTitle` attributes, if needed.

```
<p:panel id="closeableToggleable" header="PrimeFaces" footer="The
Cookbook" closable="true" toggleable="true" toggleSpeed="3000">
  <h:outputText value="Open Source Primefaces is the leading JSF
Component Suite in the industry, which is adopted widely and being
used in production ready projects around the globe." />
</p:panel>
```

There's more...

The `panel` component has the `options` facet to provide a built-in menu that would be given within the facet. The definition for a menu with two menu items would be as follows:

```
<p:panel id="panelWithMenu" header="PrimeFaces" footer="The Cookbook"
widgetVar="panel" closable="true" toggleable="true">
  <h:outputText value="Open Source Primefaces is the leading JSF
Component Suite in the industry, which is adopted widely and being
used in production ready projects around the globe." />
```

```
    <f:facet name="options">
      <p:menu>
        <p:submenu label="Settings">
          <p:menuitem value="Toggle" url="#" icon="ui-icon-newwin"
          onclick="panel.toggle()"/>
          <p:menuitem value="Remove" url="#" icon="ui-icon-close"
          onclick="panel.close()"/>
        </p:submenu>
      </p:menu>
    </f:facet>
  </p:panel>
```

The menu will render with the **Settings** icon as shown in the following screenshot. The widget variable `panel` is being used by the menu items' `onclick` events for closing and toggling the panel.

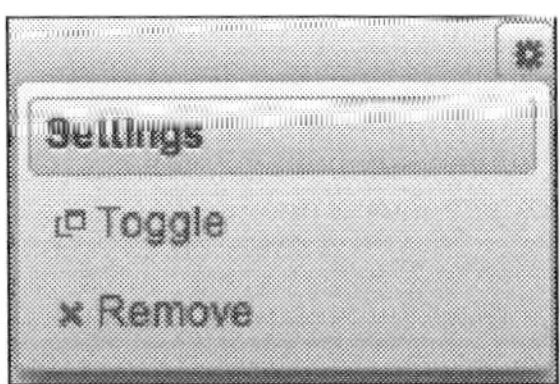

With the `toggleOrientation` attribute, it's possible to toggle the panels horizontally instead of the default vertical toggling. The value for the attribute could be either of the values `vertical` and `horizontal`.

AJAX behavior events on panel

The `panel` component supports the `close` and `toggle` AJAX behavior events that will be fired when the panel is closed or toggled. The definition of the panel with AJAX behavior events will be as follows:

```
<p:panel id="ajaxPanel" header="PrimeFaces" footer="The Cookbook"
closable="true" toggleable="true">
  <p:ajax event="close" listener="#{panelController.handleClose}"
  update="growl" />
  <p:ajax event="toggle"
  listener="#{panelController.handleToggle}" update="growl" />

  <h:outputText value="Open Source PrimeFaces is the leading JSF
  Component Suite in the industry, which is adopted widely and
  being used in production ready projects around the globe." />
</p:panel>
```

The listener methods `handleClose` and `handleToggle` receive `org.primefaces.event.CloseEvent` and `org.primefaces.event.ToggleEvent` as parameters, respectively.

```
public void handleClose(CloseEvent event) {
  MessageUtil.addInfoMessage("panel.closed", "Closed panel id:'" +
  event.getComponent().getId());
}

public void handleToggle(ToggleEvent event) {
  MessageUtil.addInfoMessage("panel.toggled", "Status:" +
  event.getVisibility().name());
}
```

To get the `id` of the closed panel, `event.getComponent().getId()` is used; and to retrieve the status of toggling, the visibility enumeration can be retrieved by using `event.getVisibility().name()`, which would be either `VISIBLE` or `HIDDEN`.

PrimeFaces Cookbook Showcase application

This recipe is available in the PrimeFaces Cookbook Showcase application on GitHub at `https://github.com/ova2/primefaces-cookbook`. You can find the details there for running the project. When the server is running, the showcase for the recipe is available at `http://localhost:8080/primefaces-cookbook/views/chapter4/panel.jsf`.

See also

- For details about the `MessageUtil` class, refer to the *Internationalization (i18n) and Localization (L10n)* section in *Chapter 1, Getting Started with PrimeFaces*

Panel grid with colspan and rowspan support

The `panelGrid` component extends the JSF `<h:panelGrid>` component with support of `colspan`, the number of columns a cell should span, and `rowspan`, the number of rows a cell should span, and the theming ability.

How to do it...

A basic definition for the panel grid would be as follows:

```
<p:panelGrid columns="2">
  <f:facet name="header">User Information</f:facet>
```

```
    <h:outputLabel for="firstname" value="First Name" />
    <p:inputText id="firstname" value="" label="firstname" />

    <h:outputLabel for="lastname" value="Last Name" />
    <p:inputText id="lastname" value="" required="true"
    label="lastname"/>

    <f:facet name="footer">
      <p:commandButton type="button" value="Save" icon="ui-icon-check"
      style="margin:0"/>
    </f:facet>
  </p:panelGrid>
```

This will render two columns with header and footer facets, as shown in the following screenshot:

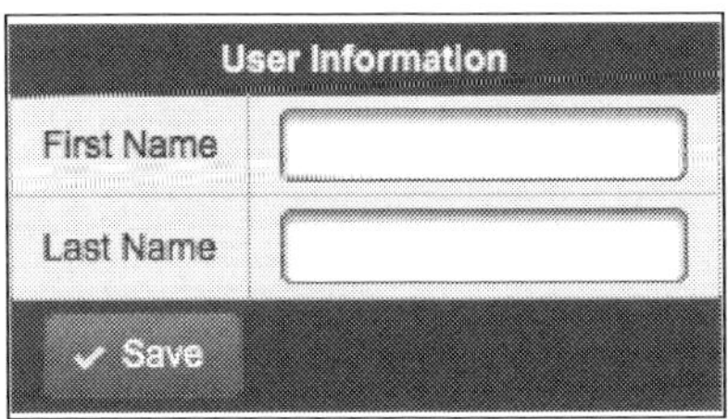

How it works...

The `p:row` and `p:column` components can be used to provide column and row spanning on the grid. They could either be used in the `header` or `footer` facets or within the content of the panel. Here is a sample with the definition and the visual result.

```
<p:panelGrid style="margin-top:20px">
  <f:facet name="header">
    <p:row>
      <p:column colspan="6">Time Chart</p:column>
    </p:row>
    <p:row>
      <p:column/>
        <p:column>Monday</p:column>
        <p:column>Tuesday</p:column>
        <p:column>Wednesday</p:column>
        <p:column>Thursday</p:column>
      <p:column>Friday</p:column>
    </p:row>
  </f:facet>
```

```
    <p:row>
      <p:column rowspan="6">Hours</p:column>
      <p:column>Science</p:column>
      <p:column>Math</p:column>
      <p:column rowspan="2"
      style="text-align:center">Project</p:column>
      <p:column>Math</p:column>
      <p:column>Arts</p:column>
    </p:row>

    <p:row>
      <p:column>Social</p:column>
      <p:column>History</p:column>
      <p:column>Sports</p:column>
      <p:column>Math</p:column>
    </p:row>

    <p:row>
      <p:column colspan="6"
      style="text-align:center">Lunch</p:column>
    </p:row>

    <p:row>
      <p:column>Math</p:column>
      <p:column>History</p:column>
      <p:column>English</p:column>
      <p:column>Science</p:column>
      <p:column>Arts</p:column>
    </p:row>

    <f:facet name="footer">
      <p:row>
        <p:column colspan="6">Duration: 40 minutes</p:column>
      </p:row>
    </f:facet>
  </p:panelGrid>
```

The sample definition given for column and row spanning will be rendered as shown in the following screenshot:

Time Chart					
	Monday	Tuesday	Wednesday	Thursday	Friday
Hours	Science	Math	Project	Math	Arts
	Social	History		Sports	Math
	Lunch				
	Math	History	English	Science	Arts
Duration: 40 minutes					

PrimeFaces Cookbook Showcase application

This recipe is available in the PrimeFaces Cookbook Showcase application on GitHub at `https://github.com/ova2/primefaces-cookbook`. You can find the details there for running the project. When the server is running, the showcase for the recipe is available at `http://localhost:8080/primefaces-cookbook/views/chapter4/panelGrid.jsf`.

Vertical stacked panels with accordion

`accordionPanel` is a container component that provides the ability to group multiple tabs.

How to do it...

A basic definition for the accordion panel with two panels would be as follows:

```
<p:accordionPanel>
  <p:tab title="Volkswagen CC">
    <h:panelGrid columns="2" cellpadding="10">
      <h:graphicImage
      library="images" name="autocomplete/CC.png" />
      <h:outputText value="The Volkswagen CC (also known as the
      Volkswagen Passat CC) is a four-door coupé version of the
      Volkswagen Passat." />
    </h:panelGrid>
  </p:tab>
```

```
      <p:tab title="Volkswagen Golf">
        <h:panelGrid columns="2" cellpadding="10">
          <h:graphicImage
          library="images" name="autocomplete/Golf.png" />
          <h:outputText value="The Volkswagen Golf is a small family
          car manufactured by Volkswagen since 1974 and marketed
          worldwide across six generations, in various body
          configurations and under various nameplates" />
        </h:panelGrid>
      </p:tab>
    </p:accordionPanel>
```

The visual output for the panel will be as follows:

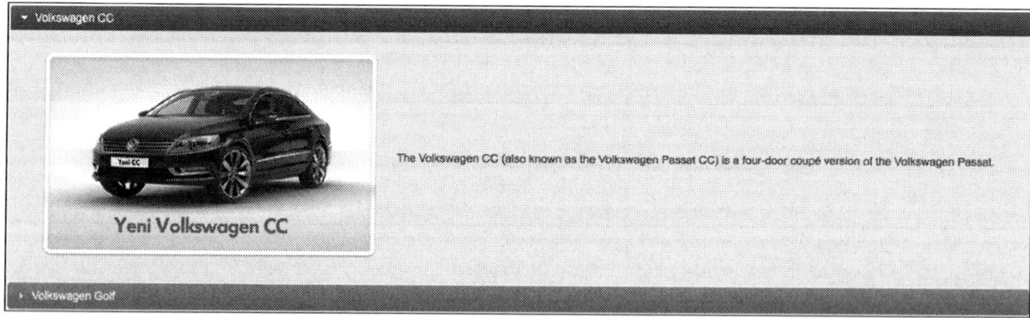

How it works...

The `multiple` attribute enables activating multiple tabs. With the value set as `enabled`, the active tab will not collapse when another tab gets activated. The default value of the attribute is `false`.

Dynamic content loading

By setting the `dynamic` attribute to `true`, it's also possible to lazily load the content of the tabs with an AJAX request when they get activated, in order to save the bandwidth and reduce the size of the page. Also, by setting the `cache` attribute to `true`, consecutive invokes on the same tab will not invoke an AJAX request.

Dynamic tabbing

Dynamic tab loading allows us to load the content of the accordion panel dynamically, by providing a data model. The component definition for providing a list of car data to `accordionPanel` would be as follows:

```
<p:accordionPanel value="#{accordionPanelController.cars}" var="car">
  <p:tab title="#{car.name}">
    <h:panelGrid columns="2" cellpadding="5">
      <p:graphicImage value=
      "/resources/images/autocomplete/#{car.name}.png" />
      <h:outputText value="#{car.name}" />
    </h:panelGrid>
  </p:tab>
</p:accordionPanel>
```

The data model here is the list of car objects that will be iterated through for rendering each panel along with the image and the name of the car.

PrimeFaces Cookbook Showcase application

This recipe is available in the PrimeFaces Cookbook Showcase application on GitHub at `https://github.com/ova2/primefaces-cookbook`. You can find the details there for running the project. When the server is running, the showcase for the recipe is available at `http://localhost:8080/primefaces-cookbook/views/chapter4/accordionPanel.jsf`.

Displaying overflowed content with scrollPanel

The `scollPanel` component provides customizable scroll bars instead of the browser's scrolls.

How to do it...

A basic definition for a scroll panel with a width of 500 pixels and a height of 500 pixels would be as follows:

```
<p:scrollPanel style="width:500px;height:500px">
  <p:dataGrid var="car" value="#{scrollPanelController.cars}"
  columns="2">
    <p:panel header="#{car.name}" style="text-align:center">
      <p:graphicImage value=
      "/resources/images/autocomplete/#{car.name}.png" />
    </p:panel>
  </p:dataGrid>
</p:scrollPanel>
```

This will render a list of car models within a data grid. The visual size of the grid will be limited to a 500 by 500 pixels view, and the content can be scrollable horizontally and vertically. By default, customized scrollbars will be rendered as shown in the following screenshot:

How it works...

The `mode` attribute defines whether the component should render customized scroll bars with the value `scrollbar` or use the browser's default ones with the value `native`.

PrimeFaces Cookbook Showcase application

This recipe is available in the PrimeFaces Cookbook Showcase application on GitHub at `https://github.com/ova2/primefaces-cookbook`. You can find the details there for running the project. When the server is running, the showcase for the recipe is available at `http://localhost:8080/primefaces-cookbook/views/chapter4/scrollPanel.jsf`.

Working with a tabbed panel

`tabView` is a tabbed panel component with powerful features such as dynamic content loading, orientations, and programmatically managing tabs.

How to do it...

A basic definition for a tabbed panel with two panels would be as follows:

```
<p:tabView id="tabView">
  <p:tab title="Volkswagen CC">
    <h:panelGrid columns="2" cellpadding="5">
      <h:graphicImage
      library="images" name="autocomplete/CC.png" />
      <h:outputText value=
      "The Volkswagen CC (also known as the Volkswagen Passat CC)
      is a four-door coupé version of the Volkswagen Passat." />
    </h:panelGrid>
  </p:tab>
  <p:tab title="Volkswagen Golf">
    <h:panelGrid columns="2" cellpadding="5">
      <h:graphicImage
      library="images" name="autocomplete/Golf.png" />
      <h:outputText value="The Volkswagen Golf is a small family
      car manufactured by Volkswagen since 1974 and marketed
      worldwide across six generations, in various body
      configurations and under various nameplates" />
    </h:panelGrid>
  </p:tab>
</p:tabView>
```

This will render two tabs with the first tab activated by default as shown in the following screenshot:

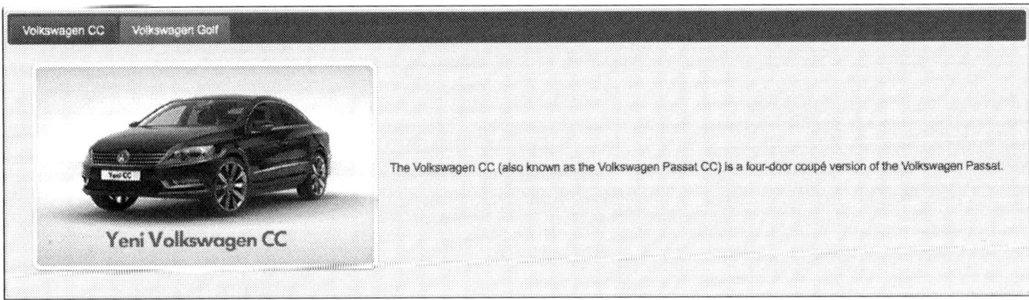

We can also enable or disable a tab within the tab view according to a business rule. If we set the `disabled` attribute to `true` in the tab, the tab will have a grayed-out caption that indicates the tab is disabled.

```
<p:tabView id="tabView4">
  <p:tab id="tab5" title="Volkswagen CC">
    <h:panelGrid columns="2" cellpadding="5">
      <h:graphicImage
      library="images" name="autocomplete/CC.png" />
      <h:outputText value="The Volkswagen CC (also known as the
      Volkswagen Passat CC) is a four-door coupé version of the
      Volkswagen Passat." />
    </h:panelGrid>
  </p:tab>
  <p:tab id="tab6" title="Volkswagen Golf" disabled="true">
    <h:panelGrid columns="2" cellpadding="5">
      <h:graphicImage
      library="images" name="autocomplete/Golf.png" />
      <h:outputText value="The Volkswagen Golf is a small family
      car manufactured by Volkswagen since 1974 and marketed
      worldwide across six generations, in various body
      configurations and under various nameplates" />
    </h:panelGrid>
  </p:tab>
</p:tabView>
```

This will be rendered as shown in the following screenshot:

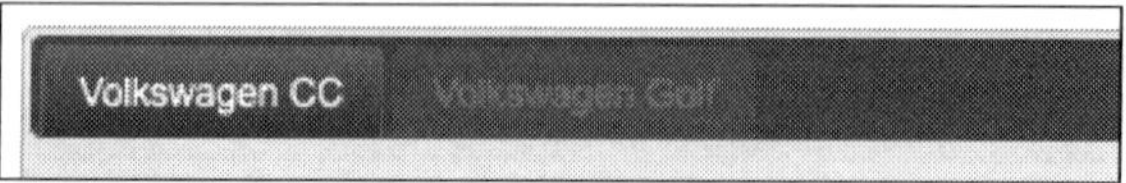

How it works...

By setting the `dynamic` attribute to `true`, it's also possible to lazily load the content of the tabs with an AJAX request when they get activated, in order to save bandwidth and reduce the size of the page. And by also setting the `cache` attribute to `true`, consecutive invokes on the same tab will not invoke an AJAX request.

Orientation of the tabs

Orientation of the tabs can be set with four positions—`top`, `bottom`, `left`, and `right`. By default, the orientation for the tabs is `top`.

Dynamic tabbing

Dynamic tab loading allows us to load the content of the tab view dynamically, by providing a data model. The component definition to provide a list of car data to `accordionPanel` would be as follows:

```
<p:tabView value="#{accordionPanelController.cars}" var="car">
  <p:tab title="#{car.name}">
    <h:panelGrid columns="2" cellpadding="5">
      <p:graphicImage value=
      "/resources/images/autocomplete/#{car.name}.png" />
    </h:panelGrid>
  </p:tab>
</p:tabView>
```

The data model here is the list of car objects that will be iterated through for rendering each tab along with the image and the name of the car.

Transition effects

Effects can be applied for content transition between the tabs, with the `effect` attribute. The possible values are as follows:

- `blind`
- `clip`
- `drop`
- `explode`
- `fade`
- `fold`
- `puff`
- `scale`
- `slide`

The effect duration can also be set with the `effectDuration` attribute. The possible values are `slow`, `normal`, and `fast`.

PrimeFaces Cookbook Showcase application

This recipe is available in the PrimeFaces Cookbook Showcase application on GitHub at `https://github.com/ova2/primefaces-cookbook`. You can find the details there for running the project. When the server is running, the showcase for the recipe is available at `http://localhost:8080/primefaces-cookbook/views/chapter4/tabView.jsf`.

Grouping of buttons and more with toolbar

`toolbar` is a horizontal grouping component that can be used for grouping commands and other components. By default, `toolbar` has two placeholders, `left` and `right`, which can be defined with the `toolbarGroup` component. There is no limit on the number of components that can be put inside the `toolbarGroup` component.

How to do it...

A definition for a toolbar with multiple groups would be as follows:

```
<p:toolbar>
  <p:toolbarGroup align="left">
    <p:commandButton
    type="push" value="New" icon="ui-icon-document" />
    <p:commandButton type="push"
    value="Open" icon="ui-icon-folder-open"/>
    <p:separator />
    <p:commandButton
    type="push" title="Save" icon="ui-icon-disk"/>
    <p:commandButton
    type="push" title="Delete" icon="ui-icon-trash"/>
    <p:commandButton
    type="push" title="Print" icon="ui-icon-print"/>
  </p:toolbarGroup>

  <p:toolbarGroup align="right">
    <p:menuButton value="Navigate">
      <p:menuitem value="Home" url="#" />
      <p:menuitem value="Logout" url="#" />
    </p:menuButton>
  </p:toolbarGroup>
</p:toolbar>
```

This definition will be visualized as shown in the following screenshot:

How it works...

The `separator` component can be used for visually separating the components from each other, such as between the components inside the `toolbarGroup` component.

PrimeFaces Cookbook Showcase application

This recipe is available in the PrimeFaces Cookbook Showcase application on GitHub at `https://github.com/ova2/primefaces-cookbook`. You can find the details there for running the project. When the server is running, the showcase for the recipe is available at http://localhost:8080/primefaces-cookbook/views/chapter4/toolbar.jsf.

Simulating the portal environment with dashboard

The `dashboard` component is a layout component with the drag-and-drop ability to support reordering of the panels.

How to do it...

A basic definition for a dashboard with six panels would be as follows:

```
<p:dashboard id="board" model="#{dashboardController.model}">
  <p:ajax event="reorder" listener=
  "#{dashboardController.handleReorder}" update="growl" />

  <p:panel id="calculator" header="Calculator">
    <h:outputText value="Content for Calculator" />
  </p:panel>

  <p:panel id="calendar" header="Calendar">
    <h:outputText value="Content for Calendar" />
  </p:panel>

  <p:panel id="contact" header="Contacts">
    <h:outputText value="Content for Contacts"  />
  </p:panel>

  <p:panel id="dictionary" header="Dictionary">
    <h:outputText value="Weather Content for Dictionary" />
  </p:panel>

  <p:panel id="weather" header="Weather">
    <h:outputText value="Content for Weather" />
  </p:panel>

  <p:panel id="translation" header="Translation">
    <h:outputText value="Content for Translation" />
  </p:panel>
</p:dashboard>
```

A data model needs to be provided in order to preserve the panel order. The data model depends on `org.primefaces.model.DefaultDashboardModel`. The model for the basic sample given would be as follows:

```
DashboardColumn column1 = new DefaultDashboardColumn();
DashboardColumn column2 = new DefaultDashboardColumn();
DashboardColumn column3 = new DefaultDashboardColumn();

column1.addWidget("calculator");
column1.addWidget("calendar");
column1.addWidget("contact");

column2.addWidget("dictionary");

column3.addWidget("weather");
column3.addWidget("translation");

model.addColumn(column1);
model.addColumn(column2);
model.addColumn(column3);
```

This dashboard definition contains three columns and six panels. The appearance will be as follows:

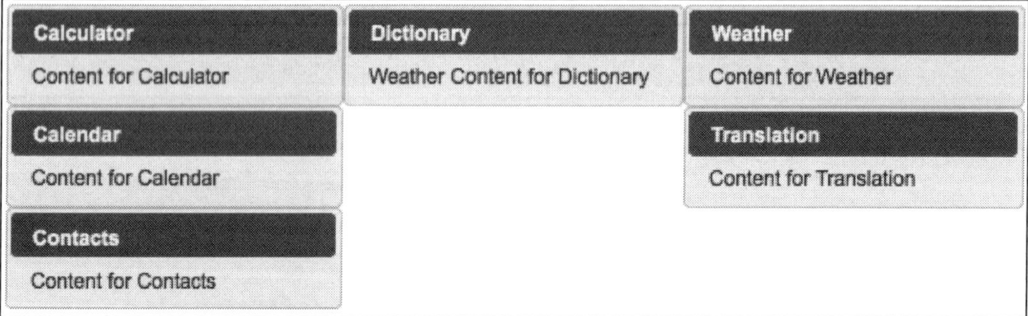

How it works...

The `dashboard` component supports the reordering AJAX behavior event that will be fired when a panel is dragged-and-dropped. The listener method `handleReorder` receives `org.primefaces.event.DashboardReorderEvent` as a parameter.

```
public void handleReorder(DashboardReorderEvent event) {
  MessageUtil.addInfoMessageWithoutKey
  ("Reordered: " + event.getWidgetId(),
```

```
        "Item index: " + event.getItemIndex() + ", Column index: " +
        event.getColumnIndex() + ", Sender column index: " +
        event.getSenderColumnIndex());
    }
```

As seen in the `handleReorder` method, the information about the drag-and-drop action is communicated to the user by adding it as a Faces message. The order number of the panel can be retrieved from the `event.getItemIndex()` method. The number of the column from which the panel has been dragged can be retrieved by `event.getColumnIndex()`, and the number of the column that the panel will be dragged onto can be retrieved from `event.getSenderColumnIndex()`.

Having fixed-sized columns

By default, if the user moves panels from one column to another and gets one column empty, it cannot be filled again by dragging panels back. To have columns of a fixed size, the `ui-dashboard-column` style should be defined with the preferred width, as shown in the following code snippet:

```
.ui-dashboard-column {
    width:200px;
}
```

PrimeFaces Cookbook Showcase application

This recipe is available in the PrimeFaces Cookbook Showcase application on GitHub at `https://github.com/ova2/primefaces-cookbook`. You can find the details there for running the project. When the server is running, the showcase for the recipe is available at `http://localhost:8080/primefaces-cookbook/views/chapter4/dashboard.jsf`.

Creating complex layouts

The `layout` component introduces a customizable border layout model that could easily be used for creating complex layouts.

How to do it...

Layout can be applied either to a full page or to a specific element. A basic definition of a full-page layout would be as follows:

```
<p:layout fullPage="true">
    <p:layoutUnit position="north" size="100" header=
    "Top" resizable="true" closable="true" collapsible="true">
```

```
        <h:outputText value="Layout content for North" />
    </p:layoutUnit>

    <p:layoutUnit position="south" size="100" header="Bottom"
    resizable="true" closable="true" collapsible="true">
        <h:outputText value="Layout content for South" />
    </p:layoutUnit>

    <p:layoutUnit position="west" size="200" header=
    "Left" resizable="true" closable="true" collapsible="true">
        <h:outputText value="Layout content for West" />
    </p:layoutUnit>

    <p:layoutUnit position="east" size="200" header=
    "Right" resizable="true" closable="true" collapsible="true">
        <h:outputText value="Layout content for Right" />
    </p:layoutUnit>

    <p:layoutUnit position="center">
        <h:outputText value="Layout content for Center" />
    </p:layoutUnit>
</p:layout>
```

This will render five panels as shown in the following screenshot:

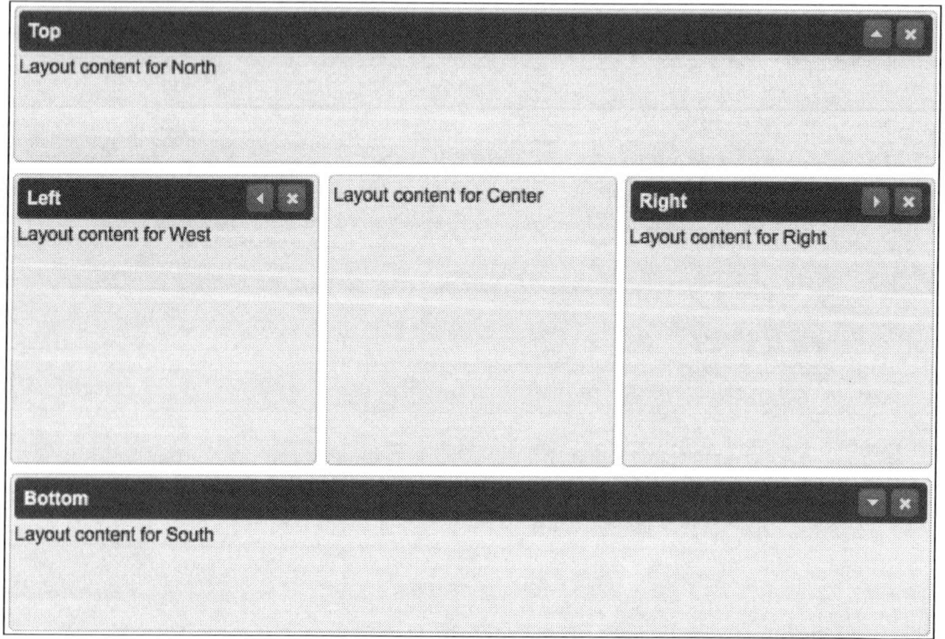

How it works...

The `fullPage` attribute defines whether the layout should span to the full page or a specific region or not. As layout is based on the border layout model, it contains five layout units: top, left, center, right, and bottom, as shown in the following screenshot. Layout units get placed to the positions respectively: top matches to north, left matches to west, bottom matches to south, right matches to east, and center unit matches to center.

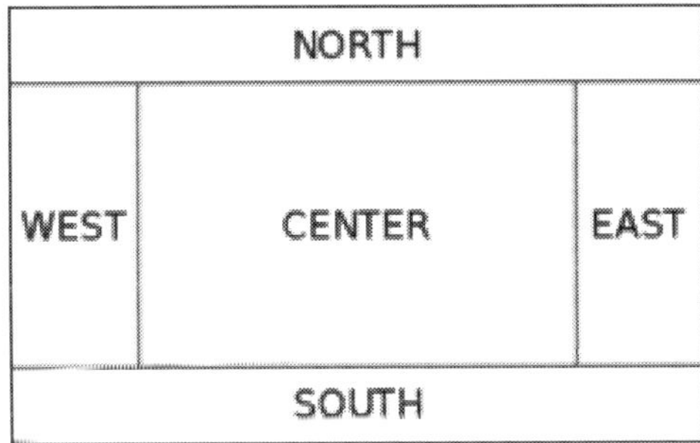

Layout can contain the `<p:layoutUnit>` components for five different positions, according to the border layout. The `position` attribute defines this positioning of the layout unit within the layout. The `layoutUnit` component can have the `resizable`, `closable`, and `collapsible` attributes for interaction.

In addition, the layout state can be preserved with the `stateful` attribute. When enabled, the layout state is saved in a cookie for the session. The `header` and `footer` attributes define the text that will be rendered for the layout unit.

```
<p:layout stateful="true">
...
</p:layout>
```

There's more...

When working with full-page layouts, using layout units within a `form` component is invalid. Instead of this, a layout unit must have a form owned by itself. Also, instead of updating the layout unit components directly, their content should be updated while doing a partial page rendering. An invalid definition for usage of the `form` component is as follows:

```
<p:layout fullPage="true">
  <h:form>
    <p:layoutUnit position="north">
      <h:outputText value="Layout content for North" />
    </p:layoutUnit>
```

```
        <p:layoutUnit position="center">
          <h:outputText value="Layout content for Center" />
        </p:layoutUnit>
      </h:form>
    </p:layout>
```

The `gutter` attribute defines the size of the space that will be left between the adjacent units, in pixels. The `minSize` and `maxSize` attributes define the minimum and maximum sizing of the layout units that will be set after resizing.

Element-based layouts

By setting the `fullPage` attribute to `false`, which is the default value, the layout can be used as a component within the page, as shown in the following screenshot:

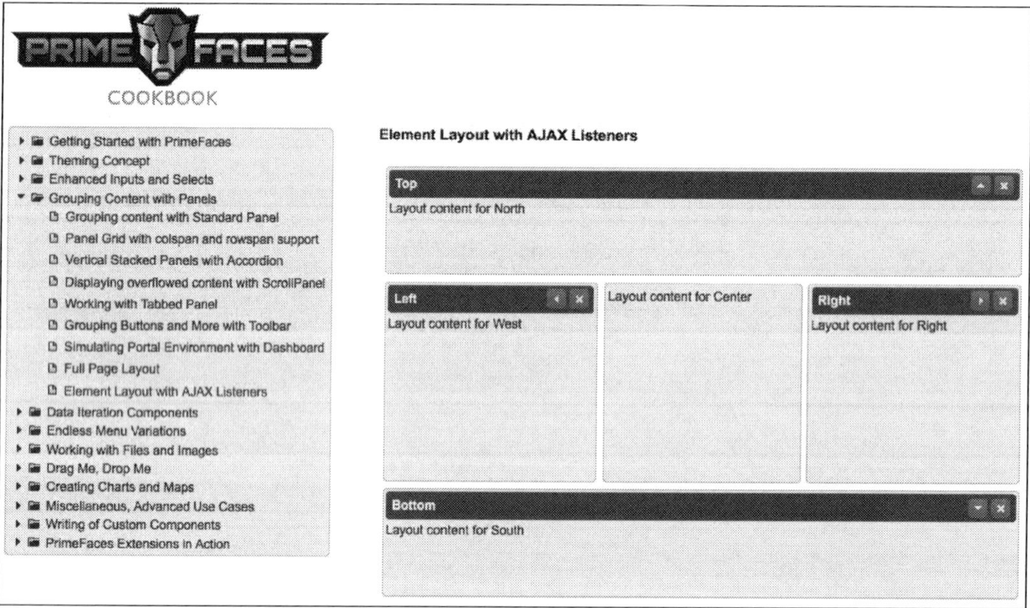

With element-based layout, CSS should be used for styling the layout component as defined in the following code snippet:

```
<p:layout id="elementLayout" style="min-width:600px;min-
height:400px;">
...
</p:layout>
```

Nested layouts

Layout unit components can also contain a layout component to provide nested layout abilities.

```
<p:layout id="elementLayout" style="min-width:600px;min-
height:400px;">
  <p:layoutUnit position="north" size="100" header=
  "Top" resizable="true" closable="true" collapsible="true">
    <h:outputText value="Layout content for North" />
  </p:layoutUnit>

  <p:layoutUnit position="south" size="100" header=
  "Bottom" resizable="true" closable="true" collapsible="true">
    <h:outputText value="Layout content for South" />
  </p:layoutUnit>

  <p:layoutUnit position="center">
    <p:layout>
      <p:layoutUnit position="north" size="100" resizable=
      "true" closable="true" collapsible="true">
        <h:outputText value="Layout content for Top of Center" />
      </p:layoutUnit>

      <p:layoutUnit position="center">
        <h:outputText value="Center of Center" />
      </p:layoutUnit>
    </p:layout>
  </p:layoutUnit>
</p:layout>
```

The visual output of the code will be as shown in the following screenshot:

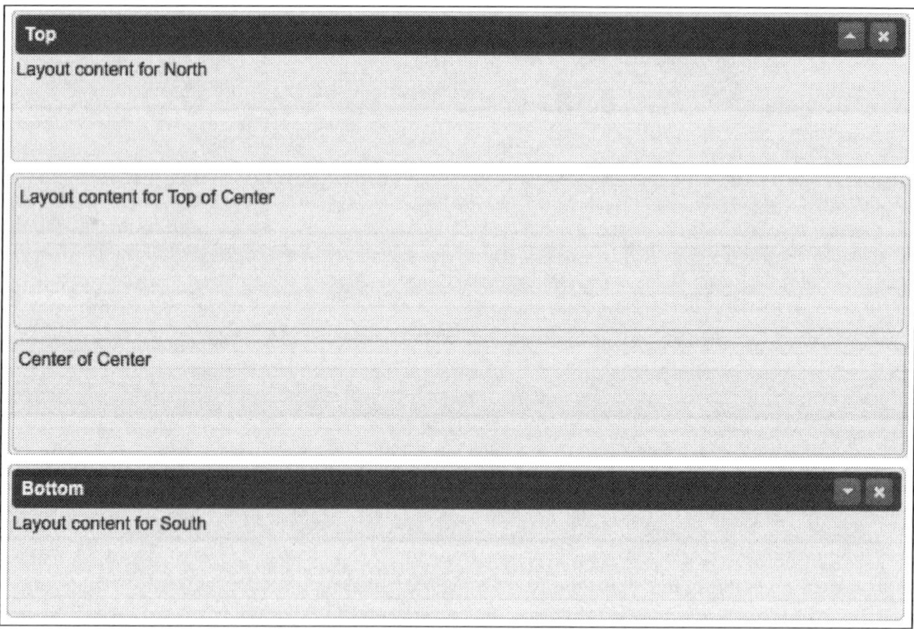

AJAX behavior events on layout

The `layout` component provides `toggle`, `close`, and `resize` AJAX behavior events, which will be fired when the layout unit is toggled, closed, or resized. The definition of the event listeners for the layout component would be as follows:

```
<p:ajax event="toggle" listener="#{layoutController.handleToggle}"
update="growl" />
<p:ajax event="close" listener="#{layoutController.handleClose}"
update="growl" />
<p:ajax event="resize" listener="#{layoutController.handleResize}"
update="growl" />
```

The listener methods `handleToggle`, `handleClose`, and `handleResize` receive `org.primefaces.event.ToggleEvent`, `org.primefaces.event.CloseEvent`, and `org.primefaces.event.ResizeEvent` as parameters respectively.

```
public void handleClose(CloseEvent event) {
  MessageUtil.addInfoMessageWithoutKey("Unit Closed", "Position:'"
  + ((LayoutUnit) event.getComponent()).getPosition());
}
```

```
public void handleToggle(ToggleEvent event) {
  MessageUtil.addInfoMessageWithoutKey(((LayoutUnit)event.
  getComponent()).getPosition() + " toggled", "Status:" +
  event.getVisibility().name());
}

public void handleResize(ResizeEvent event) {
  MessageUtil.addInfoMessageWithoutKey(((LayoutUnit)event.
  getComponent()).getPosition() + " resized", "Status:" +
  event.getComponent().getId());
}
```

The visibility of the layout unit can be retrieved from `event.getVisibility().name()`, and the position of the layout unit can be retrieved by casting the component to the layout as `((LayoutUnit) event.getComponent()).getPosition()`.

PrimeFaces Cookbook Showcase application

This recipe is available in the PrimeFaces Cookbook Showcase application on GitHub at `https://github.com/ova2/primefaces-cookbook`. You can find the details there for running the project. When the server is running, the showcase for the recipe is available at the following URLs:

- `http://localhost:8080/primefaces-cookbook/views/chapter4/fullPageLayout.jsf`
- `http://localhost:8080/primefaces-cookbook/views/chapter4/elementLayout.jsf`
- `http://localhost:8080/primefaces-cookbook/views/chapter4/nestedLayout.jsf`

5
Data Iteration Components

In this chapter we will cover:

- Selecting rows in dataTable
- Sorting and filtering data in dataTable
- In-cell editing with dataTable
- Conditional coloring in dataTable
- Handling tons of data – LazyDataModel
- Listing data with dataList
- Listing data with pickList
- Listing data with orderList
- Visualizing data with Tree
- Visualizing data with treeTable
- Exporting data in various formats
- Visualizing data with carousel
- Visualizing data with ring

Introduction

In this chapter, we will cover the basic and advanced features to visualize data with the data iteration components provided by PrimeFaces.

Selecting rows in dataTable

There are several ways to select a row or multiple rows, such as line selection or selection with radio buttons or checkboxes, from the `dataTable` component. We will cover all the possibilities in this recipe.

How to do it...

To make a single selection possible with a command component, such as `commandLink` or `commandButton`, `f:setPropertyActionListener` can be used to set the selected row as a parameter to the server side.

```
<p:dataTable id="withCommand" var="car"
value="#{dataTableController.cars}"
rowKey="#{car.name}"
selection="#{dataTableController.selectedCar}">
<p:column>
<p:commandButton value="Select" update=":mainForm:display"
oncomplete="carDialog.show()">
<f:setPropertyActionListener value="#{car}"
target="#{dataTableController.selectedCar}" />
</p:commandButton>
</p:column>
...
</p:dataTable>
```

The `selection` attribute needs to be bound to a `Car` reference in order to get the selected data.

There's more...

The `selectionMode` attribute could be used to enable the selection whenever a row is clicked. Its value should be `single` for single selection mode. The selection attribute should be bound to an instance of the `Car` class. For selecting multiple items with the modifier key (for example, *Ctrl* in Windows or *Command* in MacOS), the `selectionMode` attribute should be set to `multiple` and the selection attribute needs to be bound to an array of the `Car` reference.

```
<p:dataTable id="multipleSelection" var="car"
value="#{dataTableController.cars}" rowKey="#{car.name}"
selection="#{dataTableController.selectedCars}"
selectionMode="multiple">
...
</p:dataTable>
```

Single selection with radio buttons

The `dataTable` component supports single row selection with the help of radio buttons out of the box. This can be achieved by defining a column with the `selectionMode` attribute, set with the value `single`.

```
<p:dataTable id="withRadioButton" var="car"
value="#{dataTableController.cars}" rowKey="#{car.name}"
selection="#{dataTableController.selectedCar}">
<p:column selectionMode="single"/>
...
</p:dataTable>
```

The table will be rendered as follows:

	Year	Name
	2002	Touareg
	1974	Scirocco
	2008	CC
	1975	Polo
	1973	Passat
	1974	Golf
	1979	Jetta

View

Multiple selection with checkboxes

It's very easy to enable multiple item selection with `dataTable` by defining a column with the value of the `selectionMode` attribute set to `multiple`, as follows:

```
<p:dataTable id="multipleSelectionCheckbox" var="car"
value="#{dataTableController.cars}" rowKey="#{car.name}"
selection="#{dataTableController.selectedCars}">
<p:column selectionMode="multiple"/>
...
</p:dataTable>
```

The component will also provide a `selectAll` checkbox at the top for convenience. The appearance of the table with multiple selections will be as follows:

Year	Name
2002	Touareg
1974	Scirocco
2008	CC
1975	Polo
1973	Passat
1974	Golf
1979	Jetta

PrimeFaces Cookbook Showcase application

This recipe is available in the PrimeFaces Cookbook Showcase application on GitHub at `https://github.com/ova2/primefaces-cookbook`. You can find the details there for running the project. When the server is running, the showcase for the recipe is available at `http://localhost:8080/primefaces-cookbook/views/chapter5/dataTableSelectRow.jsf`.

Sorting and filtering data in dataTable

The `dataTable` component provides AJAX-based built-in sorting and filtering based on its columns.

How to do it...

`dataTable` provides sorting options based on AJAX, by enabling the `sortBy` attribute at column level. The following is the definition of a table that lists the `Car` data. Sorting is enabled on the `name` and `year` attributes.

```
<p:dataTable id="sorting" var="car" value="#{dataTableController.
cars}">
<p:columnheaderText="Year" sortBy="#{car.year}">
<h:outputText value="#{car.year}" />
```

```
</p:column>
<p:columnheaderText="Name" sortBy="#{car.name}">

<h:outputText value="#{car.name}" />
</p:column>
</p:dataTable>
```

The appearance of a table with sorting enabled will be like the following screenshot:

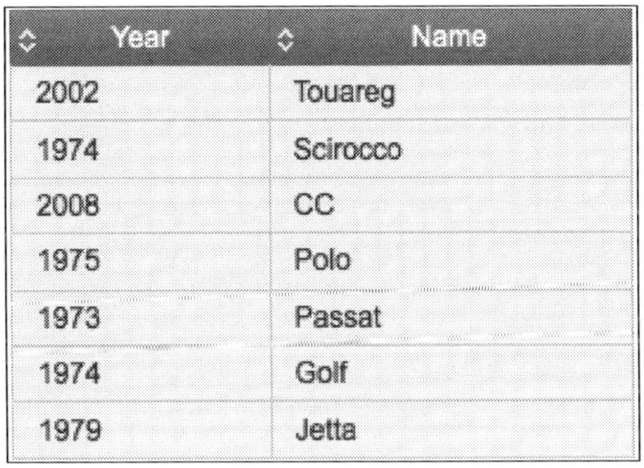

Year	Name
2002	Touareg
1974	Scirocco
2008	CC
1975	Polo
1973	Passat
1974	Golf
1979	Jetta

There's more...

`dataTable` provides filtering based on AJAX by enabling the `filterBy` attribute for the columns. The following is the definition of a table that lists the `Car` data. Filtering is enabled on the `name` and `year` attributes.

```
<p:dataTable id="filtering" var="car" value="#{dataTableController.
cars}">
<p:columnheaderText="Year" filterBy="#{car.year}">
<h:outputText value="#{car.year}" />
</p:column>
<p:columnheaderText="Name" filterBy="#{car.name}">
<h:outputText value="#{car.name}" />
</p:column>
</p:dataTable>
```

The appearance of a table with filtering enabled will be like the following screenshot:

Year	Name
2002	Touareg
1974	Scirocco
2008	CC
1975	Polo
1973	Passat
1974	Golf
1979	Jetta

Also, it is possible to set filter matching with custom matchers. The `filterMatchMode` attribute enables this built-in matcher mechanism, which is set to `startsWith` by default. Other possible values are `contains`, `exact`, and `endsWith`, which indicate how text matching will be done with the given input filter, as the attribute name implies.

The filter text field can be positioned before or after the header text by setting the `filterPosition` attribute. The values can either be `top` or `bottom` (the latter is the default value).

With the `filterMaxLength` attribute, it is possible to restrict the filter input according to the given number of characters, for example, `filterMaxLength="2"`.

It should be kept in mind that these attributes will have no effect when lazy loading is implemented for the DataModel.

For the sorting and filtering to work properly, at least a view-scoped managed bean should be used.

Options for filtering

Filtering also supports having a drop-down box as the filtering mechanism instead of the input text field. This can be achieved by providing a list with the `filterOptions` attribute. The definition of the column is given as follows:

```
<p:columnheaderText="Name" filterBy="#{car.name}"
filterOptions="#{dataTableController.carNamesAsOptions}">
<h:outputText value="#{car.name}" />
</p:column>
```

Global filtering

`dataTable` provides global filtering by invoking the client-side method `filter()`. The global filter can be positioned at the `header` of the table, as shown in the following code snippet:

```
<f:facet name="header">
<p:outputPanel>
<h:outputText value="Search all fields:" />
<p:inputText id="globalFilter" onkeyup="carsTable.filter()" />
</p:outputPanel>
</f:facet>
```

The filtering will be triggered on the `onkeyup` event by invoking the mentioned `filter()` method of the table whose `widgetVar` attribute is set to `carsTable`. The appearance of a table with global filtering will be as follows:

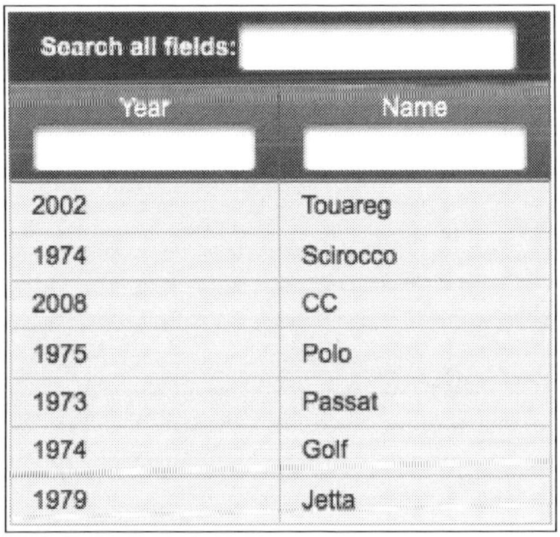

Search all fields:

Year	Name
2002	Touareg
1974	Scirocco
2008	CC
1975	Polo
1973	Passat
1974	Golf
1979	Jetta

With global filtering it is highly recommended to use filtering with a `filteredValue` attribute. Currently for backward compatibility `filteredValue` is implemented to fall back to the `viewState` method. The `viewState` method is deprecated and will be removed in the future.

PrimeFaces Cookbook Showcase application

This recipe is available in the PrimeFaces Cookbook Showcase application on GitHub at `https://github.com/ova2/primefaces-cookbook`. You can find the details there for running the project. When the server is running, the showcase for the recipe is available at `http://localhost:8080/primefaces-cookbook/views/chapter5/dataTableSortFilter.jsf`.

In-cell editing with dataTable

The `dataTable` component supports the in-cell editing feature for updating values within the table without navigating to another detail page.

How to do it...

In order to enable editing, first we need to set the `editable` attribute of the table to `true`. Each column definition that we need to be editable should contain the `p:cellEditor` helper component that will contain two facets for rendering output components; one for visualizing the data and input components, and the other for getting input data from the user. The in-place editor palette, which is the `p:rowEditor` component, also needs to be rendered as a column in order to activate editing.

```
<p:dataTable id="inCellEditing" var="car"
value="#{dataTableController.cars}" rowKey="#{car.name}"
editable="true">
<p:column headerText="Year">
<p:cellEditor>
<f:facet name="output">
<h:outputText value="#{car.year}" />
</f:facet>
<f:facet name="input">
<p:inputText value="#{car.year}" />
</f:facet>
</p:cellEditor>
</p:column>
<p:column headerText="Name">
<p:cellEditor>
<f:facet name="output">
<h:outputText value="#{car.name}" />
</f:facet>
<f:facet name="input">
<h:selectOneMenu value="#{car.name}" >
<f:selectItems
value="#{dataTableController.carNames}"
var="name"
itemLabel="#{name}"
itemValue="#{name}" />
</h:selectOneMenu>
</f:facet>
</p:cellEditor>
```

```
</p:column>
<p:column headerText="Actions">
<p:rowEditor />
</p:column>
</p:dataTable>
```

The components for the input facet could be an `inputText` component as well as a `selectOneMenu` component, which will render a dropdown list for the input.

The appearance of a data table with output facets will be as follows:

Year	Name	Actions
2002	Touareg	
1974	Scirocco	
2008	CC	
1975	Polo	
1973	Passat	
1974	Golf	
1979	Jetta	

When the pencil icon is clicked upon, the table will transit into the edit mode and the input facets will be rendered:

Year	Name	Actions
2002	Touareg	
1974	Scirocco	
2008	CC	
1975	Polo	
1973	Passat	
1974	Golf	
1979	Jetta	

Clicking on the tick "(check mark)" icon will save the edited row, and the canceling icon will revert all changes.

There's more...

The `dataTable` component supports AJAX behavior events in order to handle the interactions of the user on the row editing and cancelation of the editing actions. The definition of the AJAX behavior events should be placed within the table, as shown in the following code snippet:

```
<p:ajax event="rowEdit" listener="#{dataTableController.onEdit}"
update=":form:growl" />
<p:ajax event="rowEditCancel" listener="#{dataTableController.
onCancel}" update=":form:growl" />
```

The `onEdit` and `onCancel` methods retrieve `org.primefaces.event.RowEditEvent` as a parameter. The object that is edited can be retrieved from the event as `event.getObject()`.

```
public void onEdit(RowEditEvent event) {
MessageUtil.addInfoMessage("car.edit", ((Car) event.getObject()).
getName());
}

public void onCancel(RowEditEvent event) {
MessageUtil.addInfoMessage("car.edit.cancelled", ((Car) event.
getObject()).getName());
}
```

PrimeFaces Cookbook Showcase application

This recipe is available in the PrimeFaces Cookbook Showcase application on GitHub at `https://github.com/ova2/primefaces-cookbook`. You can find the details there for running the project. When the server is running, the showcase for the recipe is available at `http://localhost:8080/primefaces-cookbook/views/chapter5/dataTableInCellEdit.jsf`.

Conditional coloring in dataTable

The `dataTable` component provides conditional coloring on rows, which can be styled based on conditions.

How to do it...

A basic definition of a color-coded table that displays a list of cars follows:

```
<p:dataTable id="coloring" var="car"
value="#{dataTableController.cars}"
rowStyleClass="#{car.year le 1975 ? 'colored' : null}">
<p:columnheaderText="Year">#{car.year}</p:column>
<p:columnheaderText="Name">#{car.name}</p:column>
</p:dataTable>
```

The colored style definition could be as simple as the following:

```
<style type="text/css">
.colored {
background-color: #FF0000;
color: #FFFFFF;
}
</style>
```

How It works...

With the `rowStyleClass` attribute, style class can be defined for each row according the manufacturing year of the car as `rowStyleClass="#{car.year le 1975 ? 'colored' : null}"`. Arithmetic, logical, or relational operators of the JSF Expression Language can be used to define the condition.

For more on the JSF Expression Language, see `http://developers.sun.com/docs/jscreator/help/jsp-jsfel/jsf_expression_language_intro.html`.

PrimeFaces Cookbook Showcase application

This recipe is available in the PrimeFaces Cookbook Showcase application on GitHub at `https://github.com/ova2/primefaces-cookbook`. You can find the details there for running the project. When the server is running, the showcase for the recipe is available at `http://localhost:8080/primefaces-cookbook/views/chapter5/dataTableColoring.jsf`.

Handling tons of data – LazyDataModel

dataTable provides support for displaying tons of data by enabling lazy loading. In order to handle large datasets, a data model needs to be implemented based on org.primefaces.model.LazyDataModel to support pagination, sorting, filtering, and live scrolling.

How to do it...

First, the lazy attribute should be set to true for lazy loading to be enabled for the table, and the abstract load method should be implemented in org.primefaces.model.LazyDataModel. We must also implement getRowData and getRowKey when selection is enabled in the table. The lazy data model should be constructed with the list of Car instances, and it should be bound to dataTable.

```
List<Car>cars = new ArrayList<Car> (millions of cars);
LazyDataModel<Car>lazyModel = new LazyCarDataModel(cars);
```

The table calls the load method implementation with the following parameters when paging, sorting, or filtering actions occur.

- first: Index of the first data to display
- pageSize: Number of the data items to load on the page
- sortField: Name of the sort field (for example, "name" for sortBy="#{car.name}")
- sortOrder: The org.primefaces.model.SortOrder enumeration; the value could be either ASCENDING or DESCENDING
- filter: Filter the map with a field name as key (for example "name" for filterBy="#{car.name}") and the value

The definition of the table for listing Car instances with custom pagination would be as follows:

```
<p:dataTable id="lazyModel" var="car"
value="#{lazyDataTableController.lazyModel}"
paginatorTemplate="{RowsPerPageDropdown} {FirstPageLink}
{PreviousPageLink} {CurrentPageReport}
{NextPageLink} {LastPageLink}"
paginator="true" rows="10" lazy="true">

<p:column headerText="Name" sortBy="#{car.name}"
filterBy="#{car.name}">
<h:outputText value="#{car.name}" />
</p:column>
```

```
<p:column headerText="Year" sortBy="#{car.year}"
filterBy="#{car.year}">
<h:outputText value="#{car.year}" />
</p:column>
</p:dataTable>
```

PrimeFaces Cookbook Showcase application

This recipe is available in the PrimeFaces Cookbook Showcase application on GitHub at `https://github.com/ova2/primefaces-cookbook`. You can find the details there for running the project. When the server is running, the showcase for the recipe is available at `http://localhost:8080/primefaces-cookbook/views/chapter5/dataTableLazyDataModel.jsf`.

Listing data with dataList

`dataList` presents a collection of data in the list layout, with several display types and features such as AJAX pagination.

How to do it...

A simple definition for a data list with a header facet for listing countries starting with the letter "A" would be as follows:

```
<p:dataList value="#{dataListController.countriesShort}"
var="country" itemType="disc">
<f:facet name="header">
Countries starting with 'A'
</f:facet>
#{country}
</p:dataList>
```

The appearance of the component would be as follows:

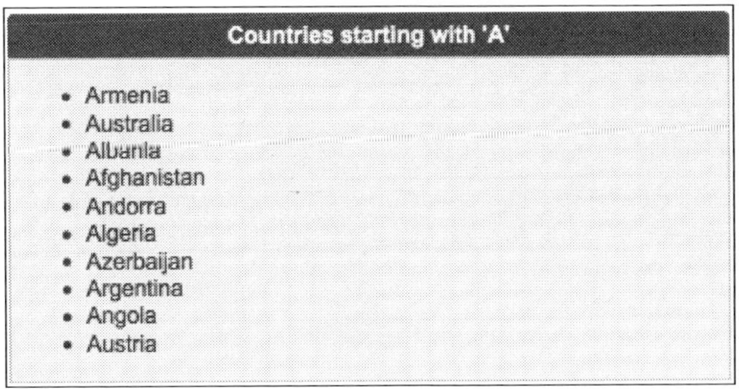

Countries starting with 'A'

- Armenia
- Australia
- Albania
- Afghanistan
- Andorra
- Algeria
- Azerbaijan
- Argentina
- Angola
- Austria

There's more...

The type attribute defines how the list should be presented. The values for the attribute can be unordered, ordered, definition, or none. The default value is unordered. When the value of the type attribute is set to ordered, the list will be rendered with numbers. This does not mean that the items of the list will be ordered according to their content. When the value of the type attribute is set to definition, it will display an inline description for each item. The detailed definition should be provided with the facet named description, as follows:

```
<p:dataList id="withDescription"
value="#{dataListController.cars}" var="car" type="definition">
Name: #{car.name}
<f:facet name="description">
<p:graphicImage
value="/resources/images/autocomplete/#{car.name}.png"
width="60" height="40" />
</f:facet>
</p:dataList>
```

itemType specifies how the items will be listed. The values for the itemType attribute can be disc, i, A, a, circle, square, and decimal. The appearance of each item type is listed as follows:

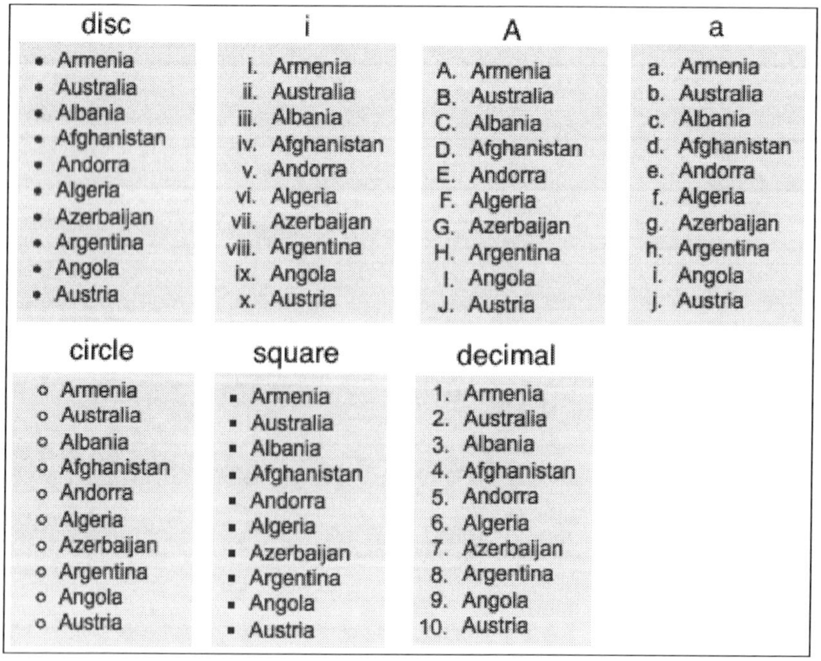

disc	i	A	a
• Armenia	i. Armenia	A. Armenia	a. Armenia
• Australia	ii. Australia	B. Australia	b. Australia
• Albania	iii. Albania	C. Albania	c. Albania
• Afghanistan	iv. Afghanistan	D. Afghanistan	d. Afghanistan
• Andorra	v. Andorra	E. Andorra	e. Andorra
• Algeria	vi. Algeria	F. Algeria	f. Algeria
• Azerbaijan	vii. Azerbaijan	G. Azerbaijan	g. Azerbaijan
• Argentina	viii. Argentina	H. Argentina	h. Argentina
• Angola	ix. Angola	I. Angola	i. Angola
• Austria	x. Austria	J. Austria	j. Austria

circle	square	decimal
○ Armenia	▪ Armenia	1. Armenia
○ Australia	▪ Australia	2. Australia
○ Albania	▪ Albania	3. Albania
○ Afghanistan	▪ Afghanistan	4. Afghanistan
○ Andorra	▪ Andorra	5. Andorra
○ Algeria	▪ Algeria	6. Algeria
○ Azerbaijan	▪ Azerbaijan	7. Azerbaijan
○ Argentina	▪ Argentina	8. Argentina
○ Angola	▪ Angola	9. Angola
○ Austria	▪ Austria	10. Austria

Pagination

dataList has a built-in pagination that is enabled by setting the paginator attribute to true. To support the pagination, the number of rows to display per page should be set with the rows attribute. Its default value is 0, which means to display all the data available. Pagination can be customized using the paginatorTemplateOption attribute, which accepts keys for specifying the content of the paginator.

- FirstPageLink
- LastPageLink
- PreviousPageLink
- NextPageLink
- PageLinks
- CurrentPageReport
- RowsPerPageDropdown

The default rendering for the pagination would be as follows:

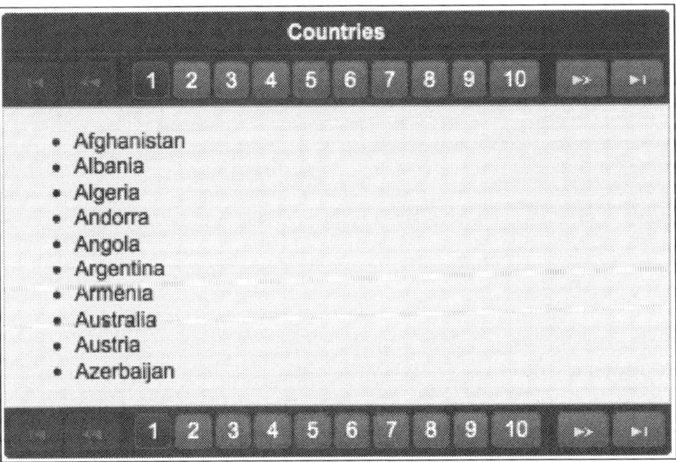

It would be the same as the pagination template, as shown in the following code snippet:

```
{FirstPageLink} {PreviousPageLink} {PageLinks} {NextPageLink}
{LastPageLink}
```

A more complex paginator definition is given as follows:

```
{CurrentPageReport} {FirstPageLink} {PreviousPageLink} {PageLinks}
{NextPageLink} {LastPageLink} {RowsPerPageDropdown}
```

This will be rendered as follows:

The {RowsPerPageDropdown} attribute has its own mechanism to produce templates, and the mechanism should be provided in order to render the dropdown. (for example, rowsPerPageTemplate="5,10,15")

Also, {CurrentPageReport} has its own template defined with the currentPageReportTemplate option.

We can use the {currentPage},{totalPages},{totalRecords},{startRecord },{endRecord} keywords within currentPageReportTemplate. The default value is {currentPage}of{totalPages}.

The pageLinks attribute defines the maximum number of page links to display. Its default value is 10. For the complex paginator definition given previously, it's set to 3. paginator can be positioned in three different locations by setting the paginatorPosition attribute as top, bottom, or both (the latter being the default value). The paginatorAlwaysVisible attribute defines whether the pagination should be hidden or not when the total data count is less than the number of rows per page.

PrimeFaces Cookbook Showcase application

This recipe is available in the PrimeFaces Cookbook Showcase application on GitHub at https://github.com/ova2/primefaces-cookbook. You can find the details there for running the project. When the server is running, the showcase for the recipe is available at http://localhost:8080/primefaces-cookbook/views/chapter5/dataList.jsf.

Listing data with pickList

`pickList` is a dual list input component that is used for transferring data between two different collections with drag-and-drop based reordering, transition effects, POJO support, client-server callbacks, and more.

How to do it...

`pickList` uses a custom data model, which is an instance of `org.primefaces.model.DualListModel` that contains two lists—one for the source and one for the target. For a `pickList` implementation that would be used to select countries, the data model could be as follows:

```
private List<String> countriesSource = new ArrayList<String>();
private List<String> countriesTarget = new ArrayList<String>();

countriesSource.add("England");
countriesSource.add("Germany");
countriesSource.add("Switzerland");
countriesSource.add("Turkey");

privateDualListModel<String> countries = new DualListModel<String>
(countriesSource, countriesTarget);
```

The definition of the component could be as follows:

```
<p:pickList id="simple" value="#{pickListController.countries}"
var="country" itemLabel="#{country}" itemValue="#{country}" />
```

The visual output of the component will be two containers—one for the source list and one for the target list—and will look as follows:

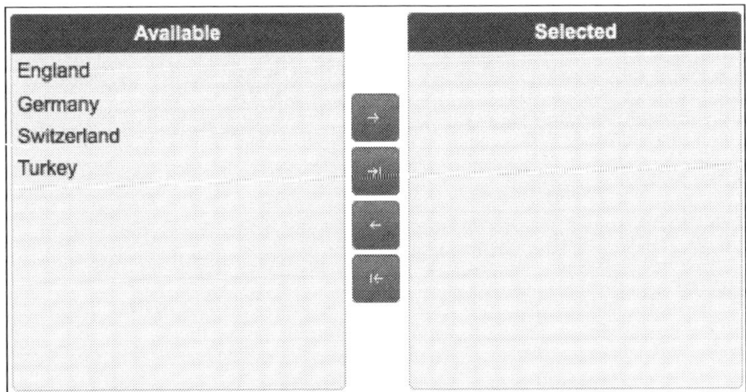

There's more...

The showSourceControls and showTargetControls attributes specify the visibility of the reorder buttons of the source list and the target list.

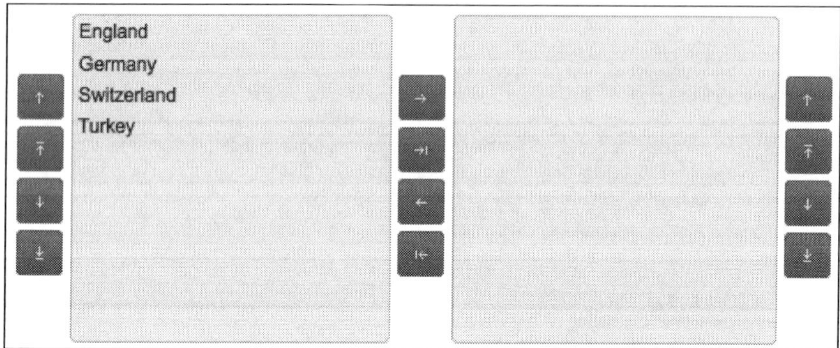

The itemDisabled attribute specifies whether an item can be picked or not. When it is set to true, the source and target list will be rendered as disabled so as to prevent the selection.

POJO support

The pickList component supports dealing with complex POJOs as well. The data model should be based on org.primefaces.model.DualListModel as it's defined with the example of strings. A converter for the Car class should also be implemented and used as defined next. The following is a definition of a data model that contains a source list and target list for the Car class:

```
DualListModel<Car> cars = new DualListModel<Car>(carsSource,
carsTarget);
```

The p:column component could be used while visualizing the instances of Car within the pickList component, to clearly identify the attributes of the class.

```
<p:pickList id="pojoSupport" value="#{pickListController.cars}"
  var="car" itemLabel="#{car.name}" itemValue="#{car}">
<f:converter converterId="org.primefaces.cookbook.converter.CarConv
  erter" />
<p:column>
<p:graphicImage
  value="/resources/images/autocomplete/#{car.name}.png"
  width="100" height="70"/>
</p:column>
```

```
<p:column>
#{car.name}
</p:column>
</p:pickList>
```

Enabling captions

It's possible to add captions at the top of the source list and the target list. The captions should be defined with `sourceCaption` and `targetCaption` as follows:

```
<p:pickList id="withCaption"
value="#{pickListController.countries}"
var="country" itemLabel="#{country}" itemValue="#{country}">
<f:facet name="sourceCaption">Available</f:facet>
<f:facet name="targetCaption">Selected</f:facet>
</p:pickList>
```

Transition effects

Effects can be applied with the `effect` attribute for content transition when a selection is moved from the source list to the target list or vice versa. The default value for the `effect` attribute is `fade`. Possible values for the attribute are as follows:

- `blind`
- `bounce`
- `clip`
- `drop`
- `explode`
- `fold`
- `highlight`
- `puff`
- `pulsate`
- `scale`
- `shake`
- `size`
- `slide`

`effectSpeed` can be used to customize the animation speed. Its default value is `fast`; other possible values are `slow` and `normal`.

Executing custom JavaScript on transfer

The `pickList` component supports the execution of a client-side callback when an item is transferred from one list to another. This could be achieved by providing a JavaScript method definition for the `onTransfer` attribute as follows:

```
<p:pickList id="withCustomScript" value="#{pickListController.
countries}" onTransfer="handleTransfer(e)"
var="country" itemLabel="#{country}" itemValue="#{country}" />
```

The definition of the `script` method for listing the values of the item that is transferred, the definition of `from` and `to` lists, and so on, is given as follows:

```
<script type="text/javascript">
function handleTransfer(e) {
alert(e.item);
alert(e.from);
alert(e.toList);
alert(e.type);
}
</script>
```

PrimeFaces Cookbook Showcase application

This recipe is available in the PrimeFaces Cookbook Showcase application on GitHub at `https://github.com/ova2/primefaces-cookbook`. You can find the details there for running the project. When the server is running, the showcase for the recipe is available at `http://localhost:8080/primefaces-cookbook/views/chapter5/pickList.jsf`.

Listing data with orderList

The `orderList` component is used to sort a collection with the support of drag-and-drop reordering, transition effects, and POJO support.

How to do it...

A basic definition for sorting a collection of strings would be as follows:

```
<p:orderList id="simple" value="#{orderListController.countries}"
var="country" itemLabel="#{country}" itemValue="#{country}" />
```

The output of the code is given as follows:

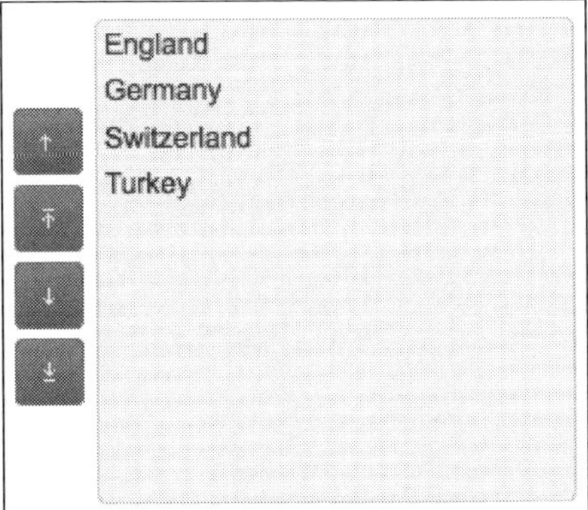

There's more...

With the `controlsLocation` attribute, we can control the position of the controls. The default value is `left`; other possible values are `right` and `none`.

Transition effects

Effects can be applied with the `effect` attribute for content transition when a selection is moved upwards or downwards. The default value of `effect` is `fade`. Possible values for the attribute are:

- `blind`
- `clip`
- `drop`
- `explode`
- `fade`
- `fold`
- `puff`
- `scale`
- `slide`

PrimeFaces Cookbook Showcase application

This recipe is available in the PrimeFaces Cookbook Showcase application on GitHub at `https://github.com/ova2/primefaces-cookbook`. You can find the details there for running the project. When the server is running, the showcase for the recipe is available at `http://localhost:8080/primefaces-cookbook/views/chapter5/orderList.jsf`.

Visualizing data with tree

The `tree` component visualizes hierarchical data in `tree` format.

How to do it...

The data for the `tree` is provided with instances of `org.primefaces.model.TreeNode`, which correspond to the nodes in the tree. A pure client-side tree might be useful to create tree-based navigation menus. A basic data model for a `tree` could be constructed as follows:

```
TreeNode root = new DefaultTreeNode("Root", null);
TreeNode node1 = new DefaultTreeNode("Node1", root);
TreeNode node2 = new DefaultTreeNode("Node2", root);

TreeNode node11 = new DefaultTreeNode("Node1.1", node1);
TreeNode node12 = new DefaultTreeNode("Node1.2", node1);

TreeNode node21 = new DefaultTreeNode("Node2.1", node2);
TreeNode node211 = new DefaultTreeNode("Node2.1.1", node21);
```

The definition of the tree will be as follows:

```
<p:tree value="#{treeDataController.root}" var="node">
<p:treeNode>
<h:outputText value="#{node}" />
</p:treeNode>
</p:tree>
```

This will be visualized as follows:

There's more...

If the hierarchical data model of the `tree` contains too many nodes, it would be useful to dynamically load the tree by setting the `dynamic` attribute to `true` in order to load a part of the tree when requested by expanding a node with a click.

Also, by enabling caching with setting the `cache` attribute to `true`, expanding a previously loaded node will not result in an AJAX request to load its children again.

```
<p:tree id="dynamic" value="#{treeDataController.root}" var="node"
dynamic="true" cache="true">
<p:treeNode>
<h:outputText value="#{node}" />
</p:treeNode>
</p:tree>
```

Node type support

It's possible to provide different visuals for each node with custom node definitions. To achieve this, the `<p:treeNode>` component could be used with defined node types. The following definition contains two node definitions—one for expandable nodes with `type="node"`, and one for the leaf nodes with `type="leaf"`. The tree nodes use the `ui-icon-minusthick` icon for leaf nodes and `ui-icon-plusthick` for expandable icons, to differentiate the nodes visually.

```
<p:tree id="customNodes" value="#{treeDataController.rootWithType}"
var="node">
<p:treeNode type="node"  icon="ui-icon-plusthick">
<h:outputText value="#{node}" />
</p:treeNode>
<p:treeNode type="leaf"  icon="ui-icon-minusthick">
<h:outputText value="#{node}" />
</p:treeNode>
</p:tree>
```

The visual output of the tree with all nodes expanded would be as follows:

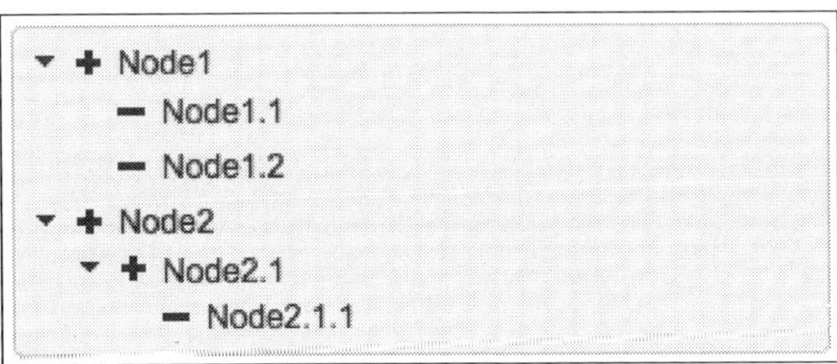

The `nodeType` attribute should match the `type` attribute in the `treeNode` component and is given while constructing the tree data model.

```
TreeNode node1 = new DefaultTreeNode("node", "Node1", root);
TreeNode node11 = new DefaultTreeNode("leaf", "Node1.1", node1);
```

Node selection

The `tree` component provides built-in selection either by single node, multiple nodes, or with checkbox selection on the nodes. The `selectionMode` attribute should be used to enable this. Its value should be `single` for the single selection mode and the `selection` attribute should be bound to an instance of `TreeNode`.

For selecting multiple nodes with the modifier key (for example, *Ctrl* in Windows or *Command* in MacOS), the `selectionMode` attribute should be set to `multiple` and the `selection` attribute needs to be bound to an array of the `TreeNode` class.

For selecting nodes with a checkbox, the `selectionMode` attribute should be set to `checkbox` and the `selection` attribute needs to be bound to an array of the `TreeNode` class.

AJAX behavior events

It's possible to invoke server-side methods instantly according to user interactions such as expanding, collapsing, or selecting the node. The declaration for the node expand event for the tree will be as follows. The definition for the other AJAX listeners will be the same as for the node expand event.

```
<p:tree id="ajaxListeners" value="#{treeDataController.root}"
var="node"
selectionMode="single"
selection="#{treeDataController.selectedNode}">
<p:ajax event="select" listener="#{treeDataController.onNodeSelect}"
update=":mainForm:growl" />

<p:treeNode>
<h:outputText value="#{node}" />
</p:treeNode>
</p:tree>
```

The list of all the possible events with their listener parameters is as follows:

Event name	Parameter of the listener method	When it gets executed
`collapse`	`org.primefaces.event.NodeCollapseEvent`	When the node is collapsed
`select`	`org.primefaces.event.NodeSelectEvent`	When the node is selected
`expand`	`org.primefaces.event.NodeExpandEvent`	When the node is expanded
`unselect`	`org.primefaces.event.NodeUnselectEvent`	When the node is unselected

Context menu support

The `tree` component easily integrates with the `contextMenu` component, and the context menu can be assigned to the rows for a right-click event. It is also possible to assign different context menus with different tree nodes, using the `nodeType` attribute.

There are two context menu definitions—one for the nodes of the tree table that could be expanded and the other one for the leaf nodes of the tree that could not be expanded. They are given as follows. The menus differ according to the given `nodeType` attribute.

```
<p:contextMenu for="withContextMenu" nodeType="node">
<p:menuitem value="View" update="dialogPanel" icon="ui-icon-
search" oncomplete="nodeDialog.show()"/>
</p:contextMenu>

<p:contextMenu for="withContextMenu" nodeType="leaf">
<p:menuitem value="View" update="dialogPanel" icon="ui-icon-
search" oncomplete="nodeDialog.show()"/>
<p:menuitem value="Delete"
actionListener="#{treeDataController.deleteNode}"
update="withContextMenu" icon="ui-icon-close"/>
</p:contextMenu>
```

The `nodeType` attribute is given while constructing the tree data model.

```
TreeNode node1 = new DefaultTreeNode("node", "Node1", root);
TreeNode node11 = new DefaultTreeNode("leaf", "Node1.1", node1);
```

The definition of `tree` would be as follows. The ID of the component should match with the attribute of the two context menus. The tree will contain two tree node definitions for the two node types—`node` and `leaf`.

```
<p:tree id="withContextMenu"
value="#{treeDataController.rootWithType}" var="node"
selectionMode="single"
selection="#{treeDataController.selectedNode}">

<p:treeNode type="node">
<h:outputText value="#{node}" />
</p:treeNode>

<p:treeNode type="leaf">
<h:outputText value="#{node}" />
</p:treeNode>
</p:tree>
```

PrimeFaces Cookbook Showcase application

This recipe is available in the PrimeFaces Cookbook Showcase application on GitHub at `https://github.com/ova2/primefaces-cookbook`. You can find the details there for running the project. When the server is running, the showcase for the recipe is available at `http://localhost:8080/primefaces-cookbook/views/chapter5/tree.jsf`.

Visualizing data with treeTable

The `treeTable` component visualizes a tree where each tree item can have some additional fields that could be displayed in a tabular format.

How to do it...

The data for the `treeTable` component is provided with instances of `org.primefaces.model.TreeNode`, which corresponds to a node in the table.

A basic implementation for a tree table with three columns would be as follows:

```
<p:treeTable id="simple" value="#{treeTableController.root}"
var="element">
<f:facet name="header">Tree Table</f:facet>
<p:column>
<f:facet name="header">Name</f:facet>
<h:outputText value="#{element.name}" />
</p:column>
<p:column>
<f:facet name="header">Column 1</f:facet>
<h:outputText value="#{element.column1}" />
</p:column>
<p:column>
<f:facet name="header">Column 2</f:facet>
<h:outputText value="#{element.column2}" />
</p:column>
</p:treeTable>
```

The model that is provided to the tree table would be a collection of the `TreeTableElement` components wrapped by the `TreeNode` instances. `TreeTableElement` is a simple class created for demonstration purposes, and is defined as follows:

```
public class TreeTableElement implements Serializable {
private String name;
private String column1;
```

```
private String column2;

    //getters&setters
}
```

The implementation of constructing the tree table would be as follows:

```
root = new DefaultTreeNode("root", null);
TreeNode node1 = new DefaultTreeNode(new TreeTableElement("Node1",
"1st Column", "2nd Column"), root);
TreeNode node2 = new DefaultTreeNode(new TreeTableElement("Node2",
"1st Column", "2nd Column"), root);
TreeNode node11 = new DefaultTreeNode(new
TreeTableElement("Node1.1", "1st Column", "2nd Column"), node1);
TreeNode node12 = new DefaultTreeNode(new
TreeTableElement("Node1.2", "1st Column", "2nd Column"), node1);
TreeNode node21 = new DefaultTreeNode(new
TreeTableElement("Node2.1", "1st Column", "2nd Column"), node2);
TreeNode node211 = new DefaultTreeNode(new
TreeTableElement("Node2.1.1", "1st Column", "2nd Column"),
node21);
```

The appearance of the tree table expanded on every node will be like the following screenshot:

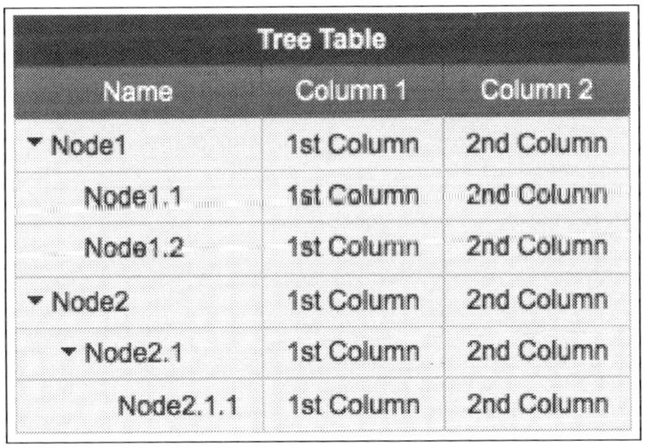

Tree Table		
Name	Column 1	Column 2
▾ Node1	1st Column	2nd Column
Node1.1	1st Column	2nd Column
Node1.2	1st Column	2nd Column
▾ Node2	1st Column	2nd Column
▾ Node2.1	1st Column	2nd Column
Node2.1.1	1st Column	2nd Column

There's more...

It's possible to make the tree table scrollable by setting the `scrollable` attribute to `true`. The `scrollWidth` and `scrollHeight` attributes can be provided to constrain the view of the tree table to a fixed width and height. Also, the width of the columns must be provided as fixed integer values when the `scrollable` attribute is set to `true` in order to preserve the layout.

Node selection

The `selectionMode` attribute should be used to enable the selection whenever a row is clicked. Its value should be `single` for the single selection mode, and the `selection` attribute should be bound to an instance of `TreeNode`. For selecting multiple items with the modifier key (for example, *Ctrl* in Windows or *Command* in MacOS), the `selectionMode` attribute should be set to `multiple` and the `selection` attribute needs to be bound to an array of the `TreeNode` class.

```
<p:treeTable id="singleSelection"
value="#{treeTableController.root}" var="element"
selection="#{treeTableController.selectedItem}"
selectionMode="single">
</p:treeTable>

<p:treeTable id="multipleSelection"
value="#{treeTableController.root}" var="element"
selection="#{treeTableController.selectedItems}"
selectionMode="multiple">
</p:treeTable>
```

AJAX behavior events

It's possible to invoke server-side methods instantly according to user interactions such as expanding, collapsing, or selecting the node. The declaration for the node expand event for the tree table would be as follows. The definition for the other AJAX listeners will be the same as for the node event `expand`.

```
<p:treeTable id="withAJAX" value="#{treeTableController.root}"
var="element">
<p:ajax event="expand"
listener="#{treeDataController.onNodeExpand}"
update="form:growl" />
...
</p:treeTable>
```

The list of all possible events with their listener parameters is as follows:

Event name	Parameter of the listener method	When it gets executed
`colResize`	`org.primefaces.event.ColumnResizeEvent`	When the column is resized
`collapse`	`org.primefaces.event.NodeCollapseEvent`	When the node is collapsed
`unselect`	`org.primefaces.event.NodeUnselectEvent`	When the node is unselected

Event name	Parameter of the listener method	When it gets executed
expand	org.primefaces.event.NodeExpandEvent	When the node is expanded
select	org.primefaces.event.NodeSelectEvent	When the node is selected

Context menu support

treeTable easily integrates with the contextMenu component, and the context menu can be assigned to the rows on a right-click event. It is possible to assign different context menus with different tree nodes, using the nodeType attribute.

There are two context menu definitions, one for the nodes of the tree table that could be expanded and the other one for the leaf nodes of the tree that could not be expanded. They are given as follows. The menus differ according to the given nodeType attribute.

```
<p:contextMenu for="withContextMenu" nodeType="node">
<p:menuitem value="View" update="dialogPanel" icon="ui-icon-
search" oncomplete="nodeDialog.show()"/>
</p:contextMenu>

<p:contextMenu for="withContextMenu" nodeType="leaf">
<p:menuitem value="View" update="dialogPanel" icon="ui-icon-
search" oncomplete="nodeDialog.show()"/>
<p:menuitem value="Delete"
actionListener="#{treeTableController.deleteNode}"
update="withContextMenu" icon="ui-icon-close"/>
</p:contextMenu>
```

The nodeType attribute is given while constructing the treeTable data model.

```
TreeNode node1 = new DefaultTreeNode("node", new
TreeTableElement("Node1", "1st Column", "2nd Column"), root);
...
TreeNode node11 = new DefaultTreeNode("leaf", new
TreeTableElement("Node1.1", "1st Column", "2nd Column"), node1);
...
```

The output of this code snippet is as follows:

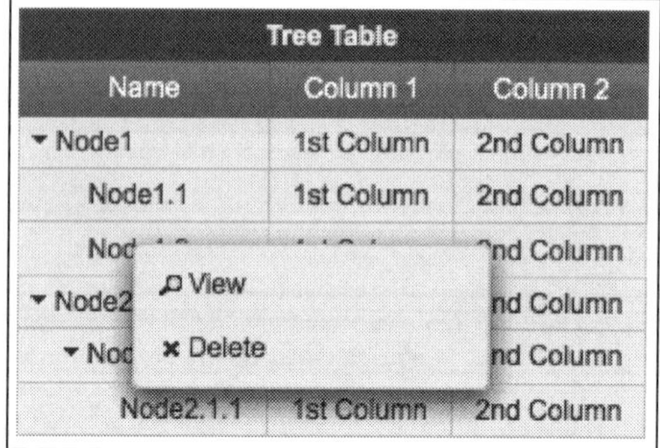

The definition of the tree table would be as follows. The ID of the component should match with the `for` attribute of the two context menus.

```
<p:treeTable id="withContextMenu"
value="#{treeTableController.root}" var="element"
selection="#{treeTableController.selectedItem}"
selectionMode="single">
<f:facet name="header">Tree Table</f:facet>
<p:column>
<f:facet name="header">Name</f:facet>
<h:outputText value="#{element.name}" />
</p:column>
<p:column>
<f:facet name="header">Column 1</f:facet>
<h:outputText value="#{element.column1}" />
</p:column>
<p:column>
<f:facet name="header">Column 2</f:facet>
<h:outputText value="#{element.column2}" />
</p:column>
</p:treeTable>
```

PrimeFaces Cookbook Showcase application

This recipe is available in the PrimeFaces Cookbook Showcase application on GitHub at `https://github.com/ova2/primefaces-cookbook`. You can find the details there for running the project. When the server is running, the showcase for the recipe is available at `http://localhost:8080/primefaces-cookbook/views/chapter5/treeTable.jsf`.

Exporting data in various formats

The `dataExporter` component allows exporting the content of the table into various formats such as XLS/XLSX, PDF, CSV, and XML. It also supports exporting the current data on a page and also only the selected data on the table by providing the ability to exclude particular columns and manipulating the exported data with pre and post processors.

How to do it...

A basic definition for having data-exporting ability with a command link that encapsulates a PDF icon would be as follows:

```
<h:commandLink>
<p:graphicImage value="/resources/images/export/pdf.png" />
<p:dataExporter type="pdf" target="countriesTable"
fileName="countries" />
</h:commandLink>
```

How it works...

In the previous definition, `target` defines the server-side ID of the table whose data will be exported. The table needs to be a PrimeFaces `dataTable` component. The `type` attribute defines the export type. The values can be `xls`, `pdf`, `csv`, or `xml`. The `fileName` attribute defines the filename of the generated export file; by default, the server-side ID of `dataTable` is used as the filename.

To Enable Excel Export, `apache-poi` should be included in the classpath, and to enable PDF Export, `itext` should be included in the classpath. See the recipe *Setting up and configuring the PrimeFaces Library* in *Chapter 1, Getting Started with PrimeFaces*, for details.

There's more...

The export could be done either with the whole data set only for the current page by setting the `pageOnly` attribute to `true` or for only the selected data by setting the `selectionOnly` attribute to `true`.

It's possible to exclude columns in the export with the `excludeColumns` attribute. A comma-separated list needs to be provided with the indexes of the columns to be excluded from the export, such as `excludeColumns="0,2,3"`. Character encoding can also be set while exporting, by setting the `encoding` attribute to the corresponding encoding value.

Pre and post processor of documents

The `dataExporter` component enables pre and post processing on the document for customization such as adding logos, captions, headers/footers, and so on. Preprocessors are executed before the data is exported, and postprocessors are processed after the data is included in the document. The `document` object is passed to the processor methods as a Java object so that it can be easily cast to the appropriate class. A preprocessor example for adding a footer for page numbers to the PDF document is given as follows:

```
<p:dataExporter type="pdf" target="countriesTable"
fileName="countries"
preProcessor="#{dataExportController.preProcessPDF}" />
```

```
public void preProcessPDF(Object document) {
Document pdf = (Document) document;
HeaderFooter footer = new HeaderFooter(new Phrase("This is page:
"), true);
pdf.setFooter(footer);
}
```

Monitoring export status

Data export is a non-AJAX process and so in order to monitor the status, PrimeFaces provides the client-side method `monitorDownload`. The method could be bound to an `onclick` event of a command component as seen in the following code snippet:

```
<h:commandLink onclick="PrimeFaces.monitorDownload(showStatus,
hideStatus)">
<p:graphicImage value="/resources/images/export/csv.png" />
<p:dataExporter type="csv" target="countriesTable"
fileName="countries" />
</h:commandLink>
```

This method will trigger two methods: `showStatus` and `hideStatus`, while the exporting process occurs. The `showStatus` and `hideStatus` methods are two simple methods for showing and hiding a dialog box component.

```
<script type="text/javascript">
function showStatus() {
statusDialog.show();
}
function hideStatus() {
statusDialog.hide();
}
</script>
```

```
<p:dialog modal="true" widgetVar="statusDialog" header="Status"
draggable="false" closable="false">
<p:graphicImage value="/resources/images/ajax-loader.gif" />
</p:dialog>
```

PrimeFaces Cookbook Showcase application

This recipe is available in the PrimeFaces Cookbook Showcase application on GitHub at `https://github.com/ova2/primefaces-cookbook`. You can find the details there for running the project. When the server is running, the showcase for the recipe is available at `http://localhost:8080/primefaces-cookbook/views/chapter5/dataExport.jsf`.

Visualizing data with carousel

The `carousel` component is for visualizing the data, to display a data set or general content with sliding effects.

How to do it...

A simple `carousel` definition for displaying a list of cars is given as follows:

```
<p:carousel id="simple" value="#{carouselController.cars}"
var="car" headerText="Cars">
<h:panelGrid columns="1">
<p:graphicImage
value="/resources/images/autocomplete/#{car.name}.png"
width="100" height="70"/>
<h:outputText value="#{car.name}" />
</h:panelGrid>
</p:carousel>
```

This will be rendered as follows:

There's more...

By default, `carousel` lists its items in pages with size 3. This can be customized with the `rows` attribute. When the `circular` attribute is set to `true`, `carousel` will scroll to the first page after the last one. The `vertical` attribute enables the `carousel` to scroll vertically, as seen in the following screenshot:

It is possible to have `carousel` start scrolling automatically after it is initialized, by setting the `autoPlayInterval` attribute to a value in milliseconds. It would make sense to make the carousel iterate in a circular manner when auto play is set.

Transition effects

The transition effect between the pages of the `carousel` can be defined as `slide` or `fade` with the `effect` attribute. Its default value is `slide`. The `effectDuration` attribute sets the speed of the scrolling animation in milliseconds with the default value `500`.

The `easing` attribute defines the animation while transiting between the elements of the `carousel`.

- `backBoth`
- `backIn`

- `backOut`
- `bounceBoth`
- `bounceIn`
- `bounceOut`
- `easeBoth`
- `easeBothStrong`
- `easeIn`
- `easeInStrong`
- `easeNone`
- `easeOut`
- `easeOutStrong`
- `elasticBoth`
- `elasticIn`
- `elasticOut`

The names of easing effects are case sensitive, so they should be defined carefully.

Sliding tabs

A carousel can also be used for general content display by sliding the tabs as defined in the following code snippet. Two tabs within the carousel will be rendered as items. Each tab will render an image along with the text definition of a car.

```
<p:carousel id="tabsCarousel" rows="1" itemStyle="width:600px;">
<p:tab id="tab1" title="Volkswagen CC">
<h:panelGrid columns="2" cellpadding="5">
<h:graphicImage library="images" name="autocomplete/CC.png"
/>
<h:outputText value="The Volkswagen CC (also known as the
Volkswagen Passat CC) is a four-door coupé version of the
Volkswagen Passat." />
</h:panelGrid>
</p:tab>
<p:tab id="tab2" title="Volkswagen Golf">
<h:panelGrid columns="2" cellpadding="5">
<h:graphicImage library="images"
name="autocomplete/Golf.png" />
```

```
<h:outputText value="The Volkswagen Golf is a small family
car manufactured by Volkswagen since 1974 and marketed
worldwide across six generations, in various body
configurations and under various nameplates" />
</h:panelGrid>
</p:tab>
</p:carousel>
```

Defining header and footer

The header and footer for the carousel can be defined by using the `headerText` and `footerText` attributes or by header and footer facets, which can take any custom content. Both definitions are demonstrated as follows:

```
<p:carousel headerText="header" footerText="footer">
...
</p:carousel>


<p:carousel>
<f:facet name="header">Header</f:facet>
<f:facet name="footer">Footer</f:facet>
...
</p:carousel>
```

PrimeFaces Cookbook Showcase application

This recipe is available in the PrimeFaces Cookbook Showcase application on GitHub at `https://github.com/ova2/primefaces-cookbook`. You can find the details there for running the project. When the server is running, the showcase for the recipe is available at `http://localhost:8080/primefaces-cookbook/views/chapter5/carousel.jsf`.

Visualizing data with ring

The `ring` component displays a list of data with a circular animation.

How to do it...

A basic definition for displaying a list of car models is as follows:

```
<p:ring id="simple" value="#{ringController.cars}" var="car"
style="width:100%">
<p:column>
<p:outputPanel style="text-align:center;" layout="block">
#{car.name}
```

```
</p:outputPanel>
</p:column>
</p:ring>
```

A collection of elements should be provided to the component as a data model. The visual output of the component will be as follows:

There's more...

The `rows` attribute defines the number of rows to display per page. The default value is `0`, meaning to display all data available. The first attribute specifies the index of the first data to display.

Effects with easing

With the `easing` attribute, it is possible to define the easing effect while transiting between the elements of `ring`. All the possible values for the easing effect are stated in the following list:

- `easeInBack`
- `easeInBounce`
- `easeInCirc`
- `easeInCubic`
- `easeInElastic`
- `easeInExpo`
- `easeInOutBack`
- `easeInOutBounce`
- `easeInOutCirc`
- `easeInOutCubic`
- `easeInOutElastic`
- `easeInOutExpo`
- `easeInOutQuad`
- `easeInOutQuart`

- `easeInOutQuint`
- `easeInQuad`
- `easeInQuart`
- `easeInQuint`
- `easeInSine`
- `easeOutBack`
- `easeOutBounce`
- `easeOutCirc`
- `easeOutCubic`
- `easeOutElastic`
- `easeOutExpo`
- `easeOutQuad`
- `easeOutQuart`
- `easeOutQuint`
- `easeOutSine`
- `swing`

To see the easing effect in action, please visit `http://jqueryui.com/demos/effect/easing.html`.

PrimeFaces Cookbook Showcase application

This recipe is available in the PrimeFaces Cookbook Showcase application on GitHub at `https://github.com/ova2/primefaces-cookbook`. You can find the details there for running the project. When the server is running, the showcase for the recipe is available at `http://localhost:8080/primefaces-cookbook/views/chapter5/ring.jsf`.

6
Endless Menu Variations

In this chapter we will cover:

- Static and dynamic positioned menus
- Creating a programmatic menu
- Context menu with nested items
- Context menu integration
- SlideMenu – menu in iPod style
- TieredMenu – submenus in nested overlays
- MegaMenu – multicolumn menu
- PanelMenu – hybrid of accordion and tree
- Accessing commands via Menubar
- Displaying checkboxes in CheckboxMenu
- Dock menu for Mac OS fans

Introduction

In this chapter we will learn about menu components. These days every website contains menus. Usually, a menu is presented to a user as a list of links to be navigated or commands to be executed. Menus are sometimes organized hierarchically, allowing navigation through different levels of the menu structure. Arranging menu items in logical groups makes it easy for users to quickly locate the related tasks. PrimeFaces' menus fulfill all major requirements. They come with various facets: static, dynamic, tiered, iPod styled, and so on, and leave nothing to be desired.

Several menu variations are covered in the recipes of this chapter. We will see a lot of recipes that will discuss menus' structure, configuration options, customizations, and integration with other components. At the end of this chapter, we should know what kind of menu to choose and how to put it on a page for various use cases.

Static and dynamic positioned menus

A menu can be positioned on a page in two ways: statically and dynamically. A menu is by default static. That means, the menu is in the normal page flow. Dynamic menu, in contrast, is not in the normal page flow and overlays other elements. In terms of CSS, it is absolutely positioned.

In this recipe, we will see how to develop these two kinds of positioned menus. But first, we will meet submenus and menu items.

How to do it...

A menu is composed of submenus and menu items. Submenus group single menu items. Grouped menu items can be presented in the same page flow or in an overlay over other elements. This behavior depends on the type of menu. The simple menu `p:menu` shows grouped menu items in the same page flow. Let's define an example structure for a static menu.

```
<p:growl id="growl"/>

<p:menu>
    <p:submenu label="JavaScript Libraries">
        <p:menuitem value="jQuery" url="http://jquery.com"/>
        <p:menuitem value="Yahoo UI" url="http://yuilibrary.com"/>
        <p:menuitem value=
        "Prototype" url="http://prototypejs.org"/>
    </p:submenu>
    <p:submenu label="Operations">
        <p:menuitem value="Save"
            actionListener=
            "#{positionedMenuController.save}" update="growl"/>
        <p:menuitem value="Update"
            actionListener=
            "#{positionedMenuController.update}" update="growl"/>
        <p:menuitem value="Delete"
            actionListener=
            "#{positionedMenuController.delete}" update="growl"/>
    </p:submenu>
</p:menu>
```

A dynamic menu is created by setting the `overlay` option to `true` and defining a trigger to show the menu. For example, a command button from the following code snippet acts as such a trigger. It will display a menu whose top-left corner is aligned with the bottom-left corner of the button when the user clicks on it.

```
<p:growl id="growl"/>

<p:menu overlay="true" trigger="btn" my="left top" at="bottom left">
    <p:menuitem value="Do something (ajax)"
        action=
        "#{positionedMenuController.doSomething}" update="growl"/>
    <p:menuitem value="Do something (non ajax)"
        action=
        "#{positionedMenuController.doSomething}" ajax="false"/>
    <p:menuitem value="Navigate" url="http://primefaces.org"/>
</p:menu>

<p:commandButton id="btn" value="Show dynamic menu" type="button"/>
```

The following screenshot shows both these types of menus. The dynamic menu is opened after the user has clicked on the button **Show dynamic menu**.

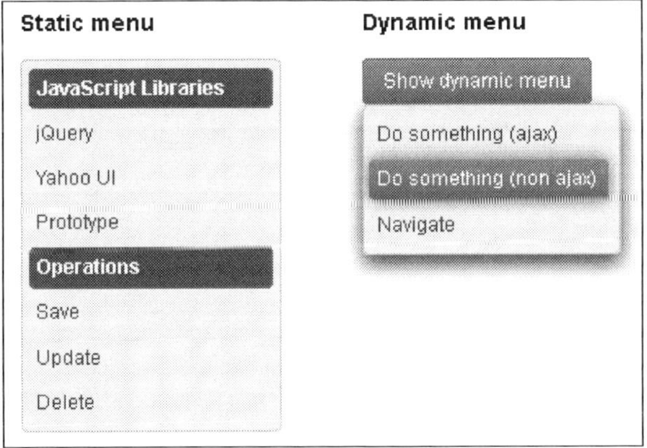

How it works...

We saw that `p:menuitem` can be placed either below `p:submenu` or directly under `p:menu`. As the menu uses menu items, it is easy to invoke actions or action listeners with or without AJAX (`ajax="false"`) as well as navigation. Navigation means a `GET` request, causing a switch to another page. This is always a full page refresh and only works when the `url` attribute on `p:menuitem` is set. In this case, the menu item is rendered as a normal HTML link element. If the `url` attribute is missing, only the `POST` requests (per AJAX or without) can be sent.

The location of the dynamic menu on a page is relative to the trigger and is defined by the `my` and `at` attributes, which take a combination of two values from the following:

- `left`
- `right`
- `bottom`
- `top`

There's more...

We can also specify an icon for the menu item and design attractive menus. There are two ways to specify an icon: either by using any predefined jQuery ThemeRoller style class (`http://jqueryui.com/themeroller`) which is a part of PrimeFaces themes or by providing our own style class for the icon attribute `<p:menuitem icon="home" .../>`.

```
.home {
   background: url(home.png) no-repeat;
   height:16px;
   width:16px;
}
```

See the *MenuItem* section in *PrimeFaces User's Guide* (`http://primefaces.org/documentation.html`) to learn more about menu item capabilities. Also consider *UI Element Guidelines* from Apple, which gives useful tips for designing menus in general (`http://developer.apple.com/library/mac/#documentation/UserExperience/Conceptual/AppleHIGuidelines/Menus/Menus.html`).

Place the most frequently used items at the top of the menu. The top of the menu tends to be the most visible part of the menu because users often see it first. Avoid combining semantically different actions/navigations in the same group. Avoid displaying an icon for every menu item. Include them only for menu items for which they add significant value. A menu that includes too many icons can appear cluttered and be hard to read.

PrimeFaces Cookbook Showcase application

This recipe is available in the demo web application on GitHub (`https://github.com/ova2/primefaces-cookbook`). Clone the project if you have not done it yet, explore the project structure, and execute the built-in Jetty Maven plugin to see this recipe in action. Follow the instructions in the `README` file if you do not know how to run Jetty.

When the server is running, the showcase for the recipe is available at `http://localhost:8080/primefaces-cookbook/views/chapter6/positionedMenus.jsf`.

Creating a programmatic menu

Programmatic menus offer a more flexible way in comparison to the declarative approach. The whole menu structure can be created in Java and bound as a model to the `p:menu` tag. Programmatic menu creation is the best choice when we load a menu definition from a database or XML file and the menu structure is not known beforehand.

In this recipe, we will learn about the PrimeFaces menu model and create a programmatic menu.

How to do it...

Every programmatically created menu instance should implement the Java interface `org.primefaces.model.MenuModel`. PrimeFaces provides a default implementation `org.primefaces.model.DefaultMenuModel` that is sufficient to use in most cases. Your own customized implementations of `MenuModel` are possible as well. Let's create a static menu from the *Static and dynamic positioned menus* recipe in a programmatic way.

```
@ManagedBean
@ViewScoped
public class ProgrammaticMenuController implements Serializable {

  private MenuModel model;

  @PostConstruct
  protected void initialize() {
    model = new DefaultMenuModel();

    // first submenu
    Submenu submenu = new Submenu();
    submenu.setLabel("JavaScript Libraries");

    // menu items
    MenuItem item = new MenuItem();
    item.setValue("jQuery");
    item.setUrl("http://jquery.com");
    submenu.getChildren().add(item);

    item = new MenuItem();
    item.setValue("Yahoo UI");
    item.setUrl("http://yuilibrary.com");
    submenu.getChildren().add(item);
```

```
        item = new MenuItem();
        item.setValue("Prototype");
        item.setUrl("http://prototypejs.org");
        submenu.getChildren().add(item);

        model.addSubmenu(submenu);

        // second submenu
        submenu = new Submenu();
        submenu.setLabel("Operations");

        // menu items
        item = new MenuItem();
        item.setValue("Save");
      item.addActionListener(FacesUtil.createMethodActionListener(
        "#{positionedMenuController.save}", Void.class, new Class[] {
        ActionEvent.class }));
        item.setUpdate("growl");
        submenu.getChildren().add(item);

        item = new MenuItem();
        item.setValue("Update");
        item.addActionListener(FacesUtil.createMethodActionListener(
        "#{positionedMenuController.update}", Void.class, new Class[]
        { ActionEvent.class }));
        item.setUpdate("growl");
        submenu.getChildren().add(item);

        item = new MenuItem();
        item.setValue("Delete");
        item.addActionListener(FacesUtil.createMethodActionListener(
        "#{positionedMenuController.delete}", Void.class, new Class[]
        { ActionEvent.class }));
        item.setUpdate("growl");
        submenu.getChildren().add(item);

        model.addSubmenu(submenu);
      }

      public MenuModel getModel() {
        return model;
      }
    }
```

The created menu can easily be bound to the corresponding component tag by means of the `model` attribute.

```
<p:menu model="#{programmaticMenuController.model}"/>
```

How it works...

After an instance of the `DefaultMenuModel` class is created, we create `Submenu` and generate the `MenuItem` instances. The `MenuItem` instances are children of `Submenu` and should be added as `submenu.getChildren().add(item)`. URLs are set by `item.setUrl()` as `String` objects. Actions or action listeners are set by `item.setActionExpression()` or `item.addActionListener()` as `MethodExpression` or `MethodExpressionActionListener` objects. The following utility methods demonstrate how to create such expression objects.

```
public static MethodExpression createMethodExpression(
    String valueExpression,
    Class<?> expectedReturnType,
    Class<?>[] expectedParamTypes) {

    FacesContext fc = FacesContext.getCurrentInstance();
    ExpressionFactory factory =
    fc.getApplication().getExpressionFactory();

    return factory.createMethodExpression(
        fc.getELContext(), valueExpression, expectedReturnType,
        expectedParamTypes);
}

public static MethodExpressionActionListener
createMethodActionListener(
    String valueExpression,
    Class<?> expectedReturnType,
    Class<?>[] expectedParamTypes) {

    return new

MethodExpressionActionListener(createMethodExpression(valueExpression,
expectedReturnType, expectedParamTypes));
}
```

There's more...

This recipe is available in the demo web application on GitHub (`https://github.com/ova2/primefaces-cookbook`). Clone the project if you have not done it yet, explore the project structure, and execute the built-in Jetty Maven plugin to see this recipe in action. Follow the instructions in the `README` file if you do not know how to run Jetty.

When the server is running, the showcase for the recipe is available at `http://localhost:8080/primefaces-cookbook/views/chapter6/programmaticMenu.jsf`.

Context menu with nested items

The context menu is displayed when the mouse is right-clicked. It replaces the native context menu in the browser and gives web applications a desktop-like feeling and behavior. PrimeFaces' context menu provides an overlay with submenus and menu items.

In this recipe, we will develop a context menu with nested items and see how to attach it to any component. As example, we will attach the context menu to a `panel` component.

How to do it...

The context menu is defined by the `p:contextMenu` tag. We would like to define two submenus—one with menu items having URLs (they send `GET` requests) and one with ajaxified menu items (they send `POST` requests). Ajaxified menu items perform the CRUD operations and update `p:growl`. The context menu is attached to `p:panel`. That means, only a right-click on the `panel` component displays the defined context menu. A click anywhere else displays the native web browser's context menu.

```
<p:growl id="growl"/>

<p:panel id="dummyPanel" header="Please click somewhere on panel to
see a context menu">
  <h:panelGroup layout="block" style="height:100px;"/>
</p:panel>

<p:contextMenu for="dummyPanel">
  <p:submenu label="JavaScript Libraries">
    <p:menuitem value="jQuery" url="http://jquery.com"/>
    <p:menuitem value="Yahoo UI" url="http://yuilibrary.com"/>
    <p:menuitem value="Prototype" url="http://prototypejs.org"/>
    </p:submenu>
  <p:separator/>
```

```
    <p:submenu label="Operations">
      <p:menuitem value="Save"
          actionListener=
          "#{contextMenuController.save}" update="growl"/>
      <p:menuitem value="Update"
          actionListener=
          "#{contextMenuController.update}" update="growl"/>
      <p:menuitem value="Delete"
          actionListener=
          "#{contextMenuController.delete}" update="growl"/>
    </p:submenu>
  </p:contextMenu>
```

The following screenshot shows what it looks like:

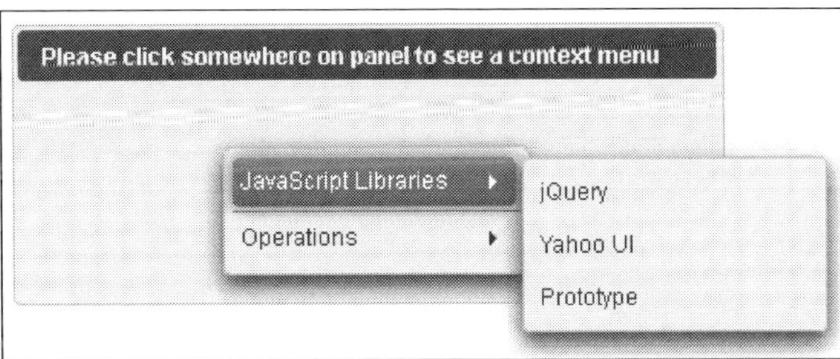

How it works...

By default, `ContextMenu` without the defined `for` attribute is attached to the whole page. That means, a right-click somewhere on the page will display the menu. The `for` attribute defines a component to which `ContextMenu` is attached. The value of `for` specifies a "search expression" in terms of `findComponent()`. The *AJAX basics with Process and Update* recipe in *Chapter 1, Getting Started with PrimeFaces*, provides more details on such expressions for `findComponent()`.

There's more...

Context menus can also be created programmatically and bound to `p:contextMenu` by the `model` attribute. Programmatic menus are discussed in the *Creating a programmatic menu* recipe of this chapter.

PrimeFaces Cookbook Showcase application

This recipe is available in the demo web application on GitHub (`https://github.com/ova2/primefaces-cookbook`). Clone the project if you have not done it yet, explore the project structure, and execute the built-in Jetty Maven plugin to see this recipe in action. Follow the instructions in the `README` file if you do not know how to run Jetty.

When the server is running, the showcase for the recipe is available at `http://localhost:8080/primefaces-cookbook/views/chapter6/contextMenu.jsf`.

See also

- Data iteration components have an exclusive integration with the context menu. Refer to the *Context menu integration* recipe to learn more about such integrations

Context menu integration

Data components such as `DataTable`, `Tree`, and `TreeTable` have a special integration with the context menu. These components can display a context menu per mouse right-click on any row in `DataTable` or any node in `Tree`.

In this recipe, we will integrate a context menu with the `Tree` component. Integration with `DataTable` or `TreeTable` is similar and well described in the *PrimeFaces User's Guide* documentation of these components (`http://primefaces.org/documentation.html`).

How to do it...

We will develop a context menu with two menu items, `View` and `Delete`. A `View` item shows the currently selected tree node and the `Delete` item removes it. We would like to implement this behavior for all tree nodes. The following listing demonstrates the `p:contextMenu` integration with `p:tree`:

```
<p:growl id="growl" showDetail="true"/>

<p:contextMenu for="fileSystem">
    <p:menuitem value="View" update="growl"
                actionListener="#{contextMenuController.viewNode}"
                icon="ui-icon-search"/>
    <p:menuitem value="Delete" update="fileSystem"
                actionListener="#{contextMenuController.deleteNode}"
                icon="ui-icon-close"/>
</p:contextMenu>
```

```
<p:tree id="fileSystem" value="#{contextMenuController.root}"
        var="node" dynamic="true"
        cache="false" selectionMode="single"
        selection="#{contextMenuController.selectedNode}">
        <p:ajax event="select"
            listener="#{contextMenuController.onNodeSelect}"/>
        <p:ajax event="unselect"
            listener="#{contextMenuController.onNodeUnselect}"/>
        <p:treeNode>
            <h:outputText value="#{node}"/>
        </p:treeNode>
</p:tree>
```

We can see the context menu over tree nodes in the picture. The clicked **View** item shows a `growl` notification.

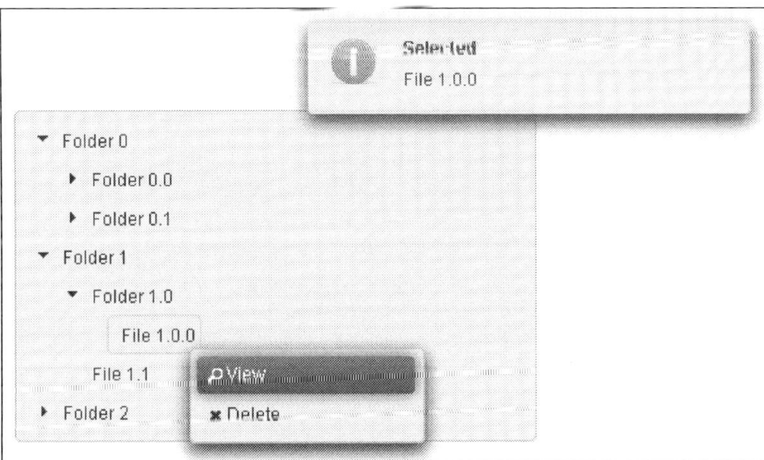

`Tree` is built up by a view-scoped managed bean `ContextMenuController`. The bean implements all listener methods.

```
@ManagedBean
@ViewScoped
public class ContextMenuController implements Serializable {

    private TreeNode root;
    private TreeNode selectedNode;

    @PostConstruct
    protected void initialize() {
        root = new DefaultTreeNode("Root", null);
```

```
        TreeNode node0 = new DefaultTreeNode("Folder 0", root);
        ...
    }

    public TreeNode getRoot() {
        return root;
    }

    public TreeNode getSelectedNode() {
        return selectedNode;
    }

    public void setSelectedNode(TreeNode selectedNode) {
        this.selectedNode = selectedNode;
    }

    public void onNodeSelect(NodeSelectEvent event) {
        selectedNode = event.getTreeNode();
    }

    public void onNodeUnselect(NodeUnselectEvent event) {
        selectedNode = null;
    }

    public void viewNode() {
        if (selectedNode == null) {
            return;
        }

        FacesMessage msg =
        new FacesMessage(FacesMessage.SEVERITY_INFO,
            "Selected", selectedNode.getData().toString());
        FacesContext.getCurrentInstance().addMessage(null, msg);
    }

    public void deleteNode() {
        if (selectedNode == null) {
            return;
        }

        selectedNode.getChildren().clear();
        selectedNode.getParent().getChildren().
        remove(selectedNode);
```

```
            selectedNode.setParent(null);
            selectedNode = null;
        }
    }
```

How it works...

When a menu item is clicked, the entire `Tree` component gets processed and the currently selected node is stored in the bean via the EL expression `#{contextMenuController.selectedNode}`. After that, an action listener is called and can access the selected node. The action listener `viewNode()` only generates a message with the name of the selected node. The subsequent AJAX response updates `p:growl`. We see a `growl` notification. The action listener `deleteNode()` deletes the selected node from the tree model. The subsequent AJAX response updates the `p:tree` (see <p:menuitem ... update="fileSystem"/>). We see an updated tree without the deleted node.

There's more...

`p:contextMenu` features an attribute `nodeType`. This attribute specifies the type of tree nodes to attach to. It matches the `type` attribute of `p:treeNode`. Hence, different menus can be attached to particular tree nodes by matching the menu's `nodeType` to the tree node's `type`.

> The matching occurs in a similar fashion to the `for` attribute of a label (`h:outputLabel` or `p:outputLabel`), linking it to an input component.

PrimeFaces Cookbook Showcase application

This recipe is available in the demo web application on GitHub (`https://github.com/ova2/primefaces-cookbook`). Clone the project if you have not done it yet, explore the project structure, and execute the built-in Jetty Maven plugin to see this recipe in action. Follow instructions in the `README` file if you do not know how to run Jetty.

When the server is running, the showcase for the recipe is available at `http://localhost:8080/primefaces-cookbook/views/chapter6/contextMenuIntegration.jsf`.

See also

- Explore data iteration components in *Chapter 5, Data Iteration Components*. You will find many tips for using `p:tree`, `p:dataTable`, and `p:treeTable`.

SlideMenu – menu in iPod style

A slide menu displays nested submenus as slides with animation similar to the iPod menu. A slide menu features the same common behaviors as every PrimeFaces' menu. It consists of (nested) submenus and menu items that can be built declaratively or programmatically by the model. The main difference to other menu types is a slide animation when displaying submenus. Positioning of the slide menu is static by default, but it can also be positioned relative to a trigger that shows the menu.

In this recipe, we will develop a slide menu with a button acting as the trigger. When the user pushes the button, the menu will be displayed in an overlay.

How to do it...

We will take `p:commandButton` as trigger. The `p:slideMenu` tag, representing a slide menu, has a `trigger` attribute that points to the ID of `p:commandButton`. The slide menu consists of submenus (slides) with menu items sending AJAX, non-AJAX (`ajax="false"`), and `GET` requests (`url` is not null).

```
<p:growl id="growl"/>

<p:commandButton id="btn" value="Show Slide Menu" type="button"/>

<p:slideMenu overlay="true" trigger="btn" my="left top"
    at="left bottom" style="width:190px;">
    <p:submenu label="CRUD Operations" icon="ui-icon-play">
        <p:menuitem value=
        "Save" actionListener="#{slideMenuController.save}"
        icon="ui-icon-disk" update="growl"/>
        <p:menuitem value=
        "Update" actionListener="#{slideMenuController.update}"
        icon="ui-icon-arrowrefresh-1-w" update="growl"/>
        <p:menuitem value=
        "Delete" actionListener="#{slideMenuController.delete}"
        icon="ui-icon-trash" update="growl"/>
    </p:submenu>
    <p:submenu label="Other Operations" icon="ui-icon-play">
        <p:menuitem value="Do something" actionListener=
        "#{slideMenuController.doSomething}"
        ajax="false" icon="ui-icon-check"/>
        <p:menuitem value="Go Home" action="/views/home"
```

```
            ajax="false" icon="ui-icon-home"/>
        </p:submenu>
        <p:submenu label="JSF Links" icon="ui-icon-extlink">
            <p:submenu label="JSF Components">
                <p:menuitem value="PrimeFaces"
                url="http://primefaces.org"/>
                <p:menuitem value="PrimeFaces Extensions"
                                           url="http://code.google.com/p/
    primefaces-extensions"/>
                <p:menuitem value=
                "RichFaces" url="http://jboss.org/richfaces"/>
            </p:submenu>
            <p:menuitem value="JSF API"
            url="http://javaserverfaces.java.net/nonav/docs/2.1"/>
        </p:submenu>
    </p:slideMenu>
```

The following screenshot shows how the slide menu looks when it is open (left part of the screenshot) and after a click on the menu item **Other Operations** (right part of the screenshot):

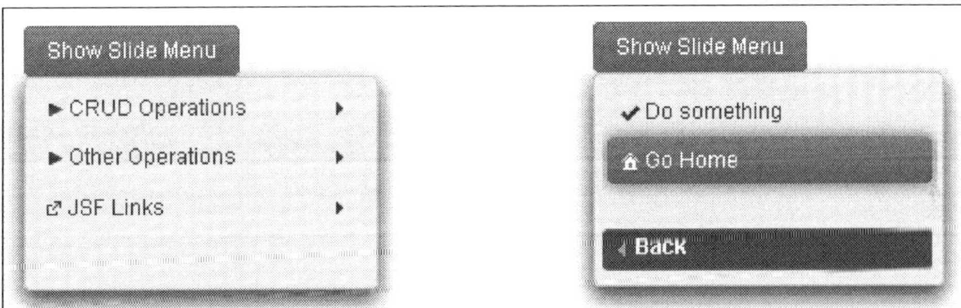

How it works...

By default, the `SlideMenu` component is positioned statically in the normal page flow. To position it dynamically, relative to a trigger component, we need to set `overlay="true"`. The preceding sample attaches a `SlideMenu` component to the button so that whenever the button is clicked the menu will display itself in an overlay. The dynamic menu's position can be controlled by the `my` and `at` attributes. `my` specifies a corner of the menu to align with the trigger element, and `at` specifies a corner of the trigger to align with the menu element.

There's more...

There is also a `triggerEvent` attribute. It defines an event name for the trigger that will show the dynamically positioned menu. The default value is `click`.

`SlideMenu` can also be opened manually by the client-side API. The menu's widget exposes the `show()` and `hide()` methods to show and hide the overlay menu respectively.

PrimeFaces Cookbook Showcase application

This recipe is available in the demo web application on GitHub (`https://github.com/ova2/primefaces-cookbook`). Clone the project if you have not done it yet, explore the project structure, and execute the built-in Jetty Maven plugin to see this recipe in action. Follow the instructions in the `README` file if you do not know how to run Jetty.

When the server is running, the showcase for the recipe is available at `http://localhost:8080/primefaces-cookbook/views/chapter6/slideMenu.jsf`.

See also

- See the *Static and dynamic positioned menus* recipe in this chapter to get some basic knowledge of statically and dynamically positioned menus

TieredMenu – submenus in nested overlays

A tiered menu displays nested submenus as overlays. Tiered menu features the same common behaviors as every PrimeFaces' menu—it consists of (nested) submenus and menu items that can be built declaratively or programmatically by model. The main difference to a default menu described in the *Static and dynamic positioned menus* recipe of this chapter is displaying with overlays. Positioning of the tiered menu is static by default, but it can also be positioned relative to a trigger that shows the menu.

In this recipe, we will develop static and dynamic tiered menus. A dynamic tiered menu will be shown after a click on a button acting as the trigger. Furthermore, we will learn about the auto-display feature.

How to do it...

The following code listing demonstrates three tiered menus: static (default), static without the auto-display feature, and dynamic. As the trigger for the dynamic menu, we will take a `p:commandButton` tag. The `p:tieredMenu` tag, representing a tiered menu, has a `trigger` attribute that points to the ID of `p:commandButton`.

```
<p:growl id="growl"/>

<h3 style="margin-top:0">Default TieredMenu</h3>

<p:tieredMenu style="width:190px;">
    <ui:include src="/views/chapter6/tieredMenuStructure.xhtml"/>
</p:tieredMenu>

<h3 style="margin-top:20px">TieredMenu without autoDisplay</h3>

<p:tieredMenu autoDisplay="false" style="width:190px;">
    <ui:include src="/views/chapter6/tieredMenuStructure.xhtml"/>
</p:tieredMenu>

<h3 style="margin-top:20px">TieredMenu on Overlay</h3>

<p:commandButton id="btn" value="Show Tiered Menu" type="button"/>

<p:tieredMenu overlay="true"
    trigger="btn" my="left top" at="left bottom" style="width:190px;">
    <ui:include src="/views/chapter6/tieredMenuStructure.xhtml"/>
</p:tieredMenu>
```

The tiered menu consists of submenus with menu items sending AJAX, non-AJAX (`ajax="false"`), and `GET` requests (`url` is not null).

```
<p:submenu label="CRUD Operations" icon="ui-icon-play">
    <p:menuitem value=
    "Save" actionListener="#{tieredMenuController.save}"
    icon="ui-icon-disk" update="growl"/>
    <p:menuitem value=
    "Update" actionListener="#{tieredMenuController.update}"
    icon="ui-icon-arrowrefresh-1-w" update="growl"/>
    <p:menuitem value=
    "Delete" actionListener="#{tieredMenuController.delete}"
    icon="ui-icon-trash" update="growl"/>
</p:submenu>
<p:submenu label="Other Operations" icon="ui-icon-play">
    <p:menuitem value="Do something" actionListener=
    "#{tieredMenuController.doSomething}"
    ajax="false" icon="ui-icon-check"/>
```

```
        <p:menuitem value="Go Home" action=
        "/views/home" ajax="false" icon="ui-icon-home"/>
    </p:submenu>
    <p:submenu label="JSF Links" icon="ui-icon-extlink">
        <p:submenu label="JSF Components">
        <p:menuitem value="PrimeFaces" url="http://primefaces.org"/>
        <p:menuitem value="PrimeFaces Extensions"
        url="http://code.google.com/p/primefaces-extensions"/>
        <p:menuitem value=
        "RichFaces" url="http://jboss.org/richfaces"/>
        </p:submenu>
      <p:menuitem value=
      "JSF API" url="http://javaserverfaces.java.net/nonav/docs/2.1"/>
    </p:submenu>
```

The following screenshot shows how the static tiered menu looks when opening nested submenus:

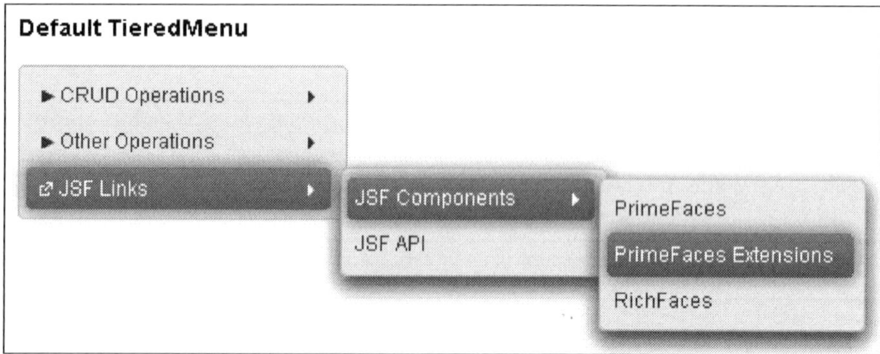

How it works...

By default, the `TieredMenu` component is positioned statically in a normal page flow. There are two modes: with and without the auto-display feature. If `autoDisplay` is set to `true` (default), the content of the submenu is displayed when the mouse is over it. A menu with `autoDisplay` set to `false` requires a click on a submenu to display its menu items.

A dynamically positioned menu is defined by setting `overlay` to `true`. The preceding sample attaches a `TieredMenu` component to the button so that whenever the button is clicked the menu will display itself in an overlay. Dynamic menu position can be controlled by the `my` and `at` attributes. `my` specifies a corner of the menu to align with the trigger element, and `at` specifies a corner of the trigger to align with the menu element.

There's more...

There is also a `triggerEvent` attribute. It defines an event name for the trigger that will show the dynamically positioned menu. The default value is `click`.

`TieredMenu` can also be opened manually by the client-side API. The menu's widget exposes the `show()` or `hide()` methods to show or hide the overlay menu.

PrimeFaces Cookbook Showcase application

This recipe is available in the demo web application on GitHub (`https://github.com/ova2/primefaces-cookbook`). Clone the project if you have not done it yet, explore the project structure, and execute the built-in Jetty Maven plugin to see this recipe in action. Follow the instructions in the `README` file if you do not know how to run Jetty.

When the server is running, the showcase for the recipe is available at `http://localhost:8080/primefaces-cookbook/views/chapter6/tieredMenu.jsf`.

See also

- See the *Static and dynamic positioned menus* recipe in this chapter to get some basic knowledge about statically and dynamically positioned menus

MegaMenu – multicolumn menu

A mega menu, sometimes also called a mega drop down menu, is designed to enhance scannability and categorization of its contents. PrimeFaces' mega menu is a horizontal navigation component that displays menu items grouped in submenus. The main advantage of such a kind of menu is that everything is visible at once—no scrolling is required.

In this recipe, we will design and implement a mega menu for an imaginary online shop selling clothes.

How to do it...

The layout of the `MegaMenu` component is grid-based. That means, root items require columns as children to define each section in a grid. Root items are direct submenus below `p:megaMenu`.

We will design four root items. The first one will show women's clothing, the second one will show men's clothing, the third one will show a color guide (pictures with available clothing colors), and the last one will show the shopping cart in a dialog.

```
<p:megaMenu>
    <p:submenu label="Women's Clothing" icon="ui-icon-person">
        <p:column>
            <p:submenu label="Shoes">
                <p:menuitem value="Size UK 3-5" url="#"/>
                <p:menuitem value="Size UK 6-8" url="#"/>
            </p:submenu>
            <p:submenu label="Jeans">
                <p:menuitem value="Curve" url="#"/>
                <p:menuitem value="Maternity" url="#"/>
                <p:menuitem value="Petites" url="#"/>
            </p:submenu>
            <p:submenu label="Nightwear">
                <p:menuitem value="Calvin Klein" url="#"/>
                <p:menuitem value="Curvy Kate" url="#"/>
            </p:submenu>
        </p:column>
        <p:column>
            <p:submenu label="Leggings">
                <p:menuitem value="Long Sleeve" url="#"/>
                <p:menuitem value="Short Sleeve" url="#"/>
            </p:submenu>
            <p:submenu label="Skirts">
                <p:menuitem value="American Apparel" url="#"/>
                <p:menuitem value="American Vintage" url="#"/>
                <p:menuitem value="Aqua" url="#"/>
                <p:menuitem value="Dagmar" url="#"/>
                <p:menuitem value="Osasis" url="#"/>
            </p:submenu>
        </p:column>
    </p:submenu>

    <p:submenu label="Men's Clothing" icon="ui-icon-person">
        // it is built in the same fashion as the p:submenu above
        ...
    </p:submenu>

    <p:submenu label="Color Guide" icon="ui-icon-image">
        <p:column>
```

```
            <h:graphicImage library="images" name="colors.gif"/>
        </p:column>
    </p:submenu>

    <p:menuitem value="Shopping Cart" onclick="wdgtShoppingCart.
    show();"
    update="shoppingCartGrp" icon="ui-icon-cart"/>
</p:megaMenu>

<p:dialog id="shoppingCart" header="Shopping Cart"
    widgetVar="wdgtShoppingCart">
    <h:panelGroup id="shoppingCartGrp" layout="block"
    style="padding:20px;">
        <h:outputText value="#{megaMenuController.items}"/>
    </h:panelGroup>
    <p:commandButton value="Close" type="button"
    onclick="wdgtShoppingCart.hide();"/>
</p:dialog>
```

The following screenshot shows the designed mega menu:

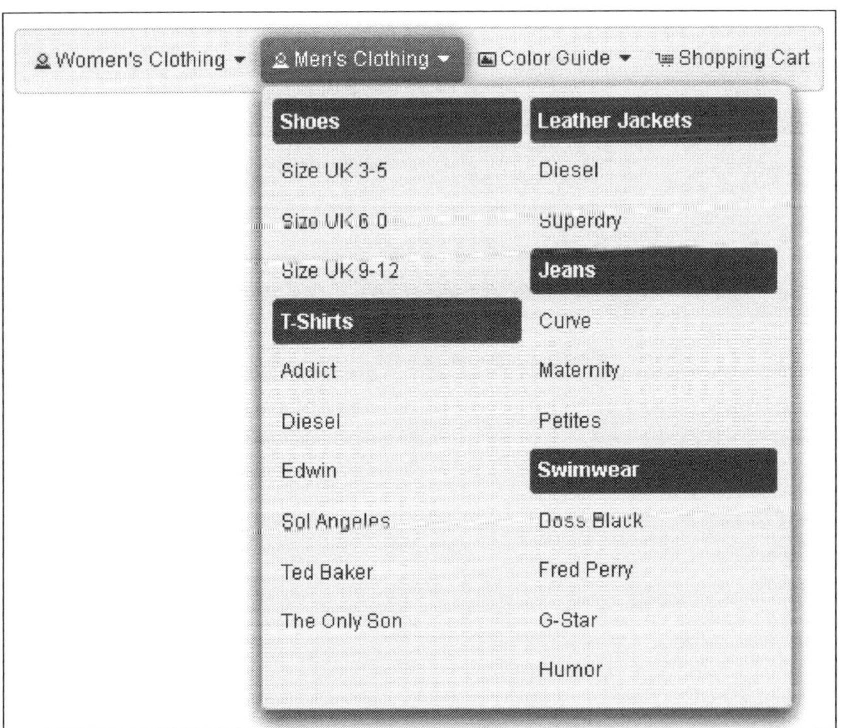

How it works...

Direct submenus of `p:megaMenu` require `p:column` to be represented in a multicolumn grid. Not only submenus, but also any content can be placed inside columns. In the preceding example, we can see `<h:graphicImage library="images" name="colors.gif"/>` below `p:column`.

Except for `p:column`, the structure of `p:megaMenu` is the same as for every PrimeFaces' menu component—it consists of submenus and menu items. A menu item as a root item is supported as well. In the designed example, it is the menu item **Shopping Cart**.

There's more...

`MegaMenu` has the auto-display feature. This feature defines whether submenus will be displayed on a mouseover event or not. If `autoDisplay` is set to `true` (default), the content of the submenu is displayed when the mouse is over it. A menu with the setting `autoDisplay="false"` requires a click on a submenu to display its menu items.

PrimeFaces Cookbook Showcase application

This recipe is available in the demo web application on GitHub (`https://github.com/ova2/primefaces-cookbook`). Clone the project if you have not done it yet, explore the project structure, and execute the built-in Jetty Maven plugin to see this recipe in action. Follow the instructions in the `README` file if you do not know how to run Jetty.

When the server is running, the showcase for the recipe is available at `http://localhost:8080/primefaces-cookbook/views/chapter6/megaMenu.jsf`.

PanelMenu – hybrid of accordion and tree

A panel menu is a hybrid of accordion and tree components used for navigations and actions. It renders a vertical menu structure with support for nested menu items.

In this recipe, we will develop a panel menu with three top submenus acting as accordion tabs and nested menu items with a tree-like look and feel.

How to do it...

A panel menu is rendered by the `p:panelMenu` tag. Top level submenus define accordion-like tabs. A click on such a tab expands or collapses the subordinated content. The menu structure is similar to every PrimeFaces' menu component—it consists of submenus and menu items. Menu items can call actions, action listeners, or trigger navigations.

```
<p:panelMenu style="width:200px">
  <p:submenu label="Ajax Operations">
    <p:menuitem value=
    "Save" actionListener="#{panelMenuController.save}"
    icon="ui-icon-disk"/>
    <p:menuitem value=
    "Update" actionListener="#{panelMenuController.update}"
    icon="ui-icon-arrowrefresh-1-w"/>
  </p:submenu>
  <p:submenu label="Non-Ajax Operations">
    <p:menuitem value=
    "Delete" actionListener="#{panelMenuController.delete}"
    ajax="false" icon="ui-icon-close"/>
  </p:submenu>
  <p:separator/>
    <p:submenu label="Navigations">
      <p:submenu label="Links" icon="ui-icon-extlink">
        <p:submenu label="Prime Products">
        <p:menuitem value="Prime UI" icon="ui-icon-home"
        url="http://primefaces.org/showcase-labs"/>
        <p:menuitem value="Prime Mobile" icon="ui-icon-signal"
        url="http://primefaces.org/showcase-labs/mobile"/>
        <p:menuitem value=
        "Prime Push" icon="ui-icon-arrowreturnthick-1-n"
        url="http://primefaces.org/showcase-labs/push"/>
      </p:submenu>
      <p:submenu label="Prime Resources">
        <p:menuitem value=
        "Docs" url="http://primefaces.org/documentation.html"
        icon="ui-icon-document"/>
        <p:menuitem value=
        "Download" url="http://primefaces.org/downloads.html"
        icon="ui-icon-arrowthick-1-s"/>
      </p:submenu>
    </p:submenu>
  </p:submenu>
</p:panelMenu>
```

The result of the preceding code listing is shown in the following screenshot. This screenshot demonstrates the same menu in two states—completely collapsed on the left side and completely expanded on the right side:

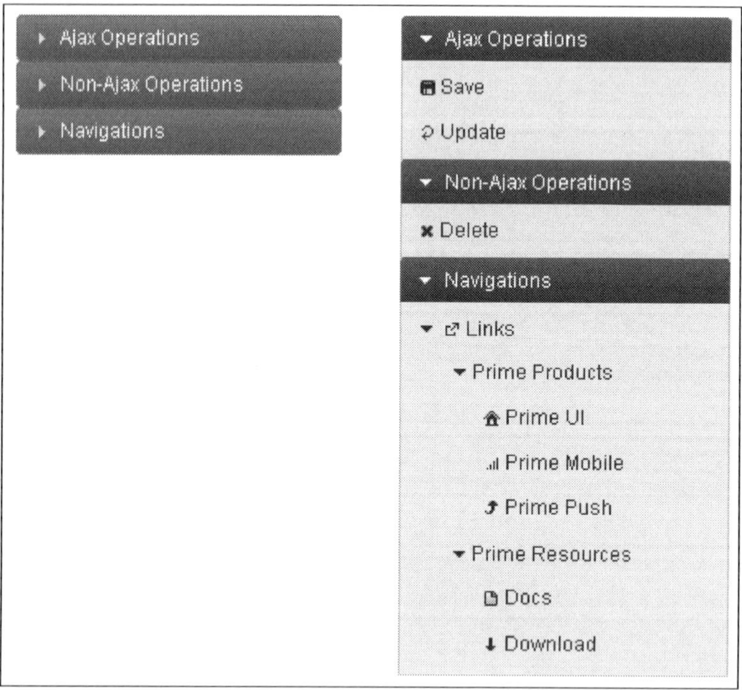

How it works...

We see that direct children of `p:panelMenu` are normally several `p:submenu` tags with labels describing the accordion-like tabs. Tabs can be styled by the `.ui-panelmenu h3` selector. In this recipe we will use the following definition:

```
.ui-panelmenu h3 {
    font-size: 1em;
}
```

As the menu uses menu items, it is easy to invoke actions or action listeners with or without AJAX (`ajax="false"`) as well as navigation. Navigation means a `GET` request, causing a switch to another page. This is always a full page refresh and only works when the `url` attribute on `p:menuitem` is set. In this case, the menu item is rendered as a normal HTML link element. If the `url` attribute is missing, only `POST` requests (per AJAX or without) can be sent.

There's more...

The PanelMenu component keeps the open or close state of submenus across web pages. The state is saved in cookies. That means, when the user enters the same page again, PanelMenu will be displayed in the same state as when he/she had last interacted with it. It is a pretty useful feature, but sometimes it is not desired if, for example, multiple users with different accounts work on the same PC. In this case, we can either call the widget method clearState() (client-side solution) or clear the cookie on logout in the response (server-side solution). The cookie name is panelMenu-<id>, where <id> is the client ID of p:panelMenu.

PrimeFaces Cookbook Showcase application

This recipe is available in the demo web application on GitHub (https://github.com/ova2/primefaces-cookbook). Clone the project if you have not done it yet, explore the project structure, and execute the built-in Jetty Maven plugin to see this recipe in action. Follow the instructions in the README file if you do not know how to run Jetty.

When the server is running, the showcase for the recipe is available at http://localhost:8080/primefaces-cookbook/views/chapter6/panelMenu.jsf.

Accessing commands via Menubar

Menubar is a horizontal navigation component with drop-down menus that are displayed on mouse over or on clicking. Menubar features the same common behaviors as every PrimeFaces' menu. It consists of (nested) submenus and menu items that can be built declaratively or programmatically by model.

In this recipe, we will build a declarative menu bar with various commands as nested and direct menu items.

How to do it...

We will create a menu bar as shown in the following screenshot:

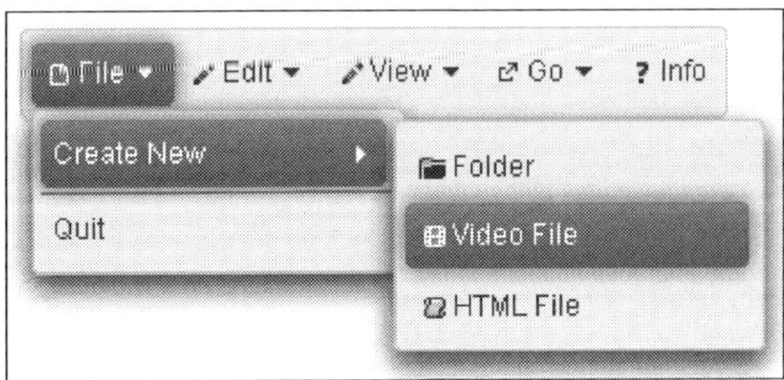

The following complete code listing shows `p:menubar` with submenus `p:submenu` and menu items `p:menuitem` inside. For instance, the submenu **Create New** contains three menu items, **Folder**, **Video File**, and **HTML File**.

```
<p:growl id="growl"/>

<p:menubar>
  <p:submenu label="File" icon="ui-icon-document">
    <p:submenu label="Create New">
      <p:menuitem value="Folder" actionListener=
      "#{menubarController.createFolder}"
        icon="ui-icon-folder-collapsed" update="growl"/>
      <p:menuitem value="Video File" actionListener=
      "#{menubarController.createVideo}"
        icon="ui-icon-video" update="growl"/>
      <p:menuitem value="HTML File" actionListener=
      "#{menubarController.createHTML}"
        icon="ui-icon-script" update="growl"/>
    </p:submenu>
    <p:separator/>
    <p:menuitem value="Quit" url="#"/>
  </p:submenu>
  <p:submenu label="Edit" icon="ui-icon-pencil">
    <p:menuitem value="Cut" actionListener=
    "#{menubarController.cut}"
      icon="ui-icon-scissors" update="growl"/>
    <p:menuitem value="Copy" actionListener=
    "#{menubarController.copy}"
      icon="ui-icon-copy" update="growl"/>
    <p:menuitem value="Paste" actionListener=
    "#{menubarController.paste}"
      icon="ui-icon-clipboard" update="growl"/>
  </p:submenu>
  <p:submenu label="View" icon="ui-icon-pencil">
    <p:menuitem value="Zoom In" actionListener=
    "#{menubarController.zoomIn}"
      icon="ui-icon-zoomin" update="growl"/>
    <p:menuitem value="Zoom Out" actionListener=
    "#{menubarController.zoomOut}"
      icon="ui-icon-zoomout" update="growl"/>
    <p:submenu label="View Mode" icon="ui-icon-search">
    <p:menuitem value="View Icons" actionListener=
    "#{menubarController.viewIcons}"
      update="growl"/>
```

```
      <p:menuitem value="View Compact" actionListener=
      "#{menubarController.viewCompact}"
        update="growl"/>
      <p:menuitem value="View Details" actionListener=
      "#{menubarController.viewDetails}"
        update="growl"/>
    </p:submenu>
    </p:submenu>
    <p:submenu label="Go" icon="ui-icon-extlink">
      <p:menuitem value=
      "Source" url="https://github.com/ova2/primefaces-cookbook"
        icon="ui-icon-star"/>
      <p:menuitem value=
      "Home" url="http://ova2.github.com/primefaces-cookbook"
        icon="ui-icon-home"/>
    </p:submenu>
    <p:menuitem value="Info" action=
    "#{menubarController.info}" ajax="false"
      icon="ui-icon-help"/>
  </p:menubar>

  <p:dialog visible="#{flash.helpVisible}" header="Info Dialog">
    PrimeFaces Menubar brings desktop menubar to JSF
    applications.<br/>
    Combine submenus and menu items to execute
    ajax, non-ajax and navigations.
  </p:dialog>
```

`Menubar` supports menu items as root items as well. In the developed example, this is the menu item **Info**. A click on **Info** shows an information dialog:

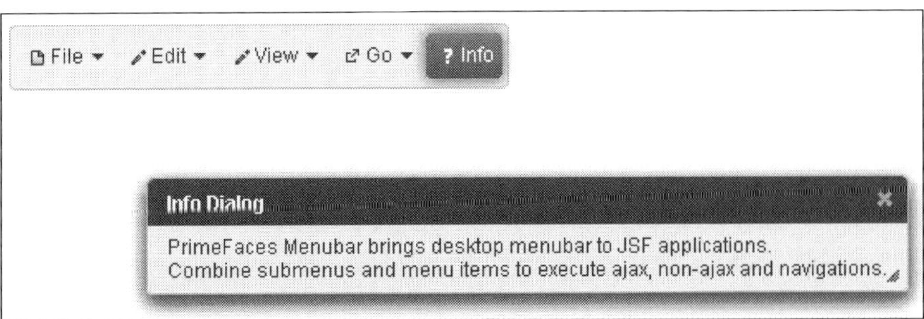

How it works...

Commands are implemented as action listeners, for example, `actionListener="#{menubarController.createFolder}"`, which updates the growl component `p:growl`. The commands in the sample are doing nothing except showing info messages. A typical command's code looks as follows:

```
public void createFolder(ActionEvent ae) {
  FacesMessage msg = new
  FacesMessage(FacesMessage.SEVERITY_INFO, "Create Folder", null);
  FacesContext.getCurrentInstance().addMessage(null, msg);
}
```

The info dialog is only visible when the EL expression `visible="#{flash.helpVisible}"` returns `true`. The non-AJAX `info` action uses the JSF `FlashScope` to pass the value (`true`) of the `helpVisible` variable to the same page with a full page request.

```
public String info() {
    FacesContext.getCurrentInstance().getExternalContext().
    getFlash().put("helpVisible", true);

    return "/views/chapter6/menubar.xhtml";
}
```

There's more...

The `Menubar` component has two modes: with and without the auto-display feature. If autoDisplay is set to `true` (default), the first level of submenus is displayed when the mouse is over the submenu. A menu with the setting `autoDisplay="false"` requires a click to display the first level of submenus.

PrimeFaces Cookbook Showcase application

This recipe is available in the demo web application on GitHub (`https://github.com/ova2/primefaces-cookbook`). Clone the project if you have not done it yet, explore the project structure, and execute the built-in Jetty Maven plugin to see this recipe in action. Follow the instructions in the `README` file if you do not know how to run Jetty.

When the server is running, the showcase for the recipe is available at `http://localhost:8080/primefaces-cookbook/views/chapter6/menubar.jsf`.

Displaying checkboxes in SelectCheckboxMenu

SelectCheckboxMenu is a multiselect input component based on checkboxes in an overlay menu. Although it is an input component, it is presented to users as a menu so that it makes sense to handle SelectCheckboxMenu in this chapter.

In this recipe, we will implement a simple and an advanced SelectCheckboxMenu component. In the advanced case, we will learn about the built-in filtering feature. Selected items should be shown in a dialog when submitting.

How to do it...

Usage of SelectCheckboxMenu is the same as for SelectManyCheckbox. Checkbox items can be attached via several f:selectItem tags or one f:selectItems tag. In the following simple example, we will use f:selectItems to display colors:

```
<p:selectCheckboxMenu value="#{checkboxMenu.selectedColors}"
                      label="Colors">
    <f:selectItems value="#{checkboxMenu.colors}"/>
</p:selectCheckboxMenu>
```

The label attribute defines a text shown to the user. The advanced SelectCheckboxMenu comes with a filtering feature. The feature gets activated by setting filter to true. The filterText attribute defines a text shown in the filter's input field when the user opens the menu. It is **Filter languages** in the following example.

```
<p:selectCheckboxMenu value="#{checkboxMenu.selectedLanguages}"
                      label="Languages" filter="true"
filterText="Filter languages">
    <f:selectItems value="#{checkboxMenu.languages}"/>
    <f:converter converterId=
    "org.primefaces.cookbook.converter.LocaleConverter"/>
</p:selectCheckboxMenu>

<p:commandButton value="Submit" update="display"
oncomplete="dlg.show()" style="margin-top:20px; display:block;"/>

<p:dialog header="Selected colors and languages" widgetVar="dlg">
    <h:panelGroup id="display">
```

```
            <p:dataList value=
            "#{checkboxMenu.selectedColors}" var="color">
                #{color}
            </p:dataList>
            <p:dataList value=
            "#{checkboxMenu.selectedLanguages}" var="lang">
                #{lang}
            </p:dataList>
        </h:panelGroup>
    </p:dialog>
```

The following screenshot shows the simple and advanced cases, as well as a dialog with the selected values:

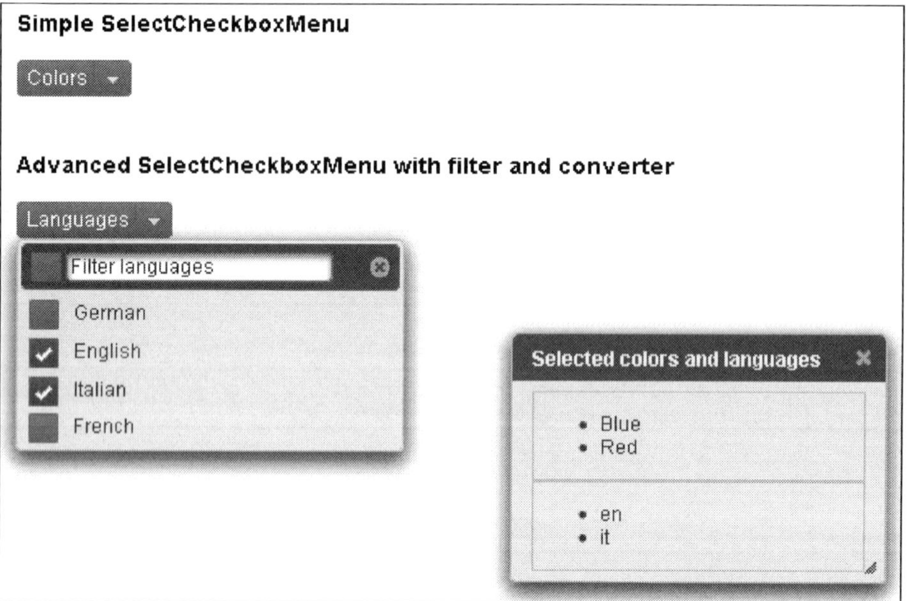

How it works...

The available checkbox items are created in the managed bean `CheckboxMenu`. Items for colors are stored in a `HashMap` class and items for languages are stored in a list of `SelectItem` objects.

```
@ManagedBean
@ViewScoped
public class CheckboxMenu implements Serializable {
```

```
    private List<SelectItem> languages;
    private Map<String, String> color;
    private List<Locale> selectedLanguages;
    private List<String> selectedColors;

    public List<SelectItem> getLanguages() {
        if (languages == null) {
            languages = new ArrayList<SelectItem>();
            languages.add(
                new SelectItem(new Locale("de"), "German"));
            ...
        }

        return languages;
    }

    public Map<String, String> getColors() {
        if (color == null) {
            color = new HashMap<String, String>();
            color.put("Red", "Red");
            ...
        }

        return color;
    }

    // getter, setter
    ...
}
```

After submitting the form, the selected items get set in the `selectedColors` and `selectedLanguages` variables respectively. Their values are displayed as lists in the dialog.

There's more...

In the advanced example, we used `LocaleConverter`—a JSF converter to convert `java.util.Locale` to `String`, and visa versa. The `LocaleConverter` class can be found on GitHub (`https://github.com/ova2/primefaces-cookbook`) in the `org.primefaces.cookbook.converter` package.

Note that filter text leverages the HTML5 attribute placeholder, so that it is not shown in browsers that do not support HTML5. Well-known browsers without HTML5 support are Internet Explorer 7 and 8.

PrimeFaces Cookbook Showcase application

This recipe is available in the demo web application on GitHub (`https://github.com/ova2/primefaces-cookbook`). Clone the project if you have not done it yet, explore the project structure, and execute the built-in Jetty Maven plugin to see this recipe in action. Follow the instructions in the `README` file if you do not know how to run Jetty.

When the server is running, the showcase for the recipe is available at `http://localhost:8080/primefaces-cookbook/views/chapter6/checkboxMenu.jsf`.

Dock menu for Mac OS fans

The PrimeFaces dock menu transforms images into a Mac-like dock menu, with icons that expand on rollover. Thus, the `Dock` component mimics the well-known `dock` interface of Mac OS X. The component consists of menu items and can be built declaratively or programmatically by model.

In this recipe we will develop a dock menu with social media icons.

How to do it...

Menu items should be direct children of `p:dockMenu`. We will take advantage of the `url` attribute, which is # in this sample, but represents a valid URL in the real world.

```
<p:dock id="dock" position="bottom">
  <p:menuitem value="Digg"
    icon="/resources/images/dock/digg.png" url="#"/>
  <p:menuitem value="Facebook"
    icon="/resources/images/dock/facebook.png" url="#"/>
  <p:menuitem value="LinkedIn"
    icon="/resources/images/dock/linkedin.png" url="#"/>
  <p:menuitem value="Picasa"
    icon="/resources/images/dock/picasa.png" url="#"/>
  <p:menuitem value="Skype"
    icon="/resources/images/dock/skype.png" url="#"/>
  <p:menuitem value="Twitter"
    icon="/resources/images/dock/twitter.png" url="#"/>
  <p:menuitem value="Wordpress"
    icon="/resources/images/dock/wordpress.png" url="#"/>
</p:dock>
```

The following screenshot shows the implemented menu. When the mouse is over the dock items, the icons are zoomed in.

How it works...

The dock menu can be placed in two locations—page top or page bottom. The default location is page bottom. To place it at the top of the page, set `position` to `top`. The path to an icon is defined by the `icon` attribute. The path is relative to the web root.

The configuration of the zoom effect is done via the `maxWidth` and `proximity` attributes. The `maxWidth` attribute specifies the maximum width of items. The default value is 50 px. `proximity` specifies the distance to enlarge. The default value is 90 px.

There's more...

The theme of all samples in this book is `home`. The text of the dock's menu items in this theme is pale-colored. The following style can be used to paint items similar to the background color of the social media icons.

```
#dock .ui-widget-header a {
    color: #e98d03;
}
```

PrimeFaces Cookbook Showcase application

This recipe is available in the demo web application on GitHub (`https://github.com/ova2/primefaces-cookbook`). Clone the project if you have not done it yet, explore the project structure, and execute the built-in Jetty Maven plugin to see this recipe in action. Follow the instructions in the `README` file if you do not know how to run Jetty.

When the server is running, the showcase for the recipe is available at `http://localhost:8080/primefaces-cookbook/views/chapter6/dockMenu.jsf`.

7
Working with Files and Images

In this chapter we will cover:

- Basic, automatic, and multiple file upload
- Uploading a file with drag-and-drop
- Downloading files
- Cropping images
- Displaying a collection of images
- Capturing images with photoCam
- Comparing images

Introduction

In this chapter, we will cover the management of file operations such as uploading and downloading, and image operations such as capturing, cropping, and comparing, with advanced use cases.

Basic, automatic, and multiple file upload

The `fileUpload` component provides a file upload mechanism with enhanced features as compared to the basic HTML `<input type="file">` file upload definition. The component provides an HTML5-powered UI with capabilities such as drag-and-drop, uploading multiple files, and progress tracking, and it will also support legacy browsers (for IE v6, v7, v8, and v9) for compatibility by degrading gracefully.

How to do it...

Firstly, the PrimeFaces FileUpload Filter must be defined in the `web.xml` file to parse incoming multipart file upload requests. It should map to the Faces Servlet definition.

```
<filter>
  <filter-name>PrimeFaces FileUpload Filter</filter-name>
  <filter-class>
    org.primefaces.webapp.filter.FileUploadFilter
  </filter-class>
</filter>
<filter-mapping>
  <filter-name>PrimeFaces FileUpload Filter</filter-name>
  <servlet-name>Faces Servlet</servlet-name>
</filter-mapping>
```

The filter has two default settings, which are threshold size and temporary file upload location. These settings can also be configured with initial parameters as follows:

```
<filter>
  <filter-name>PrimeFaces FileUpload Filter</filter-name>
  <filter-class>
    org.primefaces.webapp.filter.FileUploadFilter
  </filter-class>
  <init-param>
   <param-name>thresholdSize</param-name>
    <param-value>51200</param-value>
  </init-param>
  <init-param>
    <param-name>uploadDirectory</param-name>
    <param-value>/Users/primefaces/temp</param-value>
  </init-param>
</filter>
```

The `thresholdSize` parameter sets the minimum size in bytes for files that will be written directly to disk, and the `uploadDirectory` parameter sets the directory used to temporarily store those files. If the files are smaller than the `thresholdSize` parameter, they will be stored in the memory. In addition, dependencies for `commons-fileupload` and `commons-io` should be declared in the project. The Maven dependency definitions with the latest available versions at the time of writing this book are stated here. Please check for possible new releases on the `commons-fileupload` and `commons-io` projects at `http://commons.apache.org/fileupload/download_fileupload.cgi` and `http://commons.apache.org/io/download_io.cgi` respectively.

```
<dependency>
  <groupId>commons-fileupload</groupId>
```

```
    <artifactId>commons-fileupload</artifactId>
    <version>1.2.2</version>
  </dependency>
  <dependency>
    <groupId>commons-io</groupId>
    <artifactId>commons-io</artifactId>
    <version>2.4</version>
  </dependency>
```

The `fileUpload` component provides the `mode` attribute, which can be either `simple` or `advanced`, that makes the component work in the simple mode like a normal HTML upload component, or in advanced mode with HTML5 features. The default mode of the component is advanced.

The simple file upload component within a form definition is as follows:

```
<h:form enctype="multipart/form-data">
  <p:fileUpload value="#{fileController.file}" mode="simple" />
  <p:commandButton value="Submit" ajax="false"/>
</h:form>
```

The component will be rendered with an input text field and a **Browse...** button as shown in the following screenshot:

The file will get uploaded once the form is submitted, that is, the command button gets clicked.

The definition of the advanced file upload with a richer UI is as follows:

```
<p:fileUpload value="#{fileController.file}"
fileUploadListener="#{fileController.handleFileUpload}" />
```

The default visual rendering of the preceding example is as follows:

With the advanced file upload, the `fileUploadListener` attribute is being used to handle the uploaded file. The method bound with the attribute will be called with a parameter of `org.primefaces.event.FileUploadEvent`.

A sample method definition for retrieving the uploaded file and adding a Faces message is as follows:

```
public void handleFileUpload(FileUploadEvent event) {
  UploadedFile file = event.getFile();
  MessageUtil.addInfoMessage("upload.successful", file.getFileName() +
" is uploaded.");
}
```

Defining multiple advanced file upload components within the same form is not supported at the moment.

There's more...

Texts for the `upload` and `cancel` buttons can be customized with the `uploadLabel` and `cancelLabel` attributes. The `showButtons` attribute configures the visibility of the `upload` and `cancel` buttons in the button bar of the component. The `auto` attribute enables automatic file upload. When a file is selected or dragged-and-dropped, it will be uploaded automatically.

Restricting file upload by type

The `fileUpload` component allows us to restrict the file selection only to the types configured with the `allowTypes` attribute. The `allowTypes` attribute accepts a JavaScript regular expression that will be used to match against the name of the file to be uploaded. The following definition only accepts image files with an extension `gif`, `jpg`, `jpeg`, or `png`:

```
<p:fileUpload fileUploadListener="#{fileController.handleFileUpload}"
  allowTypes="/(\.|\/)(gif|jpe?g|png)$/" />
```

When an incorrect type of file is selected or dragged-and-dropped onto the `upload` component, the component renders an error message to alert the user to the wrong file type. The following screenshot shows the error message that occurred when a file with type `flv` was selected for upload:

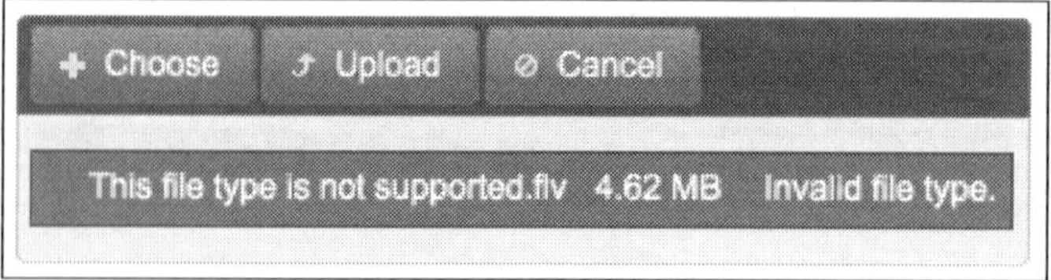

The error message **Invalid file type** can also be customized with the `invalidFileMessage` attribute.

Limiting maximum size

With the `sizeLimit` attribute, it's possible to restrict the maximum file upload size. The following definition limits the file size to a maximum of 10 KB.

```
<p:fileUpload fileUploadListener="#{fileController.handleFileUpload}"
sizeLimit="10240" />
```

The following screenshot shows the error message that occurred when a file with size 4.62 MB was selected for upload:

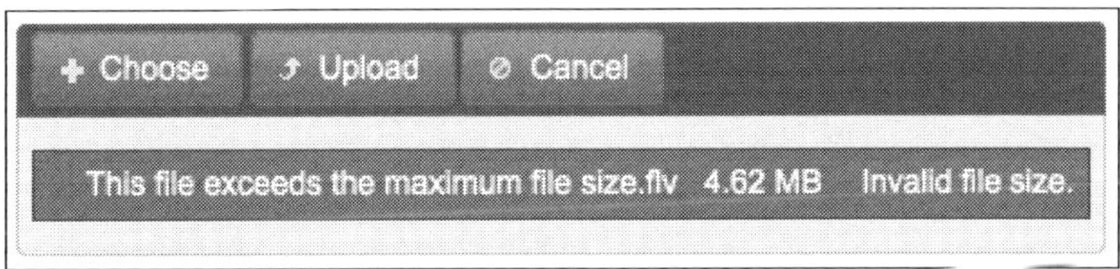

The error message **Invalid file size** can also be customized with the `invalidSizeMessage` attribute.

Uploading multiple files

By default, selecting multiple files for uploading, via browsing after clicking on the **Choose** button, is not supported by the component. Setting the `multiple` attribute to `true` enables multiple upload for the advanced file upload component. In multiple mode, files get uploaded in the selected order and the method bound with the `fileUploadListener` attribute gets called for each uploaded file.

```
<p:fileUpload id="multipleUpload" value="#{fileController.file}"
multiple="true"
fileUploadListener="#{fileController.handleFileUpload}" />
```

Handling with client-side callbacks

The `fileUpload` component supports hooking custom JavaScript methods when the upload process starts and ends. The following code snippet shows the `upload` component definition with the `onstart` and `oncomplete` attributes showing a progress dialog box while doing the upload:

```
<p:fileUpload fileUploadListener="#{fileController.handleFileUpload}"
onstart="showStatus()" oncomplete="hideStatus()" />
```

The `showStatus` and `hideStatus` methods are two simple methods for showing and hiding a dialog box component, which is also a PrimeFaces component.

```
<script type="text/javascript">
  function showStatus() {
```

```
      statusDialog.show();
    }
    function hideStatus() {
      statusDialog.hide();
    }
  </script>

  <p:dialog modal="true" widgetVar="statusDialog" header="Status"
  draggable="false" closable="false">
    <p:graphicImage value="/resources/images/ajax-loader.gif" />
  </p:dialog>
```

PrimeFaces Cookbook Showcase application

This recipe is available in the PrimeFaces Cookbook Showcase application on GitHub at `https://github.com/ova2/primefaces-cookbook`. You can find the details there for running the project. When the server is running, the showcase for the recipe is available at the URLs listed in the following table:

Showcase example	URL
Basic file upload	`http://localhost:8080/primefaces-cookbook/views/chapter7/fileUploadBasic.jsf`
Multiple file upload	`http://localhost:8080/primefaces-cookbook/views/chapter7/fileUploadMultiple.jsf`
Filtering file types for file upload	`http://localhost:8080/primefaces-cookbook/views/chapter7/fileUploadFiltering.jsf`
Limiting file size for file upload	`http://localhost:8080/primefaces-cookbook/views/chapter7/fileUploadSizeLimit.jsf`
Client-side callback for file upload	`http://localhost:8080/primefaces-cookbook/views/chapter7/fileUploadCallback.jsf`

See also

- For details about the `MessageUtil` class, see the *Internationalization (i18n) and Localization (L10n)* recipe in *Chapter 1, Getting Started with PrimeFaces*

Uploading a file with drag-and-drop

In supported browsers, a file can also be dragged-and-dropped for uploading with `fileUpload`, and the component itself will be the drop zone.

How to do it...

The `dragDropSupport` attribute defines whether or not to enable drag-and-drop from the filesystem. By default, the value of this attribute is `true`. In order to provide drag-and-drop support, the `fileUpload` component should be in advanced mode, which is the default mode. The definition of the `fileUpload` component for uploading files with drag-and-drop would be as follows:

```
<p:fileUpload id="upload" value="#{fileController.file}"
  dragDropSupport="true"
  update="growl"
  fileUploadListener="#{fileController.handleFileUpload}" />
```

How it works...

The `fileUploadListener` attribute defines the method that will be invoked when a file is uploaded.

There's more...

For applying features like restricting file upload type, limiting maximum size limit, and so on please refer to the Basic, automatic, and multiple file upload recipe.

PrimeFaces Cookbook Showcase application

This recipe is available in the PrimeFaces Cookbook Showcase application on GitHub at `https://github.com/ova2/primefaces-cookbook`. You may find the details in there for running the project. When the server is running, the showcase for the recipe is available at `http://localhost:8080/primefaces-cookbook/views/chapter7/fileUploadDND.jsf`.

Downloading files

The `fileDownload` component can be used to stream binary contents such as files to requesting browsers, by wrapping the components with any JSF command component such as a button or link.

How to do it...

The value of the `fileDownload` component should be an instance of `org.primefaces.model.StreamedContent`. The concrete class `org.primefaces.model.DefaultStreamedContent` could be used for simple purposes. The following is the backing bean implementation for the file download example along with the component definition.

```
public class FileController implements Serializable {
    private StreamedContent file;
    public FileController() {
        InputStream stream = this.getClass().
        getResourceAsStream("/chapter7/PFSamplePDF.pdf");
        file = new DefaultStreamedContent(stream,
        "application/pdf", "PFSample.pdf");
    }

    public StreamedContent getFile() {
        return file;
    }

    public StreamedContent getDownloadFile() {
        return downloadFile;
    }
}

<p:commandButton value="Download" ajax="false">
    <p:fileDownload value="#{fileController.file}" />
</p:commandButton>
```

How it works...

By default, the disposition of the downloadable content will be done with a download dialog box, which is the `attachment` mode, but setting the `contextDisposition` attribute could also configure this. The other possible mode is the `inline` mode where the browser will try to open the file without any prompt.

There's more...

Since file download progress is non-AJAX, the `ajax` attribute for PrimeFaces command components that are used for wrapping the `fileDownload` component, should be set to `false`.

Content disposition is not part of the HTTP standard, but it's widely adopted by the browsers.

Monitoring download status

File download is a non-AJAX process, so in order to monitor the status PrimeFaces provides the client-side `monitorDownload` method. The method can be bound to an `onclick` event of a command component as seen the following code snippet:

```
<h:commandLink onclick="PrimeFaces.monitorDownload(showStatus,
hideStatus)">
  <p:graphicImage value=
  "/resources/images/download/fileDownload.png" />
  <p:fileDownload value=
  "#{fileController.downloadFile}" />
```

```
</h:commandLink>
```

This method will trigger two methods, `showStatus` and `hideStatus`, when the download process occurs.

The `showStatus` and `hideStatus` methods are two simple methods for showing and hiding a dialog box component. These methods are described in the following code snippet:

```
<script type="text/javascript">
  function showStatus() {
    statusDialog.show();
  }
  function hideStatus() {
    statusDialog.hide();
</script>

<p:dialog modal="true" widgetVar="statusDialog" header="Status"
draggable="false" closable="false">
  <p:graphicImage value="/resources/images/ajax-loader.gif" />
</p:dialog>
```

PrimeFaces Cookbook Showcase application

This recipe is available in the PrimeFaces Cookbook Showcase application on GitHub at `https://github.com/ova2/primefaces-cookbook`. You can find the details there for running the project. When the server is running, the showcase for the recipe is available at `http://localhost:8080/primefaces-cookbook/views/chapter7/fileDownload.jsf`.

Cropping images

The `imageCropper` component provides image cropping functionality by allowing to us crop a certain region of an image, which could either be a local image or an external image. After cropping, a new image is created. It contains the cropped region and it is assigned to a `CroppedImage` instance.

How to do it...

The `org.primefaces.model.CroppedImage` class belongs to the PrimeFaces API, and the structure of the class is as follows:

```
public class CroppedImage {
  String originalFilename;
  byte[] bytes;
  int left;
  int top;
```

```
    int width;
    int height;
}
```

A simple definition of the image cropper for cropping a local image would be as shown in the following code line. The value of the component is bound with an instance of `CroppedImage`.

```
<p:imageCropper value="#{imageController.croppedImageSimple}"
image="/resources/images/crop/primefaces.jpg" />
```

When hovered on the image, the cursor of the mouse will change to crosshairs for making the crop region selection. When the region is selected, it will be highlighted with a dashed canvas and the section left outside the region will be grayed out.

How it works...

The `action` method for the actual crop is defined in the following code snippet. This method retrieves the cropped image and converts it to an instance of the `org.primefaces.model.StreamedContent` class to display the image with the `p:graphicImage` component.

```
StreamedContent graphicText

public String cropSimple() throws IOException {
  graphicText = new DefaultStreamedContent(new
  ByteArrayInputStream(croppedImage.getBytes()));
  return null;
}
```

Then the cropped image could be easily displayed by using the following code snippet:

```
<p:commandButton value="Crop" action="#{imageController.cropSimple}"
update="localCroppedImage"/>
```

The `graphicText` property created within the `cropSimple` method is an instance of `StreamedContent`, and it will be visualized with the `p:graphicImage` component. The backing bean containing the `graphicText` property should be defined in the session scope. The reason behind that is that the image will be fetched in a separate request from the rest of the page content and in order to retrieve the cropped image, the content should be stored in the session context.

One other possible implementation for cropping the image could be for saving the image to the disk and showing the saved image via a media display component such as `graphicImage`.

```
public String cropWithSave() {
  ServletContext servletContext =
  (ServletContext) FacesContext.getCurrentInstance().
  getExternalContext().getContext();
  String newFileName = servletContext.getRealPath("") +
  File.separator + "resources" + File.separator + "images" +
  File.separator + "cropped.jpg";
  FileImageOutputStream imageOutput;
  try {
    imageOutput =
    new FileImageOutputStream(new File(newFileName));
    imageOutput.write(croppedImageSimple.getBytes(), 0,
    croppedImageSimple.getBytes().length);
    imageOutput.close();
  }
  catch (Exception e) {
    throw new FacesException
    ("Error in writing cropped image.", e);
  }
  return null;
}
```

There's more...

The initial coordinates of the cropped region drawn on the canvas of the image can be defined with the `initialCoords` attribute. The notation of the attribute should follow the x,y,w,h format, where x and y stand for the x and y coordinate values, and w and h stand for width and height.

The `backgroundColor` attribute defines the color of the background container with a default value of black. The `backgroundOpacity` attribute defines the opacity of the outer image while cropping. Its default value is `0.6`, and the value should be between `0` and `1`.

The `minSize` and `maxSize` attributes define the minimum width and height for the cropped region in pixels with the notation `[width, height]`.

The `aspectRatio` attribute defines the ratio of the cropped region as width is to height. To make it a square, the value should be set to `1`.

The `imageCropper` component provides the ability to crop external images as well. By providing the absolute URL to the image with the `image` attribute, it is possible to crop the image.

PrimeFaces Cookbook Showcase application

This recipe is available in the PrimeFaces Cookbook Showcase application on GitHub at `https://github.com/ova2/primefaces-cookbook`. You can find the details there for running the project. When the server is running, the showcase for the recipe is available at `http://localhost:8080/primefaces-cookbook/views/chapter7/cropImage.jsf`.

Displaying a collection of images

The `galleria` component can be used to display a collection of images.

How to do it...

A basic definition for the `galleria` component for viewing a static list of car images would be as follows:

```
<p:galleria>
  <p:graphicImage value="/resources/images/autocomplete/CC.png" />
  <p:graphicImage value=
  "/resources/images/autocomplete/Golf.png" />
  <p:graphicImage value=
  "/resources/images/autocomplete/Polo.png" />
  <p:graphicImage value=
  "/resources/images/autocomplete/Touareg.png" />
</p:galleria>
```

How it works...

The definition of the `gelleria` component renders a car image in a panel and four other small images in a filmstrip right below it. This component also provides built-in iteration effects for transition to occur between the images.

It is also possible to visualize a list of car images that is bound through the value attribute of the galleria component as follows:

```
<p:galleria value="#{galleriaController.cars}" var="car">
  <p:graphicImage value=
  "/resources/images/autocomplete/#{car.name}.png" />
</p:galleria>
```

There's more...

The rendering for the filmstrip can be enabled or disabled with the showFilmstrip attribute. The width and height of the panel can be set with the panelWidth and panelHeight attributes. The width and height of each frame of the filmstrip can be set with the frameWidth and frameHeight attributes.

Transition effects

While iterating through the images, it is possible to apply transition effects. The effect attribute can have the values fade (the default), flash, pulse, or slide. The effectSpeed attribute can also be used to decide on the duration of the transition. Its default value is 800 milliseconds.

The transitionInterval attribute defines the delay in milliseconds between the transition of panels. Its default value is 4000.

Customizing filmstrip

It is possible to set the position of the filmstrip according the position of the panel. The filmstripPosition attribute could be set to left, right, top, or bottom to position the strip respectively to the panel.

The filmstripStyle attribute defines if the frames for the filmstrip should all be shown, should be rendered with a scroll mechanism, or neither. Its values can be show all or scroll.

The rendering for a car list with a filmstrip positioned on the right will be as shown in the following screenshot:

Enabling captions and overlays

By setting the `showOverlays` attribute to `true`, it is possible to render an overlay panel on top of the image panels. The content of the overlay panel can be defined with the `<p:galleriaOverlay>` helper component. The following is the definition for rendering a list of car images with the overlay panel and for stating the model and the brand year of the car:

```
<p:galleria value="#{galleriaController.cars}" var="car"
showOverlays="true">
  <p:graphicImage value=
  "/resources/images/autocomplete/#{car.name}.png"
  title="#{car.name}" />
  <p:galleriaOverlay title="#{car.name}">
    Model #{car.name}, Year: #{car.year}
  </p:galleriaOverlay>
</p:galleria>
```

For each frame in the filmstrip, the caption will also be rendered at the bottom of the frame. Setting the `showCaptions` attribute to `true` for the `galleria` component enables this. The `title` attribute for each frame image is being used for the caption to be viewed.

Viewing custom content

It is also possible to view custom content within the panel beside the images. Here is the definition for listing a car image along with the brand name and year within the panel. The `p:galleriaContent` helper component is being used to define what to render within the panel.

```
<p:galleria id="withCustomContent" value="#{galleriaController.cars}"
var="car"
  frameWidth="140" frameHeight="80"
```

```
    panelWidth="400" panelHeight="300">
    <p:graphicImage
    value="/resources/images/autocomplete/#{car.name}.png"
    title="#{car.name}" />

    <p:galleriaContent>
      <h:panelGrid  columns="2" cellpadding="5">
        <f:facet name="header">
          <p:graphicImage
          value="/resources/images/autocomplete/#{car.name}.png" />
        </f:facet>

        <h:outputText value="Name: " />
        <h:outputText id="name" value="#{car.name}"/>

        <h:outputText value="Year: " />
        <h:outputText id="number" value="#{car.year}"/>
      </h:panelGrid>
    </p:galleriaContent>
  </p:galleria>
```

The rendering of the `galleria` component will be as shown in the following screenshot:

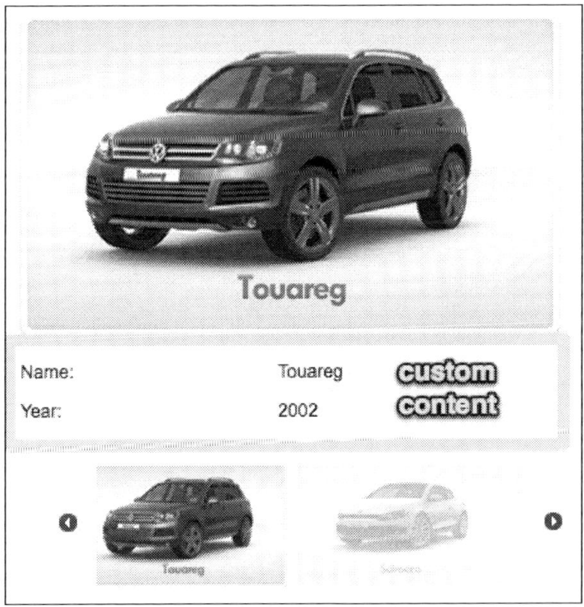

PrimeFaces Cookbook Showcase application

This recipe is available in the PrimeFaces Cookbook Showcase application on GitHub at `https://github.com/ova2/primefaces-cookbook`. You can find the details there for running the project. When the server is running, the showcase for the recipe is available at `http://localhost:8080/primefaces-cookbook/views/chapter7/displayImageCollection.jsf` and `http://localhost:8080/primefaces-cookbook/views/chapter7/displayImageCollection2.jsf`.

Capturing images with photoCam

The `photoCam` component supports taking images with the attached camera and sending them to the JSF backend data model.

How to do it...

A simple definition for capturing an image with the `photoCam` component would be as follows:

```
<p:photoCam widgetVar="pc" listener="#{photoCamController.onCapture}"
update="capturedImage"/>

<p:graphicImage id="capturedImage" value="#{photoCamController.
capturedImage}" />update="capturedImage"/>

<p:commandButton type="button" value="Capture" onclick="pc.
capture()"/>
```

How it works...

The captured image is triggered via the client-side JavaScript method `capture`. The button declared in the preceding sample invokes the `capture` method via the `widget` variable defined for the `photoCam` component. A method expression, which will be invoked when an image is captured, is bound to the `listener` attribute. This method will handle the image captured on the server side. A sample definition for the method is as follows:

```
StreamedContent capturedImage;

public void onCapture(CaptureEvent captureEvent) {
  byte[] data = captureEvent.getData();
  capturedImage = new DefaultStreamedContent(new
  ByteArrayInputStream(data));
}
```

Since `capturedImage` is an instance of `StreamedContent` and it will be visualized with the `p:graphicImage` component, the backing bean containing the `capturedImage` object should be defined in the session scope. The reason behind that is that the image will be fetched in a separate request from the rest of the page content and in order to retrieve the captured image, the content should be stored in the session context.

One other possible implementation for capturing the image could be saving the image to the disk and showing the saved image via a media display component such as `graphicImage`.

```
public void onCaptureWithSave(CaptureEvent captureEvent) {
  byte[] data = captureEvent.getData();
  ServletContext servletContext = (ServletContext)
  FacesContext.getCurrentInstance().getExternalContext().
  getContext();
  String newFileName = servletContext.getRealPath("") +
  File.separator + "resources" + File.separator + "images" +
  File.separator + "captured.png";
  FileImageOutputStream imageOutput;
  try {
    imageOutput = new FileImageOutputStream(new
    File(newFileName));
    imageOutput.write(data, 0, data.length);
    imageOutput.close();
  }
  catch(Exception e) {
    throw new FacesException
    ("Error in writing captured image.", e);
  }
}
```

In order to capture the image, the user might need to authorize the settings of the Flash Player by allowing access to the camera and the microphone. The user will be notified with a dialog box before viewing the current image, as shown in the following screenshot:

Currently Internet Explorer does not support the `photoCam` component.

`photoCam` requires human intervention in order to take an image and upload it.

`photoCam` does not provide you with a video stream, but just single frames taken manually.

There's more...

If you are getting the **Form too large** error while capturing an image through `photoCam` (this could be monitored with Firebug or some other tool while calling the HTTP request), configuration needs to be done on the form's content size in order to increase the value, which is 200,000 bytes in the default configuration for the Jetty container. This could be configured via the system property definition. The following code snippet is the Maven configuration definition for the `jetty-maven-plugin` object that resides in `pom.xml`.

For Jetty 7 and above, the configuration is as follows:

```
<configuration>
    ...
  <systemProperties>
    <systemProperty>
  <name>org.eclipse.jetty.server.Request.maxFormContentSize</name>
      <value>-1</value>
```

```
      </systemProperty>
    </systemProperties>
  </configuration>
```

For Jetty 6, the content size should be configured as follows:

```
  <configuration>
      ...
    <systemProperties>
      <systemProperty>
    <name>org.mortbay.jetty.Request.maxFormContentSize</name>
        <value>-1</value>
      </systemProperty>
    </systemProperties>
  </configuration>
```

`-1` represents that there is no limit on the content size. If you encounter the same error for other web containers, please check the respective manuals for the same configuration.

PrimeFaces Cookbook Showcase application

This recipe is available in the PrimeFaces Cookbook Showcase application on GitHub at `https://github.com/ova2/primefaces-cookbook`. You can find the details there for running the project. When the server is running, the showcase for the recipe is available at `http://localhost:8080/primefaces-cookbook/views/chapter7/captureImage.jsf`.

Comparing images

The `imageCompare` component supports comparing two images by providing the user with a slider to drag over the images.

How to do it...

A basic definition for comparing two images of the maps of a sample city would be as follows:

```
  <p:imageCompareleftImage="/resources/images/compare/istanbulMap.png"
    rightImage="/resources/images/compare/istanbulSatellite.png"
    width="700"
    height="400" />
```

How it works...

The `leftImage` attribute defines the image placed on the left side, and the `rightImage` attribute defines the one to be placed on the right side. The `width` and `height` attributes should be provided in order to compare images properly by mapping them on top of each other. The rendering of the `imageCompare` component with the two images with the slider rendered on top of it will be as shown in the following screenshot:

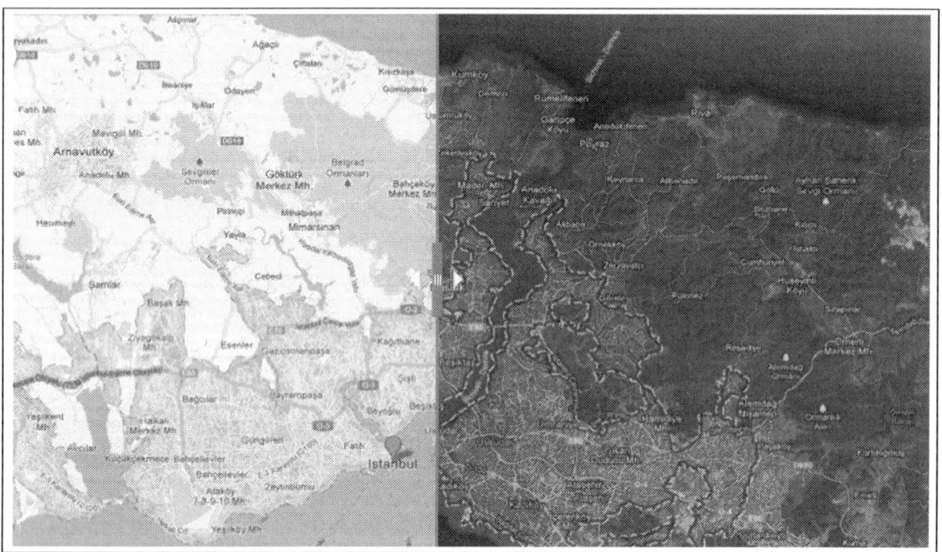

There's More

The style and the style class of the image container element can also be set with the style and styleClass attribute respectively.

PrimeFaces Cookbook Showcase application

This recipe is available in the PrimeFaces Cookbook Showcase application on GitHub at `https://github.com/ova2/primefaces-cookbook`. You can find the details there for running the project. When the server is running, the showcase for the recipe is available at `http://localhost:8080/primefaces-cookbook/views/chapter7/compareImage.jsf`.

8
Drag Me, Drop Me

In this chapter we will cover:

- Making a component draggable
- Restricting dragging by axis, grid, and containment
- Snapping to the edges of the nearest elements
- Defining droppable targets
- Restricting dropping by tolerance and acceptance
- AJAX-enhanced drag-and-drop
- Integrating drag-and-drop with data iteration components

Introduction

Drag-and-drop is an action, meaning *grabbing* an object and *dragging* it to a different location. Components capable of being dragged and dropped enrich the Web and make a solid base for modern UI patterns. The drag-and-drop utilities in PrimeFaces allow us to create draggable and droppable user interfaces efficiently. They make it abstract for developers to deal with the implementation details on a browser level.

In this chapter, we will learn about PrimeFaces' drag-and-drop utilities—`Draggable` and `Droppable`. AJAX-enhanced drag-and-drop and a special integration with data iteration components will be explained as well.

Making a component draggable

Any component can be enhanced with draggable behavior. To enable draggable functionality on any PrimeFaces component, we always need a component called `Draggable`.

In this recipe, we will see how to make a component draggable and learn some basic features of `Draggable`. To demonstrate these features, we will make several `p:panel` components draggable.

How to do it...

A component can be made draggable by using `p:draggable`. The component ID must match the `for` attribute of the `p:draggable` component. If the `for` attribute is omitted, the `parent` component will be selected as a draggable target. Let's make some `panel` components draggable and apply some basic features:

```
<p:panel id="pnl" header="Draggable panel with default settings">
    <h:outputText value="Drag me around"/>
</p:panel>
<p:draggable for="pnl"/>

<p:panel id="hpnl" header="Draggable panel by handle">
    <h:outputText value="I can be only dragged by my header"/>
</p:panel>
<p:draggable for="hpnl" handle=".ui-panel-titlebar"/>

<p:panel id="cpnl" header="Draggable panel with clone">
    <h:outputText value="I display a clone as helper while being
    dragged"/>
</p:panel>
<p:draggable for="cpnl" helper="clone"/>

<p:panel id="rpnl" header="Draggable panel with revert">
    <h:outputText value="I will be returned to my start position
    when dragging stops"/>
</p:panel>
<p:draggable for="rpnl" revert="true"/>

<p:panel id="opnl" header="Draggable panel with opacity">
    <h:outputText value="I use opacity for helper while being
    dragged"/>
</p:panel>
<p:draggable for="opnl" opacity="0.5"/>
```

The following screenshot shows the five panels. The last panel is being dragged. Its opacity has been changed to `0.5` after dragging starts.

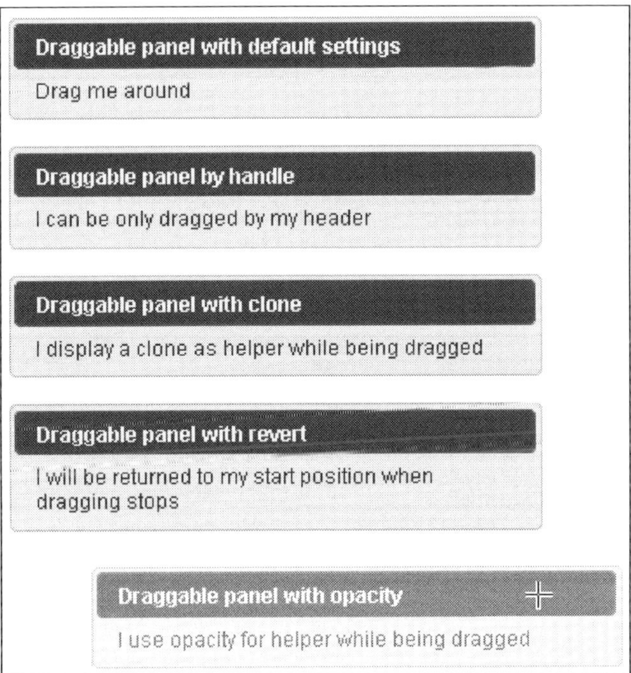

How it works...

By default, any point in a dragged component can be used as a handle. To restrict the drag start click to a specified element(s), we can use the `handle` option, which is a jQuery selector. The second panel is dragged by using its header only.

By default, the actual component is used as a drag indicator. The `helper` option allows keeping the component at its original location during dragging. This can be achieved with `helper` set to `clone` as for the third panel.

If the `revert` option is set to `true`, the component will return to its starting position when dragging stops and the draggable component is not dropped onto a matching droppable component. The fourth panel features this behavior.

Opacity for `helper` while it is being dragged is another useful option to give the user a visual feedback. The opacity of the fifth panel is reduced when dragging.

There's more...

Other basic features are related to the attributes `cursor` and `stack`. `cursor` is a CSS cursor that is to be displayed when dragging. It is handy to set its value to `move`. `stack` is a jQuery selector. It controls the `z-index` of the set of draggable elements that match the selector and always brings them to the front. That means, the draggable component always overlays other draggables.

PrimeFaces Cookbook Showcase application

This recipe is available in the demo web application on GitHub (`https://github.com/ova2/primefaces-cookbook`). Clone the project if you have not done it yet, explore the project structure, and execute the built-in Jetty Maven plugin to see this recipe in action. Follow the instructions in the `README` file if you do not know how to run Jetty.

When the server is running, the showcase for the recipe is available under `http://localhost:8080/primefaces-cookbook/views/chapter8/draggable.jsf`.

See also

- Refer to the *Restricting dragging by axis, grid, and containment* and *Snapping to the edges of the nearest elements* recipes discussed later in this chapter to learn advanced features of `Draggable`

Restricting dragging by axis, grid, and containment

The dragging behavior can be limited with some configurable constraints.

In this recipe, we will see how to drag an element either horizontally or vertically, on a grid or inside a certain section on the page.

How to do it...

The next example demonstrates three draggable panels and one draggable image. The first panel can be dragged only horizontally, the second one only vertically, and the third panel is dragged on a grid. Dragging on a grid means the dragging helper snaps to a grid—every specific x and y pixels. The image is placed within an `h:panelGroup` tag, which acts as a container for dragging. The image cannot go outside of this container.

```
<p:panel id="hpnl" header="Only horizontal draggable panel">
    <h:outputText value="I can be only dragged horizontally."/>
</p:panel>
```

```
<p:draggable for="hpnl" axis="x"/>

<p:panel id="vpnl" header="Only vertical draggable panel">
    <h:outputText value="I can be only dragged vertically"/>
</p:panel>
<p:draggable for="vpnl" axis="y"/>

<p:panel id="gpnl" header="Draggable panel in grid [40,50]">
    <h:outputText value="I can be only dragged in a grid"/>
</p:panel>
<p:draggable for="gpnl" grid="40,50"/>

<h:outputText value="The image below can be only dragged within its
parent's boundaries"/>
<h:panelGroup layout="block"
    styleClass="dragContainer ui-widget-content">
    <h:graphicImage id="pic" library="images" name="logo.png"/>
</h:panelGroup>
<p:draggable for="pic" containment="parent"/>
```

The following screenshot shows the result achieved with the preceding code snippet. Especially, we can see that the image has stayed in its boundaries although the cursor has gone outside.

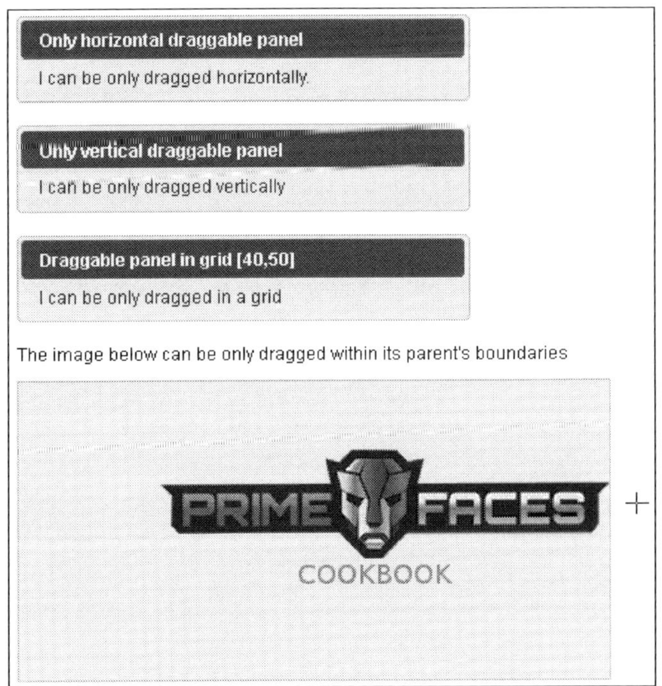

How it works...

Horizontal or vertical dragging is possible by setting the `axis` attribute as `axis="x"` or `axis="y"`, which means the draggable element can be dragged only horizontally or only vertically respectively.

Dragging on a grid is defined by the `grid` attribute. The value for dragging on a grid takes comma-separated dimensions. For instance, `grid="40,50"` means the draggable element can be dragged in only 40 pixel steps horizontally and 50 vertically.

The `containment` attribute constraints dragging within the boundaries of the containment element. Possible string values are `parent`, `document`, `window`, and `[x1, y1, x2, y2]`. The setting `containment="parent"` in the preceding example means the draggable element cannot go outside of its parent.

PrimeFaces Cookbook Showcase application

This recipe is available in the demo web application on GitHub (`https://github.com/ova2/primefaces-cookbook`). Clone the project if you have not done it yet, explore the project structure, and execute the built-in Jetty Maven plugin to see this recipe in action. Follow the instructions in the `README` file if you do not know how to run Jetty.

When the server is running, the showcase for the recipe is available under `http://localhost:8080/primefaces-cookbook/views/chapter8/advancedDraggable.jsf`.

See also

- Refer to the *Snapping to edges of the near elements* recipe to learn more advanced features of `Draggable`.

Snapping to the edges of the nearest elements

With PrimeFaces, we can snap the dragged component to the inner or outer boundaries of another component (component's DOM element).

In this recipe, we will discuss snapping and its options in detail. As an example, we will develop a big `h:panelGroup` component as a snap target and three other small `h:panelGroup` components as draggable components with various snapping options.

How to do it...

Generally, the snapping behavior is activated by setting the attribute `snap` to `true`. The snapping behavior is configurable with two options—`snapMode` and `snapTolerance`. The first option, `snapMode`, determines which edges of snap elements the draggable component will snap to. The second option, `snapTolerance`, determines a distance in pixels the draggable component must be from the element when snapping is invoked.

```
<h:panelGroup id="snaptarget" layout="block"
    styleClass="ui-widget-content"
              style="height:150px;width:450px;">
    <p class="ui-widget-header" style="margin:0;padding:5px;">
        I'm a snap target to play with me
    </p>
    <p:draggable/>
</h:panelGroup>

<h:panelGroup id="defsnap" layout="block"
    styleClass="dragSnap ui-widget-content">
    <p>I'm with default snap and snap to all edges of other
    draggable elements</p>
</h:panelGroup>
<p:draggable for="defsnap" snap="true"/>

<h:panelGroup id="outersnap" layout="block"
    styleClass="dragSnap ui-widget-content">
    <p>I only snap to the outer edges - try with the big box</p>
</h:panelGroup>
<p:draggable for="outersnap" snap="true" snapMode="outer"/>

<h:panelGroup id="innersnap" layout="block"
    styleClass="dragSnap ui-widget-content">
    <p>I only snap to the inner edges - try with the big box</p>
</h:panelGroup>
<p:draggable for="innersnap" snap="true" snapMode="inner"
snapTolerance="15"/>
```

The following screenshot shows the snapping for the last `h:panelGroup` tag. The component can be snapped only to the inner edges of the snap target when it is being dragged.

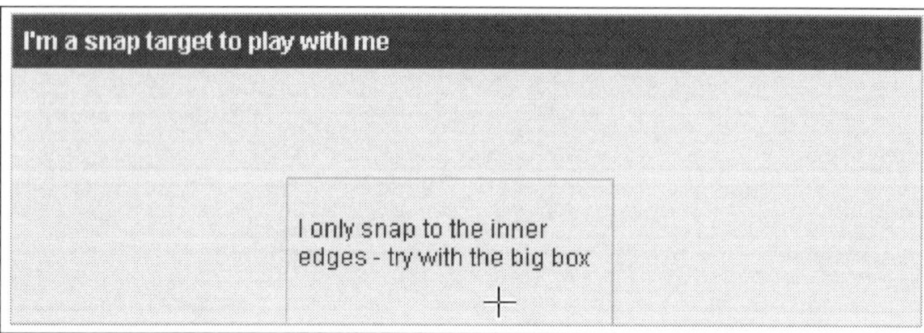

How it works...

The snapping is enabled by setting `snap` to `true`. If the `snap` attribute is set to `false` (default), no snapping occurs. The first small `h:panelGroup` has no snapping options. It snaps to the inner as well as outer boundaries of other draggable components. The second `h:panelGroup` sets `snapMode` and can only snap to the outer boundaries. Possible values of `snapMode` are `inner`, `outer`, and `both`. The third `h:panelGroup` also has a custom `snapTolerance` parameter in addition to `snapMode` set to `inner`. This is the distance in pixels from the snap element's edges at which snapping should occur. The default value is 20 pixels, but we set it to `15`.

In the current PrimeFaces implementation, a draggable component with snap set to `true` snaps to all other draggable components. This is a little bit different from jQuery's `Draggable` (`http://jqueryui.com/demos/draggable`), where we can also specify the elements that the draggable component will snap to when it is close to an edge of such an element.

PrimeFaces Cookbook Showcase application

This recipe is available in the demo web application on GitHub (`https://github.com/ova2/primefaces-cookbook`). Clone the project if you have not done it yet, explore the project structure, and execute the built-in Jetty Maven plugin to see this recipe in action. Follow the instructions in the `README` file if you do not know how to run Jetty.

When the server is running, the showcase for the recipe is available under `http://localhost:8080/primefaces-cookbook/views/chapter8/snapping.jsf`.

Defining droppable targets

Any component can be enhanced with a droppable behaviour. Droppable components are targets for draggable ones. To enable droppable functionality on any PrimeFaces component, we always need a component called `Droppable`.

In this recipe, we will see how to define droppable targets and learn a client-side callback `onDrop`.

How to do it...

A component can be made droppable by using `p:droppable`. The component ID must match the `for` attribute of `p:droppable`. If the `for` attribute is omitted, the parent component will be selected as a droppable target. We will take two `h:panelGroup` components and make them droppable and draggable respectively. In addition, we will define a client-side callback that gets invoked when a draggable component is dropped. This can be accomplished by the `onDrop` attribute, which points to a JavaScript function.

```
<h:panelGroup id="drop" layout="block" styleClass="ui-widget-content"
              style="height:150px;width:300px;">
    <p class="ui-widget-header" style="margin:0;padding:5px;">
      Drop here</p>
    <p:droppable onDrop="handleDrop"/>
</h:panelGroup>

<br/>

<h:panelGroup id="drag" layout="block"
    styleClass="dragDiv ui-widget-content">
    <p>Drag me to my target</p>
</h:panelGroup>
<p:draggable for="drag"/>
```

The client-side callback highlights the droppable `h:panelGroup` component and adds the text `Dropped!` to the paragraph tag `p` when invoked.

```
function handleDrop(event, ui) {
    $(event.target).addClass("ui-state-highlight").find("p").
    html("Dropped!");
}
```

The following screenshot shows the result after dropping the draggable `h:panelGroup` component onto the droppable one:

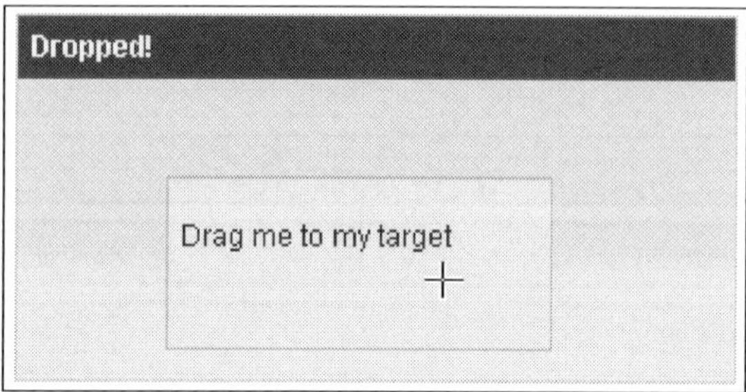

How it works...

The `onDrop` callback gets two parameters: `event` and `ui`, which are objects holding information about the drag-and-drop event. The droppable target is accessible by `event.target`. We use this fact to add the style class `ui-state-highlight` to the target. This class is defined by jQuery ThemeRoller.

The `event` parameter is the original browser event, and `ui` is a prepared object with the following properties:

- `ui.draggable`: This is the current draggable element, an jQuery object
- `ui.helper`: This is the current draggable helper, an jQuery object
- `ui.position`: This is the current position of the draggable helper `{ top: , left: }`
- `ui.offset`: This is the current absolute position of the draggable helper `{ top: , left: }`

See also

- The most important style classes defined by jQuery ThemeRoller are described in the *Understanding the structural and skinning CSS* recipe in *Chapter 2, Theming Concept*
- Advanced configuration and use cases of `Droppable` will be discussed in the *Restricting dropping by tolerance and acceptance*, *AJAX-enhanced drag-and-drop*, and *Integrating drag-and-drop with data iteration components* recipes discussed later in this chapter

PrimeFaces Cookbook Showcase application

This recipe is available in the demo web application on GitHub (`https://github.com/ova2/primefaces-cookbook`). Clone the project if you have not done it yet, explore the project structure, and execute the built-in Jetty Maven plugin to see this recipe in action. Follow the instructions in the `README` file if you do not know how to run Jetty.

When the server is running, the showcase for the recipe is available under `http://localhost:8080/primefaces-cookbook/views/chapter8/droppable.jsf`.

Restricting dropping by tolerance and acceptance

Droppable behavior is highly configurable. There are a lot of options to restrict dropping. They are useful in matching the draggable and droppable components more precisely.

In this chapter, we will meet options for tolerance and acceptance. We will take several `h:panelGroup` components and make them droppable with different tolerance and acceptance values.

How to do it...

Tolerance specifies which mode to use for testing if a draggable component is over a droppable target. There are four different tolerance modes. They can be chosen by the `tolerance` attribute of `p:droppable`. The following code snippet shows four `h:panelGroup` components with settings for tolerance:

```
<h:panelGrid columns="4">
  <h:panelGroup id="dropFit" layout="block" styleClass="dropTarget
  ui-widget-content">
  <p class="ui-widget-header">Drop here (tolerance = fit)</p>
    <p:droppable onDrop="handleDrop" tolerance="fit"/>
  </h:panelGroup>

  <h:panelGroup id="dropIntersect" layout="block"
  styleClass="dropTarget ui-widget-content">
    <p class="ui-widget-header">Drop here (tolerance =
    intersect)</p>
    <p:droppable onDrop="handleDrop" tolerance="intersect"/>
  </h:panelGroup>
```

```
    <h:panelGroup id="dropPointer" layout="block"
    styleClass="dropTarget ui-widget-content">
      <p class="ui-widget-header">Drop here (tolerance =
      pointer)</p>
      <p:droppable onDrop="handleDrop" tolerance="pointer"/>
    </h:panelGroup>

    <h:panelGroup id="dropTouch" layout="block"
    styleClass="dropTarget ui-widget-content">
      <p class="ui-widget-header">Drop here (tolerance = touch)</p>
      <p:droppable onDrop="handleDrop" tolerance="touch"/>
    </h:panelGroup>
  </h:panelGrid>

  <br/>

  <h:panelGroup id="drag" layout="block"
    styleClass="dragDiv ui-widget-content">
    <p>Drag me to my target</p>
    <p:draggable/>
  </h:panelGroup>
```

The `scope` attribute is used for acceptance. Its aim is to group sets of the draggable and droppable components. Only a draggable component with the same scope value as a droppable one will be accepted during drag-and-drop. The following code snippet shows two draggable `h:panelGroup` components with different scope values. Only one can be dropped onto the droppable `h:panelGroup` component with the ID `dropTarget2`.

```
  <h:panelGroup id="dropTarget2" layout="block"
      styleClass="ui-widget-content"
      style="height:120px;width:300px;">
    <p class="ui-widget-header" style="margin:0;padding:5px;">
      Drop here</p>
    <p:droppable onDrop="handleDrop" scope="dnd"/>
  </h:panelGroup>

  <br/>

  <h:panelGrid columns="2">
    <h:panelGroup id="drag1" layout="block"
       styleClass="dragDiv ui-widget-content">
      <p>Drag me to my target</p>
      <p:draggable scope="dnd"/>
    </h:panelGroup>
```

```
    <h:panelGroup id="drag2" layout="block"
      styleClass="dragDiv ui-widget-content">
      <p>I'm draggable, but can't be dropped</p>
      <p:draggable scope="dummy"/>
    </h:panelGroup>
  </h:panelGrid>
```

The following screenshot demonstrates that the `handleDrop` callback is not invoked when the `h:panelGroup` with `scope` set to `dummy` gets dropped onto the `h:panelGroup` with `scope` set to `dnd`.

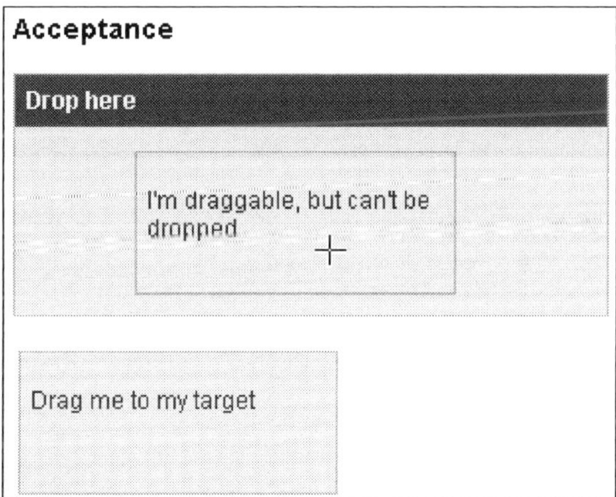

How it works...

The following table lists four tolerance modes that define the way of accepting a `Draggable`:

Mode	Description
`fit`	Draggable component should overlap the droppable component entirely
`intersect`	Draggable component should overlap the droppable component by at least 50 percent
`pointer`	Mouse pointer should overlap the droppable
`touch`	Draggable should overlap the droppable by any amount

There's more...

In additional to `scope`, there is also the `accept` attribute. This is the jQuery selector that defines the accepted components. Only the draggable components matching the selector will be accepted by the droppable component.

PrimeFaces Cookbook Showcase application

This recipe is available in the demo web application on GitHub (`https://github.com/ova2/primefaces-cookbook`). Clone the project if you have not done it yet, explore the project structure, and execute the built-in Jetty Maven plugin to see this recipe in action. Follow the instructions in the `README` file if you do not know how to run Jetty.

When the server is running, the showcase for the recipe is available under `http://localhost:8080/primefaces-cookbook/views/chapter8/advancedDroppable.jsf`.

AJAX-enhanced drag-and-drop

The user's client-side drag-and-drop interactions can be posted to the server. Drag-and-drop has only one (default) AJAX behavior event provided by the droppable component, which is processed when a valid draggable component is dropped. That is the `drop` event. If we define a listener, it will be invoked by passing an event instance of the type `org.primefaces.event.DragDrop` as parameter. This parameter holds information about the dragged-and-dropped components. By means of this information, the server-side state of the draggable/droppable items can be updated.

In this recipe, we will develop a workflow simulating a process of pizza ordering. The pizza ordering should occur by drag-and-drop. Users should be able to select any available Turkish pizza and drag-and-drop it onto the order list. The remove functionality, capable of drag-and-drop, should be included as well. For this purpose, we will implement a trash for the items removed from the pizza items in the order list.

How to do it...

We will make the five pizza image tags `h:graphicImage` draggable.

```
<p:growl id="growl" escape="false"/>

<h:panelGrid id="selectPizza" columns="1">
    <h:outputText value="Kiymali Pide" styleClass="text"/>
    <h:graphicImage id="pizza1" styleClass="pizzaimage"
        library="images" name="dragdrop/pizza1.png"
        title="Kiymali Pide"/>
```

```
        <h:outputText value="Kusbasi Pide" styleClass="text"/>
        <h:graphicImage id="pizza2" styleClass="pizzaimage"
            library="images" name="dragdrop/pizza2.png"
            title="Kusbasi Pide"/>

        <h:outputText value="Sucuklu Ve Yumurtali Pide"
        styleClass="text"/>
        <h:graphicImage id="pizza3" styleClass="pizzaimage"
            library="images" name="dragdrop/pizza3.png"
            title="Sucuklu Ve Yumurtali Pide"/>

        <h:outputText value="Peynirli Pide" styleClass="text"/>
        <h:graphicImage id="pizza4" styleClass="pizzaimage"
            library="images" name="dragdrop/pizza4.png"
            title="Peynirli Pide"/>

        <h:outputText value="Ispanakli Pide" styleClass="text"/>
        <h:graphicImage id="pizza5" styleClass="pizzaimage"
            library="images" name="dragdrop/pizza5.png"
            title="Ispanakli Pide"/>
</h:panelGrid>

<p:draggable for="pizza1" helper="clone" revert="true" cursor="move"/>
<p:draggable for="pizza2" helper="clone" revert="true" cursor="move"/>
<p:draggable for="pizza3" helper="clone" revert="true" cursor="move"/>
<p:draggable for="pizza4" helper="clone" revert="true" cursor="move"/>
<p:draggable for="pizza5" helper="clone" revert="true" cursor="move"/>
```

Two `h:panelGroup` tags will be made droppable. One `h:panelGroup` tag is intended to be used for the order list and one for items removed from the order list. Droppable `p:droppable` tags will get AJAX behaviors `p:ajax` attached with corresponding listeners in each case. One listener should be invoked on pizza ordering and another on pizza removal.

```
<h:panelGroup id="order" layout="block" styleClass="ui-widget-content"
              style="width:350px; padding:1px;">
   <p class="ui-widget-header" style="margin:0;padding:5px;">Order</p>

    <h:panelGroup layout="block" style="padding:10px;"
                  rendered="#{empty ajaxDragDrop.orderedPizza}">
        Please drag and drop any available pizza to order it
    </h:panelGroup>
```

```
        <p:dataList id="orderedPizza"
            value="#{ajaxDragDrop.orderedPizza}" var="op"
            rendered="#{not empty ajaxDragDrop.orderedPizza}">
            <h:panelGroup id="op" styleClass="text" layout="block">
                <f:attribute name="pizza" value="#{op}"/>
                <h:outputText value="#{op}"/>
            </h:panelGroup>

            <p:draggable for="op" revert="true" cursor="move"
            scope="trash"/>
        </p:dataList>

        <p:droppable id="drop1" for="order" accept=".pizzaimage"
                    tolerance="touch"
                    activeStyleClass="ui-state-default"
                    hoverStyleClass="ui-state-hover">
            <p:ajax listener="#{ajaxDragDrop.onPizzaOrder}"
            update="order growl"/>
        </p:droppable>
    </h:panelGroup>

    <p:commandButton value="Send order" action="#{ajaxDragDrop.sendOrder}"
                     update="growl" style="margin:10px 0 20px 0;"/>

    <h:panelGroup id="trash" layout="block" styleClass="ui-widget-content"
                  style="width:350px; padding:1px;">
        <p class="ui-widget-header"
        style="margin:0;padding:5px;">Trash</p>

        <h:panelGroup layout="block" style="padding:10px;"
                      rendered="#{empty ajaxDragDrop.removedPizza}">
            Drag and drop a pizza from the ordered list to remove it
        </h:panelGroup>

        <p:dataList value="#{ajaxDragDrop.removedPizza}" var="rp"
                    rendered="#{not empty ajaxDragDrop.removedPizza}">
            <h:panelGroup styleClass="text" layout="block">
                <h:outputText value="#{rp}"/>
            </h:panelGroup>
        </p:dataList>
```

```
    <p:droppable id="drop2" for="trash" scope="trash"
                tolerance="touch"
                activeStyleClass="ui-state-default"
                hoverStyleClass="ui-state-hover">
        <p:ajax listener="#{ajaxDragDrop.onPizzaRemove}"
        update="order trash growl"/>
    </p:droppable>
</h:panelGroup>
```

The corresponding managed bean `AjaxDragDrop` adds an ordered pizza to the `orderedPizza` list, and moves the pizza to the `removedPizza` list when it gets removed. This happens in the listeners `onPizzaOrder` and `onPizzaRemove` respectively.

```
@ManagedBean
@ViewScoped
public class AjaxDragDrop implements Serializable {

    private List<String> orderedPizza = new ArrayList<String>();
    private List<String> removedPizza = new ArrayList<String>();

    public List<String> getOrderedPizza() {
        return orderedPizza;
    }

    public List<String> getRemovedPizza() {
        return removedPizza;
    }

    public void onPizzaOrder(DragDropEvent event) {
        HtmlGraphicImage image = (HtmlGraphicImage)
        event.getComponent().findComponent(event.getDragId());
        String pizza = image != null ? image.getTitle() : "";

        orderedPizza.add(pizza);

        FacesMessage msg = new
        FacesMessage(FacesMessage.SEVERITY_INFO,
         "Selected pizza: " + pizza, null);
        FacesContext.getCurrentInstance().addMessage(null, msg);
    }
```

```
    public void onPizzaRemove(DragDropEvent event) {
        DataList dataList = (DataList)
        event.getComponent().findComponent("orderedPizza");
        dataList.invokeOnComponent
        (FacesContext.getCurrentInstance(), event.getDragId(),
            new ContextCallback() {

                public void invokeContextCallback(FacesContext fc,
                UIComponent component) {
                    HtmlPanelGroup panelGroup = (HtmlPanelGroup)
                    component;
                    String pizza = panelGroup != null ? (String)
                    panelGroup.getAttributes().get("pizza") : "";

                    orderedPizza.remove(pizza);
                    removedPizza.add(pizza);

                    FacesMessage msg = new
                    FacesMessage(FacesMessage.SEVERITY_INFO,
                            "Removed pizza: " + pizza, null);
                    fc.addMessage(null, msg);
                }
            });
    }

    public String sendOrder() {
        StringBuilder sb = new StringBuilder("You have ordered:");
        for (String pizza : orderedPizza) {
            sb.append("<br/>");
            sb.append(pizza);
        }

        FacesMessage msg = new FacesMessage
        (FacesMessage.SEVERITY_INFO, sb.toString(), null);
        FacesContext.getCurrentInstance().addMessage(null, msg);

        return null;
    }
}
```

The following screenshots demonstrate the entire workflow.

The first screenshot shows the dragging process from the list of available pizzas to the order list:

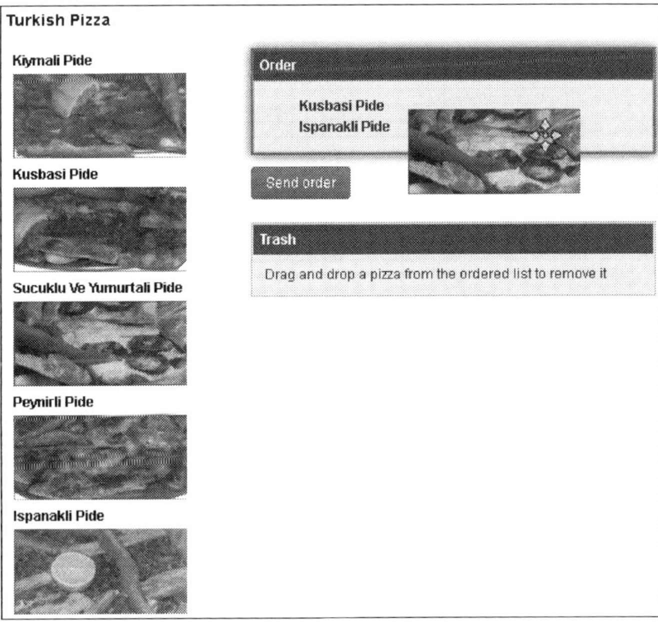

The second screenshot shows what happens when the dragged pizza image is dropped on the order list. A growl component is displayed with the currently selected pizza name.

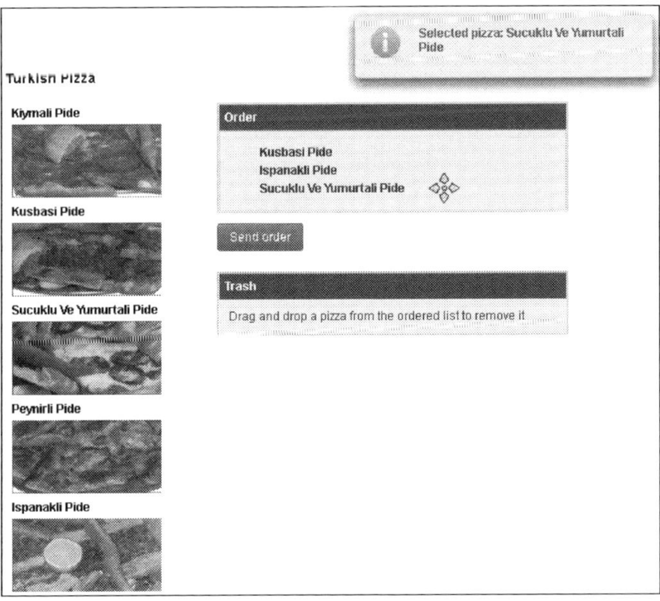

The last screenshot demonstrates the removal process. One pizza has been dragged from the order list and dropped onto the trash list.

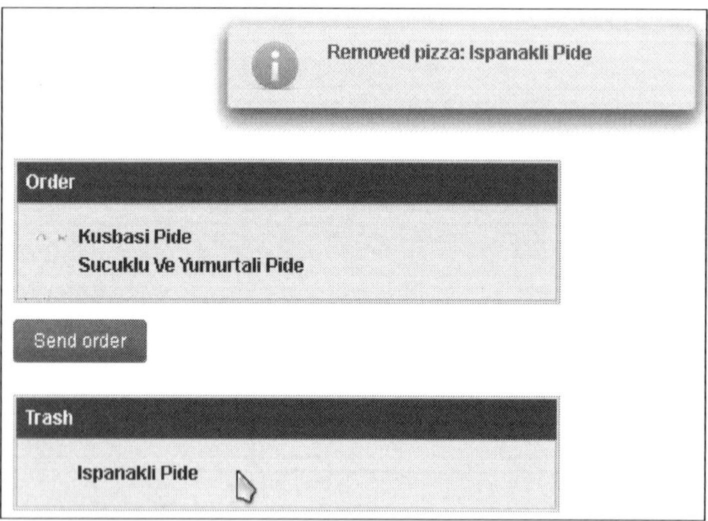

How it works...

To make `h:graphicImage` draggable, we use `p:draggable` with proper options: `helper="clone"`, `revert="true"`, and `cursor="move"`. The draggable images have the `title` attributes set to the pizza names. This is important for getting the dropped pizza's name in the `onPizzaOrder` listener by means of the `findComponent()` call. The draggable `h:panelGroup` tag in the order list has, in contrast to `h:graphicImage`, `f:attribute` set with the pizza name as value. This allows us to get the dropped pizza's name from the component's attribute map in the `onPizzaRemove` listener by means of the `invokeOnComponent()` call. Client IDs of the draggable/droppable components can be accessed by `getDragId()` / `getDropId()` on a `DragDropEvent` instance.

> Refer to the JSF 2 API documentation (`http://javaserverfaces.java.net/nonav/docs/2.1/javadocs/javax/faces/component/UIComponent.html`) to read more about `findComponent()` and `invokeOnComponent()`.

Last but not least, we use different ways to accept `Draggable`. In the case of images, we set `accept` to `.pizzaimage`. The `accept` attribute defines a jQuery selector for the accepted draggable components. In the case of items in the order list, we set `scope` to `trash`. The `scope` attribute is an alternative way to match the droppable and accepted draggable components. What is easier to use in each particular case depends on the code.

There's more...

We used two style classes with `p:droppable`:

- `activeStyleClass` set to `ui-state-default`
- `hoverStyleClass` set to `ui-state-hover`

They are used for better visual effects when dragging/dropping. If `activeStyleClass` is specified, the class will be added to the droppable component while an acceptable draggable component is being dragged. If `hoverStyleClass` is specified, the class will be added to the droppable component while an acceptable draggable component is being dragged over it.

PrimeFaces Cookbook Showcase application

This recipe is available in the demo web application on GitHub (`https://github.com/ova2/primefaces-cookbook`). Clone the project if you have not done it yet, explore the project structure, and execute the built-in Jetty Maven plugin to see this recipe in action. Follow the instructions in the `README` file if you do not know how to run Jetty.

When the server is running, the showcase for the recipe is available under `http://localhost:8080/primefaces-cookbook/views/chapter8/ajaxDragDrop.jsf`.

Integrating drag-and-drop with data iteration components

The `Droppable` component has a special integration with the data iteration components extending `javax.faces.component.UIData`. Such PrimeFaces components are `DataTable`, `DataGrid`, `DataList`, `Carousel`, `Galleria`, `Ring`, and `Sheet`. The component tag `p:droppable` defines a datasource option as an ID of the data iteration component that needs to be connected with `Droppable`.

In this recipe, we will introduce a `DataGrid` component containing some imaginary documents and make these documents draggable in order to drop them onto a recycle bin. The `DataGrid` component will act as a data source for the droppable Recycle Bin.

How to do it...

For the purpose of better understanding the developed code, pictures come first.

The first screenshot shows what happens when we start to drag a document. The **Recycle Bin** area gets highlighted.

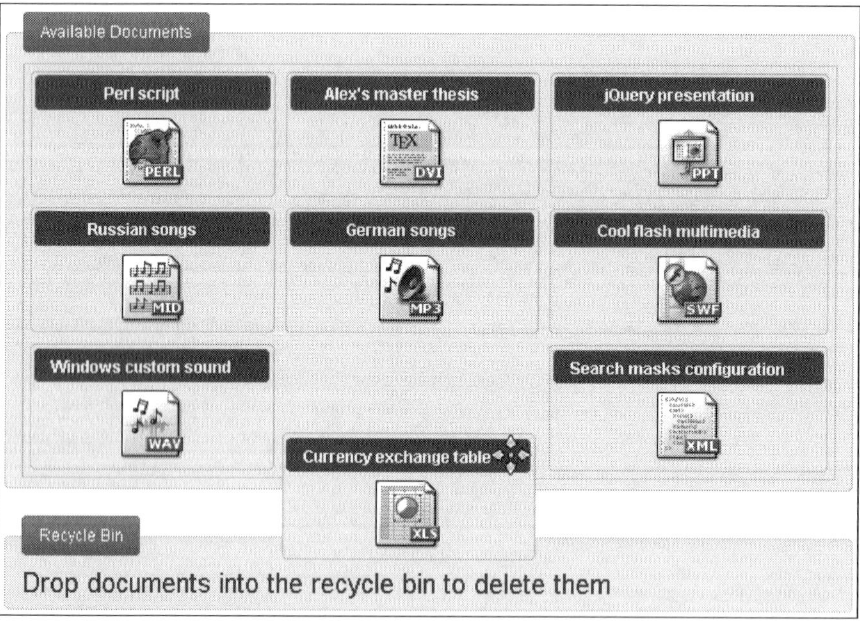

What it looks like after dropping three documents onto the Recycle Bin is reproduced in the following screenshot:

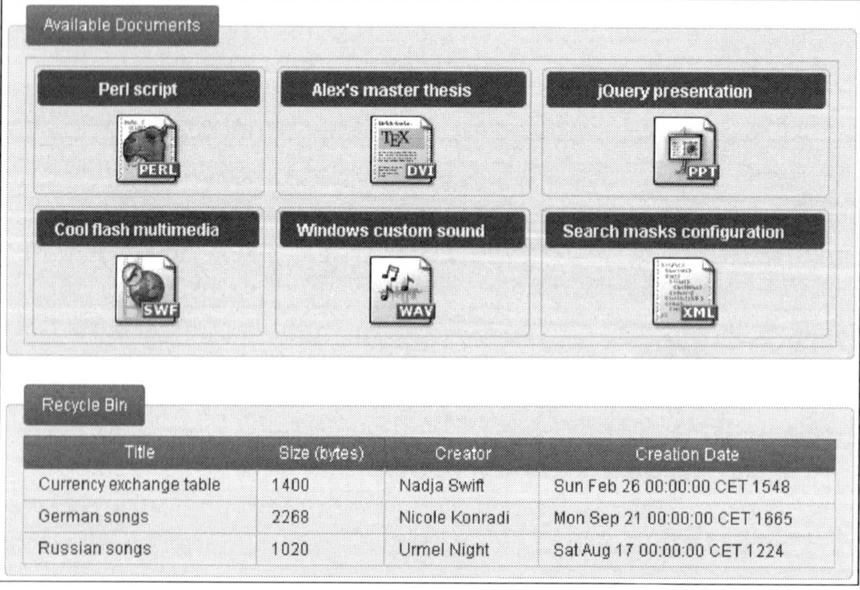

Available documents are represented as images within a `p:dataGrid`. They are placed in the `Panel` components, which are made draggable. The dragging occurs via the panel's titlebar. The titlebar contains the document's title (name). The Recycle Bin is represented by a `p:fieldset` tag with the ID `deletedDocs`. `Fieldset` is made droppable. It also contains a `p:dataTable` with currently deleted document items. Whenever a document is being dragged-and-dropped onto the Recycle Bin, an AJAX listener is invoked. The dropped document gets removed from the list of all available documents and gets added to the list of deleted documents. Data iteration components will be updated after that in order to display the correct data. The code snippet, in XHTML, looks as follows:

```
<p:fieldset legend="Available Documents">
  <p:dataGrid id="availableDocs" var="doc"
    value="#{integrationDragDrop.availableDocs}" columns="3">
    <p:column>
      <p:panel id="pnl" header="#{doc.title}"
      style="text-align:center">
      <h:graphicImage library="images"
      name="dragdrop/#{doc.extension}.png"/>
    </p:panel>
    <p:draggable for="pnl" revert="true"
    handle=".ui-panel-titlebar"
      stack=".ui-panel" cursor="move"/>
    </p:column>
  </p:dataGrid>
</p:fieldset>

<p:fieldset id="deletedDocs" legend="Recycle Bin"
  style="margin-top:20px">
  <p:outputPanel id="dropArea">
    <h:outputText value="Drop documents into the recycle bin to
      delete them"rendered="#{empty integrationDragDrop.deletedDocs}"
      style="font-size:20px;"/>

    <p:dataTable var="doc"
       value="#{integrationDragDrop.deletedDocs}"
       rendered="#{not empty integrationDragDrop.deletedDocs}">

      <p:column headerText="Title">
        <h:outputText value="#{doc.title}"/>
      </p:column>
      <p:column headerText="Size (bytes)">
        <h:outputText value="#{doc.size}"/>
      </p:column>
      <p:column headerText="Creator">
```

```
            <h:outputText value="#{doc.creator}"/>
          </p:column>
          <p:column headerText="Creation Date">
            <h:outputText value="#{doc.creationDate}"/>
          </p:column>
        </p:dataTable>
      </p:outputPanel>
    </p:fieldset>

    <p:droppable id="droppable" for="deletedDocs" tolerance="touch"
      activeStyleClass="ui-state-highlight" datasource="availableDocs">
      <p:ajax listener="#{integrationDragDrop.onDocumentDrop}"
        update="dropArea availableDocs"/>
    </p:droppable>
```

The model class `Document` contains the document properties. `getter / setter` has been omitted for brevity.

```
public class Document implements Serializable {

    private String title;
    private int size;
    private String creator;
    private Date creationDate;
    private String extension;

    public Document(String title, int size, String creator, Date
    creationDate, String extension) {
        this.title = title;
        this.size = size;
        this.creator = creator;
        this.creationDate = creationDate;
        this.extension = extension;
    }

    // getter / setter
    ...
}
```

The managed bean `IntegrationDragDrop` creates available documents (they can be loaded from a document management system, database, or filesystem), holds two lists for the data iteration components, and provides the AJAX listener `onDocumentDrop`.

```
@ManagedBean
@ViewScoped
```

```
public class IntegrationDragDrop implements Serializable {

  private List<Document> availableDocs = new
  ArrayList<Document>();
  private List<Document> deletedDocs = new
  ArrayList<Document>();

  @PostConstruct
  public void initialize() {
    availableDocs.add(new Document(
    "Perl script", 120, "Sara Schmidt", getCreationDate(),
    "perl"));
    ...
    availableDocs.add(new Document(
    "Search masks configuration", 33, "Andrew Andreev",
    getCreationDate(), "xml"));
  }

  public List<Document> getAvailableDocs() {
    return availableDocs;
  }

  public List<Document> getDeletedDocs() {
    return deletedDocs;
  }

  public void onDocumentDrop(DragDropEvent ddEvent) {
    Document doc = (Document) ddEvent.getData();

    deletedDocs.add(doc);
    availableDocs.remove(doc);
  }

  private Date getCreationDate() {
    Random random = new Random();
    int day = random.nextInt(30);
    int month = random.nextInt(Calendar.DECEMBER + 1);
    int year = random.nextInt(2012);
    GregorianCalendar calendar = new GregorianCalendar(year,
    month, day);

    return calendar.getTime();
  }
}
```

How it works...

We make the second `p:fieldset` tag droppable and connect it to the `p:dataList` tag with the ID `availableDocs`. This is done by setting `datasource` to `availableDocs` on `p:droppable`. The AJAX listener `onDocumentDrop`, attached by the `p:ajax` tag, is invoked on the `drop` event. Thanks to `datasource`, we can now access the dropped document instance by passing it to the listener event object `Document doc = (Document) ddEvent.getData()`.

PrimeFaces Cookbook Showcase application

This recipe is available in the demo web application on GitHub (`https://github.com/ova2/primefaces-cookbook`). Clone the project if you have not done it yet, explore the project structure, and execute the built-in Jetty Maven plugin to see this recipe in action. Follow the instructions in the `README` file if you do not know how to run Jetty.

When the server is running, the showcase for the recipe is available under `http://localhost:8080/primefaces-cookbook/views/chapter8/dragDropIntegration.jsf`.

9
Creating Charts and Maps

In this chapter we will cover the following:

- Creating a line chart
- Creating a bar chart
- Creating a pie chart
- Creating a bubble chart
- Creating a donut (doughnut) chart
- Creating a meter gauge chart
- Creating an OHLC chart
- Updating live data in charts with polling
- Interacting with charts through AJAX
- Creating dynamic image streaming programmatically
- Mapping with Google Maps

Introduction

In this chapter, we will cover creating charts with PrimeFaces' extensive charting features and creating maps based on Google Maps. PrimeFaces offers basic and advanced charting with its easy-to-use and user-friendly charting infrastructure. Along with the basic charting, live data updating of charts and the interaction with charts via the AJAX mechanism will also be covered. Throughout the chapter, we will cover mapping abilities such as drawing polylines, polygons, and handling markers and events.

Creating a line chart

The `lineChart` component visualizes series of point data as lines in a graph.

How to do it...

A simple definition for a line chart with two series of data to display is as follows:

```
<p:lineChart value="#{chartController.model}" style="height:250px" />
```

The chart will be rendered as follows:

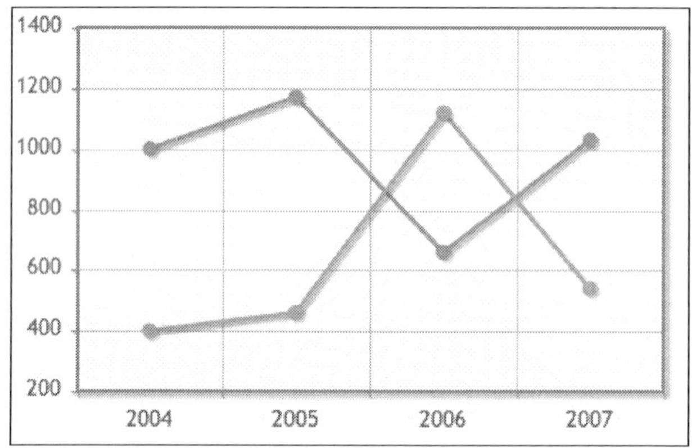

The model that binds to the component should be an instance of `org.primefaces.model.chart.CartesianChartModel`. The definition of data with two sample series is shown next:

```
CartesianChartModel model = new CartesianChartModel();

ChartSeries sales = new ChartSeries();
sales.setLabel("Sales");
sales.set("2004", 1000);
sales.set("2005", 1170);
sales.set("2006", 660);
sales.set("2007", 1030);

ChartSeries expenses = new ChartSeries();
expenses.setLabel("Expenses");
expenses.set("2004", 400);
expenses.set("2005", 460);
expenses.set("2006", 1120);
expenses.set("2007", 540);
```

```
model.addSeries(sales);
model.addSeries(expenses);
```

`CartesianChartModel` is a wrapper class that contains a list of `org.primefaces.model.chart.ChartSeries`. The `ChartSeries` class defines the actual data in a hash map along with a label string.

```
public class ChartSeries implements Serializable {
    private String label;
    private Map<Object,Number> data = new LinkedHashMap<Object,
    Number>();
    ...
}
```

There's more...

The `title` attribute defines the title of a chart. By default, the title is positioned at the top of the chart.

Positioning the legend

By default, the chart component does not show any legends for its lines. By specifying the `legendPosition` attribute, the legend can be activated and its position can be set to cardinal or intermediate directions, as `nw`, `w`, `sw`, `ne`, `e`, or `se`. The content of the legend will be the label that is set to the chart series.

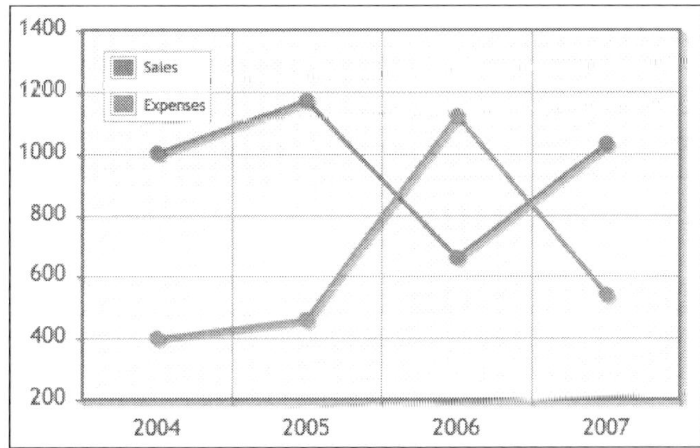

The `legendCols` and `legendRows` attributes control the appearance of the legend grid. By default, legends will be rendered in a grid with one column.

Labels and positioning

The `xaxisLabel` and `yaxisLabel` attributes define the labeling on the axes.

```
<p:lineChart value="#{lineChartController.model}" xaxisLabel="Year"
yaxisLabel="Amount" />
```

The `xaxisAngle` and `yaxisAngle` attributes define the angle of the ticks on the X or Y axis. With the following definition, the labels for the ticks will be rendered with 45 degrees tilt.

```
<p:lineChart value="#{lineChartController.model}" xaxisAngle="45"
yaxisAngle="45" />
```

The appearance of the chart definition given above will be as follows:

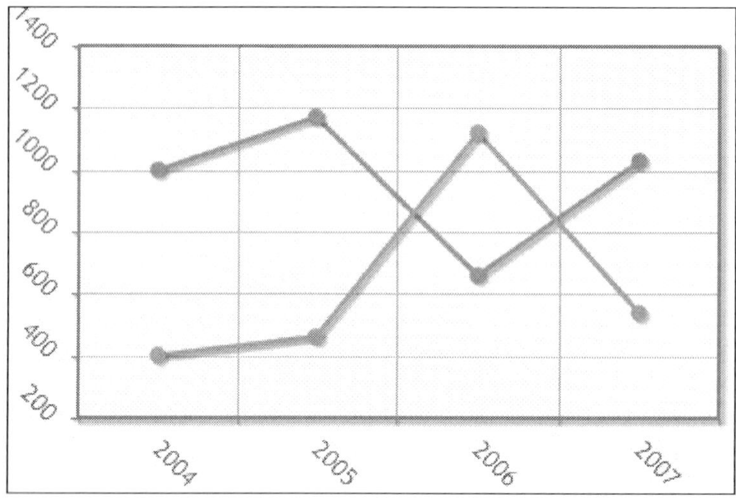

Minimum and maximum values on the axes

It is possible to constrain the values to be shown on the chart according to the X or Y axis. The `minX` attribute defines the minimum value and the `maxX` attribute defines the maximum value for the X axis. The `minY` and `maxY` attributes constrain the minimum and maximum values on the Y axis.

```
<p:lineChart value="#{lineChartController.model}" minY="400"
maxY="800" />
```

The output will be rendered as follows:

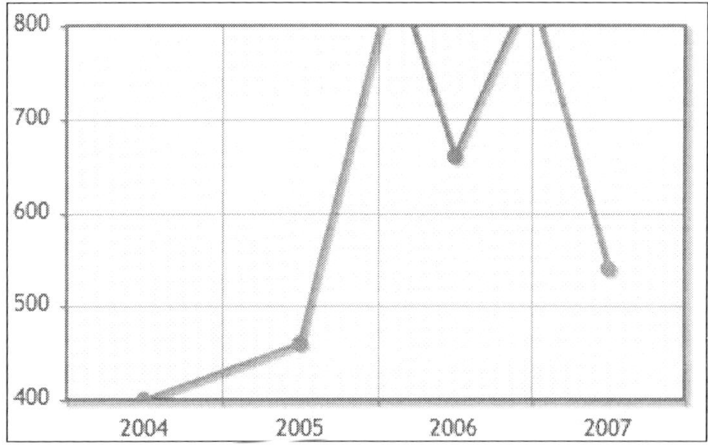

Breaking lines at null values

The `breakOnNull` attribute states whether line segments should be broken at null value or not. Its default value is `false`. For a two-series sample data set, which contains null values as given in the following code snippet, the output will be as given in the following image when `breakOnNull` is set to `true`.

```
ChartSeries sales = new ChartSeries();
sales.setLabel("Sales");
sales.set("2004", 1000);
sales.set("2005", null);
sales.set("2006", null);
sales.set("2007", 1030);

ChartSeries expenses = new ChartSeries();
expenses.setLabel("Expenses");
expenses.set("2004", 400);
expenses.set("2005", null);
expenses.set("2006", 1120);
expenses.set("2007", 540);
```

The output of this will be rendered as shown in the following screenshot:

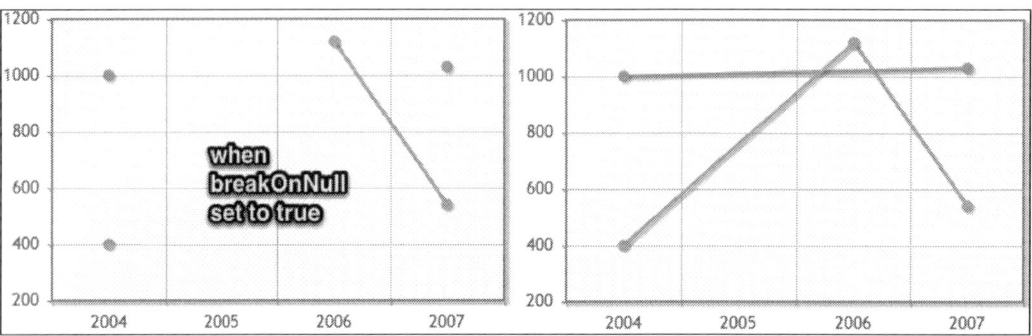

Styling lines

With the `seriesColors` attribute, it is possible to define a list of colors in a hexadecimal format, separated with commas. The colors of the lines will be picked up respectively, according to the given hex values.

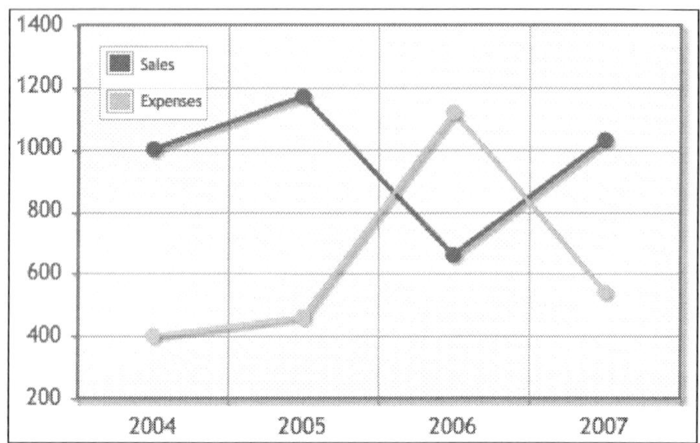

By default, the lines appear to have a shadow to give it a 3D effect. The `shadow` attribute controls this effect with its default value, `true`.

Filling under lines

By setting the `fill` attribute to `true`, it is possible to fill under the lines vertically starting from the X axis.

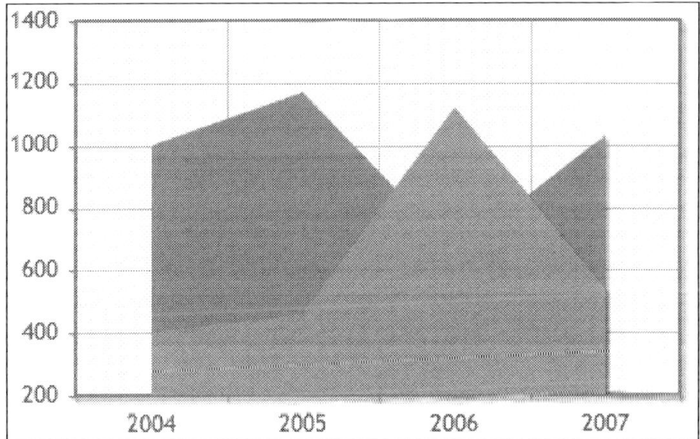

The `stacked` attribute defines whether the lines should be stacked on top of each other by adding the data sets.

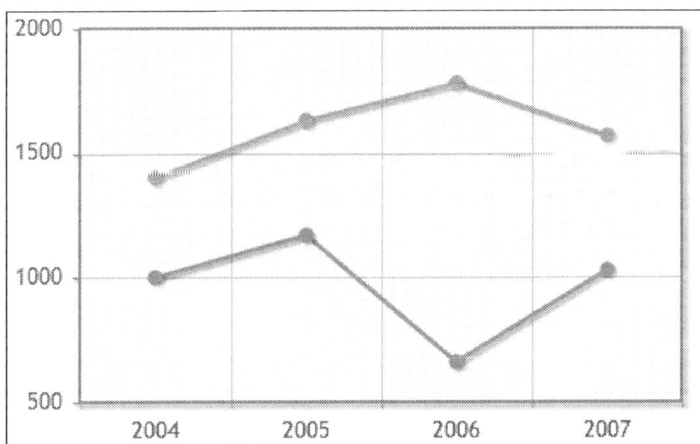

Customizing data tips

The chart component displays tips on each data point by default, shown in the following screenshot. The content of the tip is in the pattern `[index, value-of-the-axis]`.

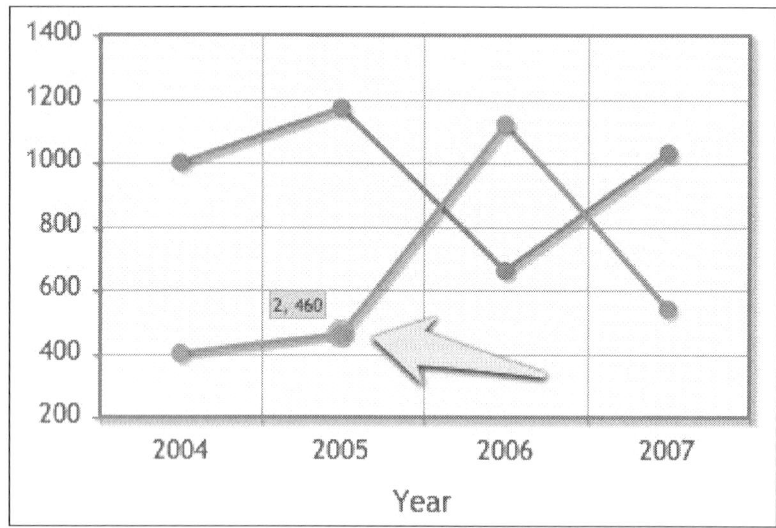

With the `showDataTip` attribute, it is possible to configure the default behavior, and the `datatipFormat` attribute customizes the content that will be displayed as the tip. The following definition uses a server-side method to define the format of the tip, which is an HTML snippet. This definition states that only the value of the Y axis will be shown as the tip, so it hides the first value with CSS.

```
<p:lineChart value="#{lineChartController.model}"
  showDatatip="true"
  datatipFormat="#{lineChartController.datatipFormat}" />

public String getDatatipFormat() {
  return "<span style=\"display:none;\">%s</span><span>%s</span>";
}
```

Animating and zooming

The chart component animates the plotting when the `animate` attribute is set to `true`. The duration of the animation effect is 1000 ms by default. With the `zoom` attribute set to `true`, the chart will provide users with the ability to zoom by selecting a region on the plot canvas, as seen in the following screenshot:

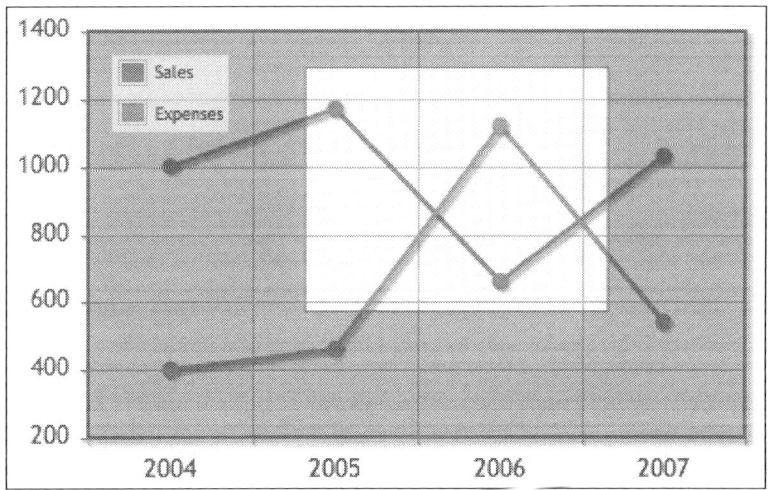

PrimeFaces Cookbook Showcase application

This recipe is available in the PrimeFaces Cookbook Showcase application on GitHub at `https://github.com/ova2/primefaces-cookbook`. You can find the details there for running the project. When the server is running, the showcase for the recipe is available at `http://localhost:8080/primefaces-cookbook/views/chapter9/lineChart.jsf`.

Creating a bar chart

The `barChart` component visualizes the series of point data as bars in a graph.

How to do it...

A simple definition for a bar chart to display two series of data is shown in the following code snippet:

```
<p:barChart value="#{barChartController.model}" style="height:250px"
title="Company Performance" />
```

The chart will be rendered as shown in the following screenshot:

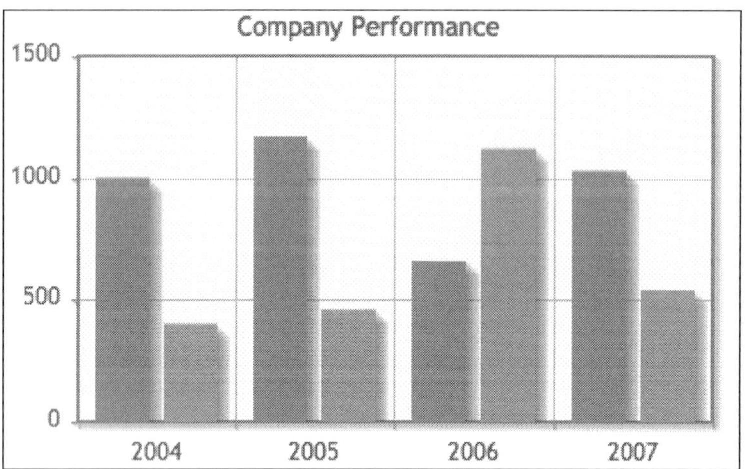

The model that binds to the component should be an instance of the `org.primefaces.model.chart.CartesianChartModel` class. The definition of data with two sample series is shown in the following code snippet:

```
CartesianChartModel model = new CartesianChartModel();

ChartSeries sales = new ChartSeries();
sales.setLabel("Sales");
sales.set("2004", 1000);
sales.set("2005", 1170);
sales.set("2006", 660);
sales.set("2007", 1030);

ChartSeries expenses = new ChartSeries();
expenses.setLabel("Expenses");
expenses.set("2004", 400);
expenses.set("2005", 460);
expenses.set("2006", 1120);
expenses.set("2007", 540);

model.addSeries(sales);
model.addSeries(expenses);
```

`CartesianChartModel` is a wrapper class that contains a list of `org.primefaces.model.chart.ChartSeries` classes. The `ChartSeries` class defines the actual data in a hash map along with a label string.

```
public class ChartSeries implements Serializable {
    private String label;
    private Map<Object,Number> data = new LinkedHashMap<Object,
Number>();
    ...
}
```

There's more...

The `title` attribute defines the title of a chart. By default, the title is positioned at the top of the chart.

Positioning the legend

By default, a chart component doesn't show any legends for its bars. By specifying the `legendPosition` attribute, the legend can be activated and its position can be set to cardinal or intermediate directions, as `nw`, `w`, `sw`, `ne`, `e`, or `se`. The content of the legend will be the label that is set to the chart series.

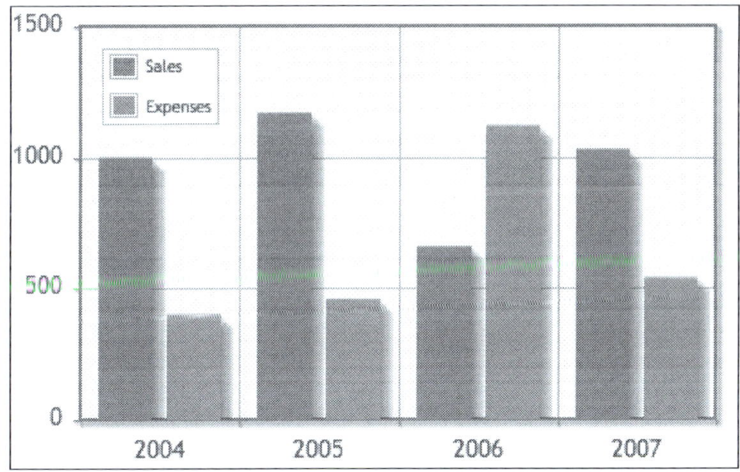

The `legendCols` and `legendRows` attributes control the appearance of the legend grid. By default, the legends will be rendered in a grid with one column.

Labels and positioning

The attributes `xaxisLabel` and `yaxisLabel` define the labeling on the axes.

```
<p:barChart value="#{barChartController.model}" xaxisLabel="Year"
yaxisLabel="Amount" />
```

The attributes `xaxisAngle` and `yaxisAngle` define the angle of the ticks on the X or Y axis. With the definition given as follows, the labels for the ticks will be rendered with 45 degrees tilt.

```
<p:barChart value="#{barChartController.model}" xaxisAngle="45"
yaxisAngle="45"  />
```

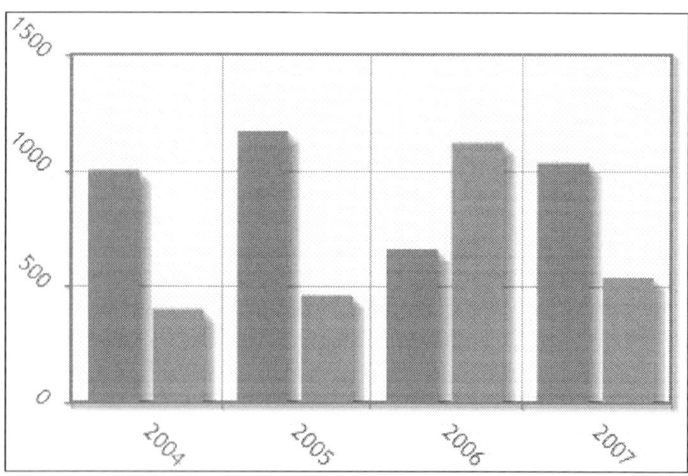

Styling bars

With the `seriesColors` attribute, it is possible to define a list of colors separated with commas in a hexadecimal format. The colors of the bars will be picked up respectively, according to the given hex values.

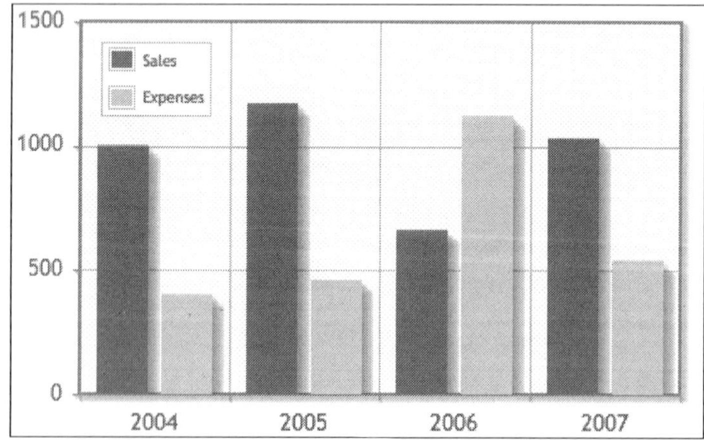

By default, the bars have a shadow effect to give a 3D appearance. The `shadow` attribute controls this effect with its default value, `true`.

Orientation

The `orientation` attribute defines the orientation of the bars in the plot. Its value can be `vertical` (which is the default value) or `horizontal`.

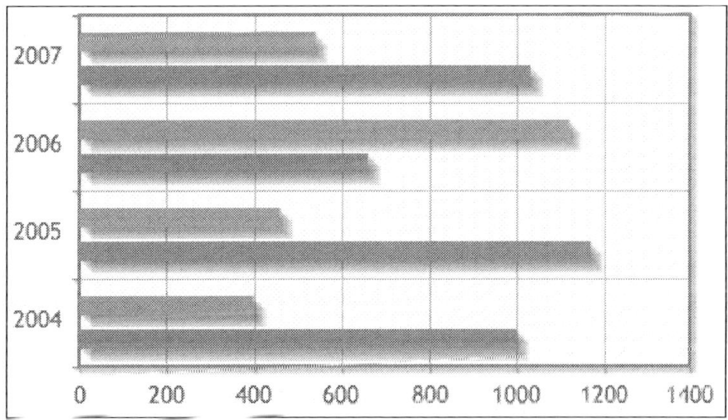

Stacked bar chart

The `stacked` attribute defines the corresponding values for each series to be merged as one bar, stacked onto each other.

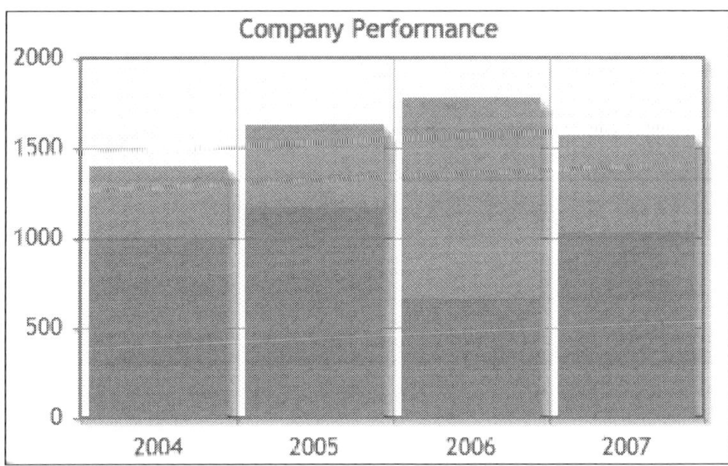

Customizing data tips

The chart component displays tips on each data point by default. The content of the tip is in the `[index, value-of-the-axis]` pattern in the `vertical` mode. With the `showDataTip` attribute it is possible to configure the default behavior, and the `datatipFormat` attribute customizes the content that will be displayed as the tip. The following definition uses a server-side method to define the format of the tip, which is an HTML snippet. This definition states that only the value of the Y axis will be shown as the tip, so it hides the first value with CSS.

```
<p:barChart value="#{barChartController.model}" showDatatip="true"
  datatipFormat="#{barChartController.datatipFormat}" />

public String getDatatipFormat() {
  return "<span style=\"display:none;\">%s</span><span>%s</span>";
}
```

Animating and zooming

The `chart` component animates the plotting when the `animate` attribute is set to `true`. The duration of the animation effect is 1000 ms by default. With the `zoom` attribute set to `true`, the chart will provide zooming to the user by selecting a region on the plot canvas, as shown in the following screenshot:

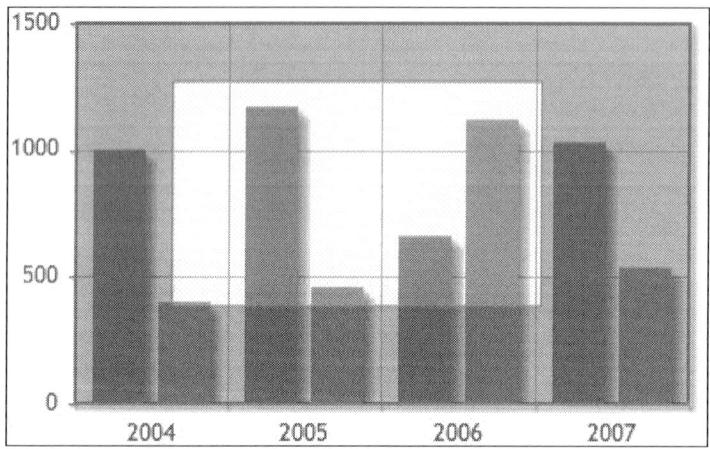

PrimeFaces Cookbook Showcase application

This recipe is available in the PrimeFaces Cookbook Showcase application on GitHub at `https://github.com/ova2/primefaces-cookbook`. You can find the details there for running the project. When the server is running, the showcase for the recipe is available at `http://localhost:8080/primefaces-cookbook/views/chapter9/barChart.jsf`.

Creating a pie chart

The `pieChart` component visualizes category data as a pie chart.

How to do it...

A simple definition for a pie chart with categories of data for displaying hours spent per day is shown as follows:

```
<p:pieChart value="#{pieChartController.model}" style="height:250px"
title="Hours per Day" />
```

The chart will be rendered as follows:

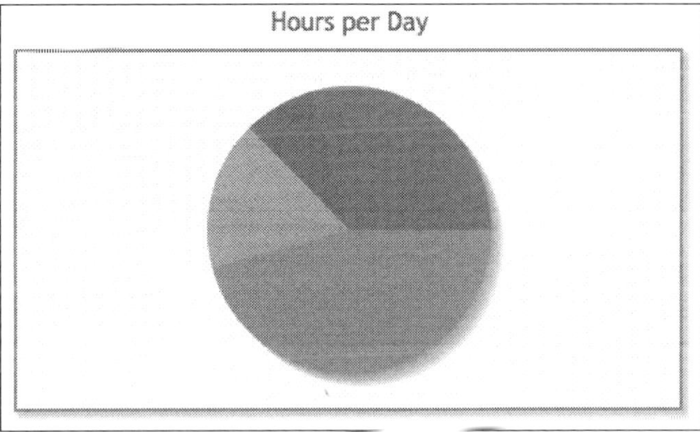

The model that binds to the component should be an instance of `org.primefaces.model.chart.PieChartModel`. The definition of the model along with the categories is given in the following code snippet:

```
PieChartModel model = new PieChartModel();

model.set("Work", 11);
model.set("Eat", 2);
model.set("Commute", 2);
model.set("Watch TV", 2);
model.set("Sleep", 7);
```

There's more...

The `title` attribute defines the title of a chart. By default, the title is positioned at the top of the chart.

Positioning the legend

By default, the `chart` component does not show any legends for its slices. By specifying the `legendPosition` attribute, the legend can be activated and its position can be set to cardinal or intermediate directions, as `nw`, `w`, `sw`, `ne`, `e`, or `se`. The content (text) of the legends will be the categories that are set to the pie chart series.

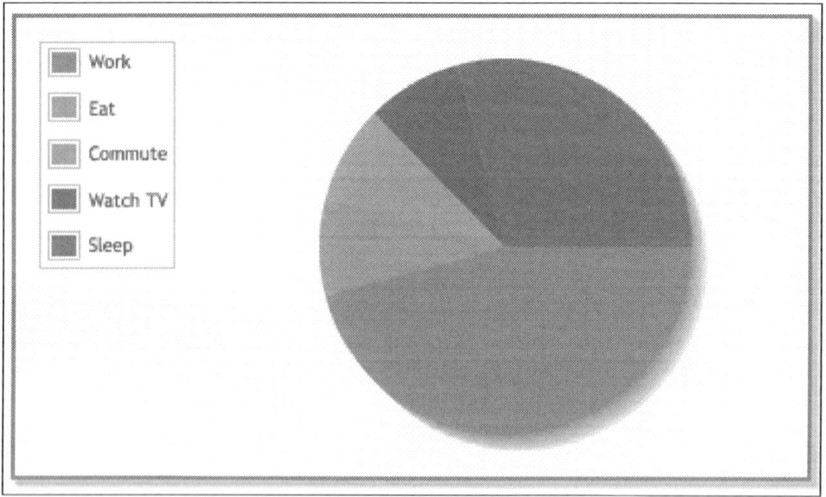

The `legendCols` and `legendRows` attributes control the appearance of the legend grid. By default, legends will be rendered in a grid with one column.

Styling slices

With the `seriesColors` attribute, it is possible to define a list of colors in a hexadecimal format separated with commas. The colors of the slices will be picked up respectively according to the given hex values. By default, slices have a shadow effect to give a 3D appearance. The `shadow` attribute controls this effect with its default value, `true`.

Showing data labels

The `showDataLabels` attribute defines whether the label data should be displayed on each slice or not. The `dataFormat` attribute defines the format of the data. By default, its value is `percent`, which renders the percentage for each slice. Other possible values are `label` and `value`.

Adjusting pie appearance

The `pieChart` component provides features for customized look and feel. The `sliceMargin` attribute defines the gap between slices, which is the angular spacing between pie slices in degrees. By default, its value is `0`. The `diameter` attribute defines the outer diameter of the pie, which is auto-computed by default. The `fill` attribute defines whether to fill the slices or not. Its default value is `true`.

```
<p:pieChart value="#{pieChartController.model}" sliceMargin="5"
diameter="200" fill="false" />
```

The chart will be rendered as shown in the following screenshot:

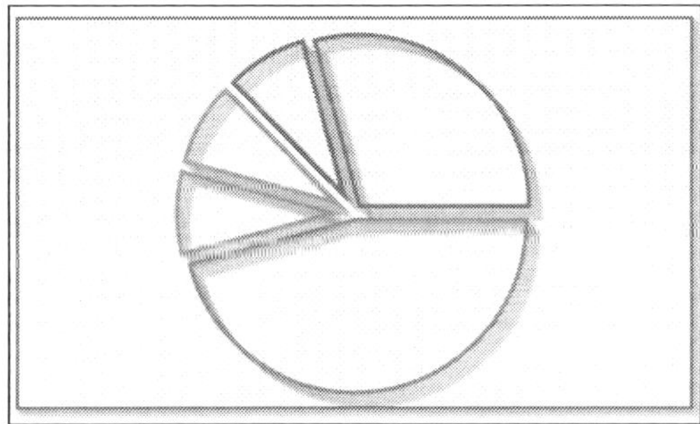

PrimeFaces Cookbook Showcase application

This recipe is available in the PrimeFaces Cookbook Showcase application on GitHub at `https://github.com/ova2/primefaces-cookbook`. You can find the details there for running the project. When the server is running, the showcase for the recipe is available at `http://localhost:8080/primefaces-cookbook/views/chapter9/pieChart.jsf`.

Creating a bubble chart

The `bubbleChart` component renders the data points displayed as colored circles with an optional text label inside.

How to do it...

A simple definition for a bubble chart to list public road mileage, the number of fatal crashes, and average annual daily traffic for a list of states is given as follows:

```
<p:bubbleChart value="#{bubbleChartController.model}"
style="height:250px" xaxisLabel="Number of Fatal Crashes"
yaxisLabel="Public Road Mileage" />
```

The chart will be rendered as shown in the following screenshot:

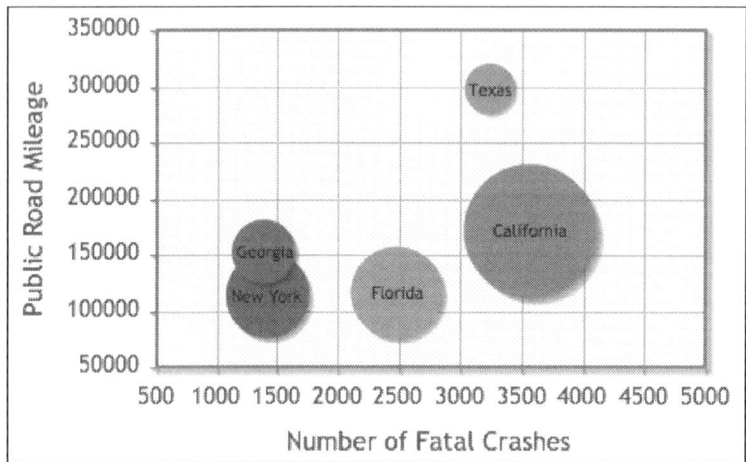

The model that binds to the component should be an instance of `org.primefaces.model.chart.BubbleChartModel`.

```
BubbleChartModel model = new BubbleChartModel();

model.add(new BubbleChartSeries("California", 3576, 170506, 4455));
model.add(new BubbleChartSeries("Texas", 3248, 296259, 1710));
model.add(new BubbleChartSeries("Florida", 2496,114422, 3104));
model.add(new BubbleChartSeries("New York", 1422, 112347, 2885));
model.add(new BubbleChartSeries("Georgia", 1403, 151746, 2179));
```

`BubbleChartModel` is a wrapper class that contains a list of `org.primefaces.model.chart.BubbleChartSeries` instances. The `BubbleChartSeries` class defines the series data. It must be in the form of a label and a triplet, which are `x`, `y`, and `radius` values.

```
public class BubbleChartSeries {
    private int x;
    private int y;
    private int radius;
    private String label;
    ...
}
```

There's more...

The `title` attribute defines the title of a chart. By default, the title is positioned at the top of the chart.

Styling bubbles

The `bubbleGradients` attribute defines whether the bubbles will be colored with gradient fills instead of flat colors. The `bubbleAlpha` attribute defines the alpha transparency to be applied to all the bubbles in the series.

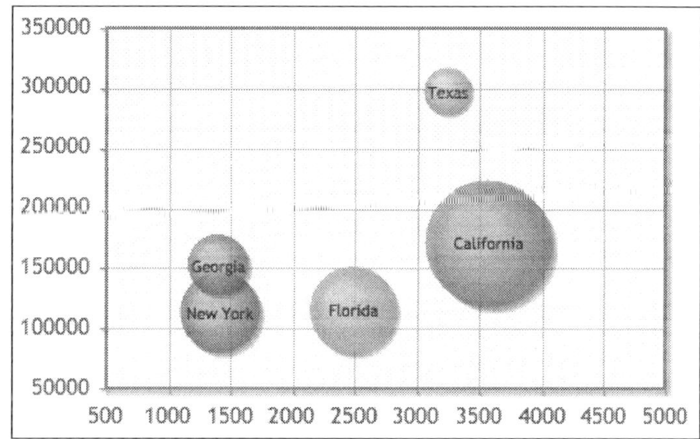

With the `seriesColors` attribute, it is possible to define a list of colors in a hexadecimal format separated with commas. The colors of the bubbles will be picked up respectively according to the given hex values. By default, the bubbles have a shadow effect to give the chart a 3D appearance. The `shadow` attribute controls this effect with its default value, `true`.

> The `bubbleGradients` attribute is not available in Internet Explorer due to the lack of `excanvas` support for radial gradient fills. This attribute will be ignored in IE.

Labels and positioning

The `xaxisLabel` and `yaxisLabel` attributes define the labeling on the axes. The attributes `xaxisAngle` and `yaxisAngle` define the angle of the ticks on the X and Y axis. In the following definition, the labels for the ticks will be rendered at 45 degrees.

```
<p:bubbleChart value="#{bubbleChartController.model}"
style="height:250px" xaxisAngle="45" yaxisAngle="45" />
```

The chart will be rendered as the following screenshot:

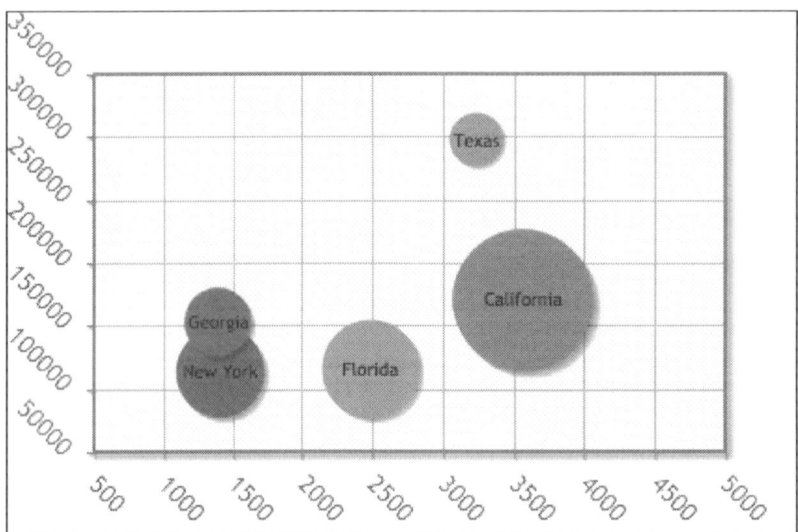

By default, the chart shows labels on each bubble. This can be prevented by setting the `showLabels` attribute to `false`.

PrimeFaces Cookbook Showcase application

This recipe is available in the PrimeFaces Cookbook Showcase application on GitHub at `https://github.com/ova2/primefaces-cookbook`. You can find the details there for running the project. When the server is running, the showcase for the recipe is available at `http://localhost:8080/primefaces-cookbook/views/chapter9/bubbleChart.jsf`.

Creating a donut (doughnut) chart

The `donutChart` component renders a multiseries of pie charts, like a combination, in one plotting.

How to do it...

A simple definition for a donut(doughnut) chart to display stock exchange options as three circles would be as follows:

```
<p:donutChart value="#{donutChartController.model}"
style="height:250px" title="Stocks by Year"  />
```

This output will be rendered as follows:

The model that binds to the component should be an instance of `org.primefaces.model.chart.DonutChartModel`.

```
DonutChartModel model = new DonutChartModel();

Map<String, Number> circle1 = new LinkedHashMap<String, Number>();
circle1.put("APPL", 150);
circle1.put("IBM", 180);
circle1.put("AMD", 30);
circle1.put("INTC", 120);
model.addCircle(circle1);

Map<String, Number> circle2 = new LinkedHashMap<String, Number>();
circle2.put("APPL", 180);
circle2.put("IBM", 90);
circle2.put("AMD", 100);
circle2.put("INTC", 80);
model.addCircle(circle2);

Map<String, Number> circle3 = new LinkedHashMap<String, Number>();
circle3.put("APPL", 210);
circle3.put("IBM", 40);
circle3.put("AMD", 80);
circle3.put("INTC", 160);
model.addCircle(circle3);
```

`DonutChartModel` is a container class that contains a list of maps, `List<Map<String,Number>>`, that contain the definitions for each circle of the doughnut.

There's more...

The `title` attribute defines the title of a chart. By default, the title is positioned at the top of the chart.

Positioning the legend

By default, the chart component does not show any legends for its slices. By specifying the `legendPosition` attribute, the legend can be activated and its position can be set to cardinal or intermediate directions, as `nw`, `w`, `sw`, `ne`, `e`, or `se`. The content of the legend will be the label that is set to the chart series. The `legendCols` and `legendRows` attributes control the appearance of the legend grid. By default, legends will be rendered in a grid with one column.

Adjusting donut appearance

With the `seriesColors` attribute, it is possible to define a list of colors in hexadecimal format separated with commas. The colors of the lines will be picked up according to the given hex values. By default, the lines have a shadow effect to give a 3D appearance. The `shadow` attribute controls this effect with its default value, `true`. The `sliceMargin` attribute defines the gap between slices, which is the angular spacing between pie slices in degrees.

By default, its value is `0`. The `fill` attribute defines whether to fill the slices or not. Its default value is `true`. The following is a definition for an adjusted doughnut appearance:

```
<p:donutChart value="#{donutChartController.model}"
style="height:250px" sliceMargin="5" fill="false" />
```

This output will be rendered as follows:

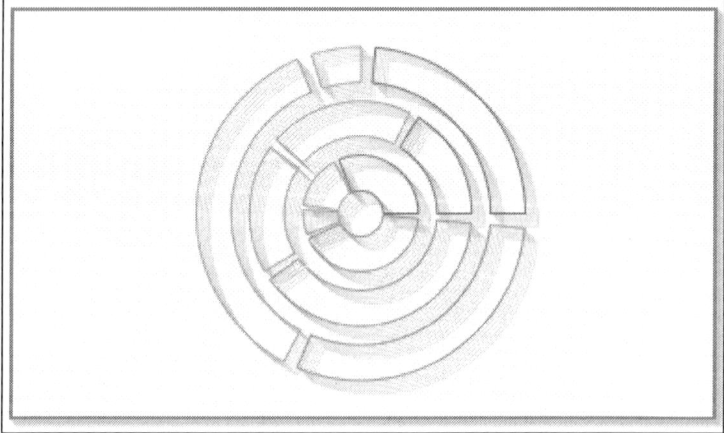

PrimeFaces Cookbook Showcase application

This recipe is available in the PrimeFaces Cookbook Showcase application on GitHub at `https://github.com/ova2/primefaces-cookbook`. You can find the details there for running the project. When the server is running, the showcase for the recipe is available at `http://localhost:8080/primefaces-cookbook/views/chapter9/donutChart.jsf`.

Creating a meter gauge chart

The `meterGauge` component visualizes data on a meter gauge display.

How to do it...

A simple definition for a meter gauge to list metric tons per year is shown as follows:

```
<p:meterGaugeChart id="simple" value="#{meterGaugeController.model}"
style="height:250px" />
```

The chart will be rendered as shown in the following screenshot:

The model that binds to the component should be an instance of `org.primefaces.model.chart.MeterGaugeChartModel`. The definition for the model with the ticks and intervals is given as follows:

```
List<Number> intervals = new ArrayList<Number>(){{
  add(22000);
  add(55000);
  add(70000);
}};
```

```
List<Number> ticks = new ArrayList<Number>(){{
  add(10000);
  add(20000);
  add(30000);
  add(50000);
  add(70000);
}};

MeterGaugeChartModel model = new MeterGaugeChartModel(52200,
intervals, ticks);
```

`MeterGaugeChartModel` is a container class for `value`, `intervals`, and `ticks` that control the gauge appearance.

There's more...

The `title` attribute defines the title of a chart. By default, the title is positioned at the top of the chart. The `label` attribute defines a gauge label and it is put between intervals and ticks.

Customizing the look of the gauge

The `showTickLabels` attribute should be set to `true` to show tick labels next to the ticks. The `labelHeightAdjust` attribute defines the number of pixels to offset the label up (-) or down (+) from its default position. The `intervalOuterRadius` attribute defines the radius of the outer circle of the interval ring. The `min` attribute defines the minimum value and the `max` attribute defines the maximum value on the gauge.

```
<p:meterGaugeChart id="custom"
      value="#{meterGaugeController.model}" style="height:250px"
      label="tons" title="Metric Tons Per Year"
      showTickLabels="false" labelHeightAdjust="-20"
      intervalOuterRadius="60" />
```

The chart will be rendered as shown in the following screenshot:

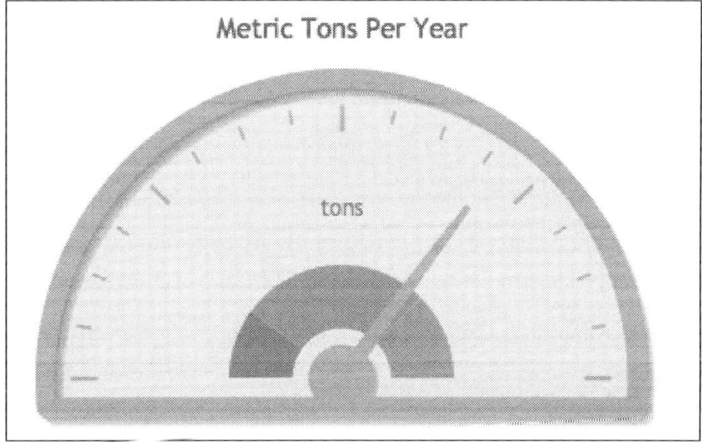

PrimeFaces Cookbook Showcase application

This recipe is available in the PrimeFaces Cookbook Showcase application on GitHub at `https://github.com/ova2/primefaces-cookbook`. You can find the details there for running the project. When the server is running, the showcase for the recipe is available at `http://localhost:8080/primefaces-cookbook/views/chapter9/meterGaugeChart.jsf`.

Creating an OHLC chart

The `ohlcChart` component visualizes the data more like a bar chart, but it's a type of chart typically used to illustrate fluctuations in the price of a financial instrument over time. For example, an **Open High Low Close** (**OHLC**) chart can display the open, high, low, and close prices of a publicly traded security on a given day, with the day as the X axis and the price as the Y axis.

How to do it...

A simple definition for an OHLC chart with the price of a stock for given days of a month is shown as follows:

```
<p:ohlcChart value="#{ohlcChartController.model}" style="height:250px"
/>
```

The output of this will be rendered as follows:

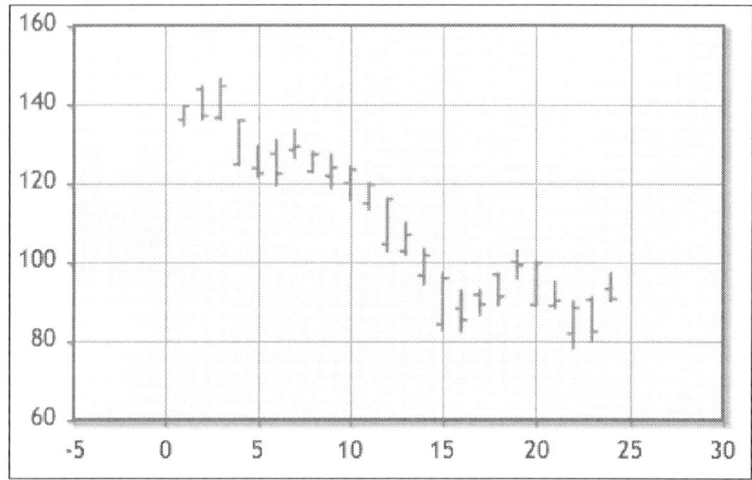

The model that binds to the component should be an instance of `org.primefaces.model.chart.OhlcChartModel`. The definition for the stock data is as follows:

```
OhlcChartModel model = new OhlcChartModel();

model.add(new OhlcChartSeries(1, 136.01, 139.5, 134.53, 139.48));
model.add(new OhlcChartSeries(2, 143.82, 144.56, 136.04, 136.97));
model.add(new OhlcChartSeries(3, 136.47, 146.4, 136, 144.67));
model.add(new OhlcChartSeries(4, 124.76, 135.9, 124.55, 135.81));
model.add(new OhlcChartSeries(5, 123.73, 129.31, 121.57, 122.5));
model.add(new OhlcChartSeries(6, 127.37, 130.96, 119.38, 122.42));
model.add(new OhlcChartSeries(7, 128.24, 133.5, 126.26, 129.19));
model.add(new OhlcChartSeries(8, 122.9, 127.95, 122.66, 127.24));
model.add(new OhlcChartSeries(9, 121.73, 127.2, 118.6, 123.9));
model.add(new OhlcChartSeries(10, 120.01, 124.25, 115.76,
  123.42));
model.add(new OhlcChartSeries(11, 114.94, 120, 113.28, 119.57));
model.add(new OhlcChartSeries(12, 104.51, 116.13, 102.61,
  115.99));
model.add(new OhlcChartSeries(13, 102.71, 109.98, 101.75,
  106.85));
model.add(new OhlcChartSeries(14, 96.53, 103.48, 94.18, 101.59));
model.add(new OhlcChartSeries(15, 84.18, 97.2, 82.57, 95.93));
model.add(new OhlcChartSeries(16, 88.12, 92.77, 82.33, 85.3));
```

```
model.add(new OhlcChartSeries(17, 91.65, 92.92, 86.51, 89.31));
model.add(new OhlcChartSeries(18, 96.87, 97.04, 89, 91.2));
model.add(new OhlcChartSeries(19, 100, 103, 95.77, 99.16));
model.add(new OhlcChartSeries(20, 89.1, 100, 88.9, 99.72));
model.add(new OhlcChartSeries(21, 88.86, 95, 88.3, 90.13));
model.add(new OhlcChartSeries(22, 81.93, 90, 78.2, 88.36));
model.add(new OhlcChartSeries(23, 90.46, 90.99, 80.05, 82.33));
model.add(new OhlcChartSeries(24, 93.17, 97.17, 90.04, 90.58));
```

`OhlcChartModel` is a wrapper class that contains a list of `org.primefaces.model.chart.OhlcChartSeries`. The `OhlcChartSeries` class defines the value and the quadrant for the OHLC—`open`, `high`, `low`, and `close`.

```
public class OhlcChartSeries implements Serializable {
    private Object value;
    private double open;
    private double high;
    private double low;
    private double close;
}
```

There's more...

The `title` attribute defines the title of a chart. By default, the title is positioned at the top of the chart.

Labels and positioning

The `xaxisLabel` and `yaxisLabel` attributes define the labeling on the axes.

```
<p:ohlcChart value="#{ohlcChartController.model}" style="height:250px"
xaxisLabel="Day" yaxisLabel="$" />
```

The `xaxisAngle` and `yaxisAngle` attributes define the angle of the ticks on the X or Y axis. With the following definition, the labels for the ticks will be rendered with 45 degrees tilt.

```
<p:ohlcChart value="#{ohlcChartController.model}" style="height:250px"
xaxisAngle="45" yaxisAngle="45" />
```

Candlestick mode

By setting the `candleStick` attribute to `true`, it is possible to render the chart bars as follows. The OHLC chart must be set to `open` in order to be rendered properly.

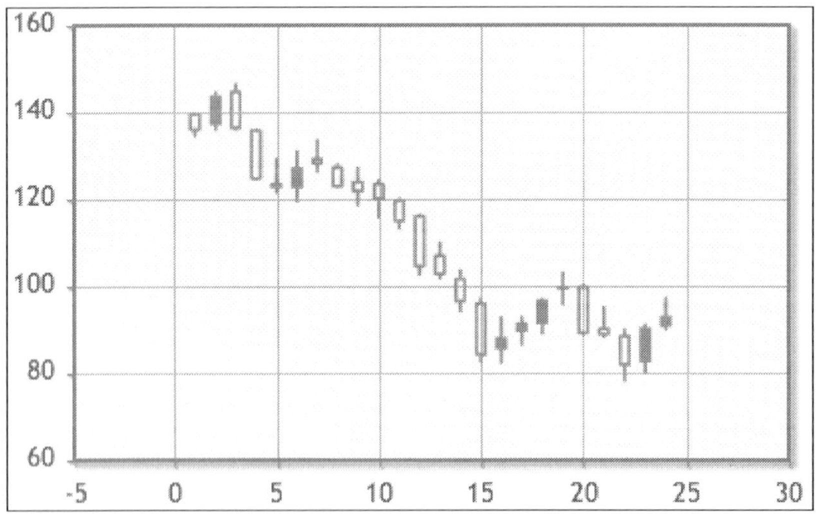

PrimeFaces Cookbook Showcase application

This recipe is available in the PrimeFaces Cookbook Showcase application on GitHub at `https://github.com/ova2/primefaces-cookbook`. You can find the details there for running the project. When the server is running, the showcase for the recipe is available at `http://localhost:8080/primefaces-cookbook/views/chapter9/ohlcChart.jsf`.

Updating live data in charts with polling

It's possible to update the chart in a timely manner with the help of the `<p:poll>` component.

How to do it...

The following definition updates the pie chart every 3 seconds:

```
<p:poll interval="3" update="live" />
<p:pieChart id="live" value="#{pieChartController.livePieModel}"
style="height:250px" />
```

The data model definition with the getter method, which will randomly create chart data, is given as follows:

```
PieChartModel liveChartModel = new PieChartModel();

liveChartModel.set("Candidate 1", 500);
liveChartModel.set("Candidate 2", 300);

public PieChartModel getLivePieModel() {
  int random1 = (int)(Math.random() * 1000);
  int random2 = (int)(Math.random() * 1000);

  liveChartModel.getData().put("Candidate 1", random1);
  liveChartModel.getData().put("Candidate 2", random2);

  return liveChartModel;
}
```

PrimeFaces Cookbook Showcase application

This recipe is available in the PrimeFaces Cookbook Showcase application on GitHub at `https://github.com/ova2/primefaces-cookbook`. You can find the details there for running the project. When the server is running, the showcase for the recipe is available at `http://localhost:8080/primefaces-cookbook/views/chapter9/pollingChart.jsf`.

Interacting with charts through AJAX

PrimeFaces' chart components support the `itemSelect` AJAX behavior event, which is fired when an item on the plotted data is clicked upon.

How to do it...

A simple definition for a bar chart, with a listener attached and two series of data to be displayed, is given as follows:

```
<p:barChart id="withAjax" value="#{barChartController.model}"
style="height:250px">
  <p:ajax event="itemSelect" listener="#{barChartController.
itemSelect}" update="growl" />
</p:barChart>
```

The listener is defined with the `p:ajax` component and will be called with the `org.primefaces.event.ItemSelectEvent` attribute.

```
public void itemSelect(ItemSelectEvent event) {
  MessageUtil.addInfoMessageWithoutKey("Item selected",
      "Series Index:" + event.getSeriesIndex() + ", Item Index: "
      + event.getItemIndex());
}
```

How it works...

`ItemSelectEvent` is a wrapper class that contains `seriesIndex`, the series that the item resides inside, and `itemIndex`, the position of the item within the series.

```
public class ItemSelectEvent extends AjaxBehaviorEvent {
  private int itemIndex;
  private int seriesIndex;
  ...
}
```

PrimeFaces Cookbook Showcase application

This recipe is available in the PrimeFaces Cookbook Showcase application on GitHub at `https://github.com/ova2/primefaces-cookbook`. You can find the details there for running the project. When the server is running, the showcase for the recipe is available at `http://localhost:8080/primefaces-cookbook/views/chapter9/chartInteraction.jsf`.

See also

For details about the `MessageUtil` class, see the *Internationalization (i18n) and Localization (L10n)* section in *Chapter 1, Getting Started with PrimeFaces*

Creating dynamic image streaming programmatically

With the `graphicImage` component, it is possible to render an image that is created programmatically in the server-side backing bean.

How to do it...

The following is an example that renders a PrimeFaces logo that is read with the resource streaming mechanism.

```
<p:graphicImage value="#{dynaImageController.graphicText}" />

public StreamedContent getGraphicText() throws IOException {
  InputStream stream =
  this.getClass().getResourceAsStream("/chapter9/primefaces.jpg");
  return new DefaultStreamedContent(stream);
}
```

How it works...

As seen, the `getGraphicText()` method returns an instance of `StreamedContent`. PrimeFaces also provides a default implementation for the stream content, which is `org.primefaces.model.DefaultStreamedContent`. The backing bean containing the `graphicText` getter method should be defined in the session scope. The reason behind this is that the image will be fetched in a separate request from the rest of the page content, and in order to retrieve the logo image the content should be stored in the session context.

> The other applicable fields in which to use programmatically created images can be listed as follows: with the JFreeChart API chart, charting images could be easily created; or with the Barbecue framework, which is the open source barcode creator Java library, barcode images can be created. In both of these use cases, the output will be rendered on the page with the `graphicImage` component.

PrimeFaces Cookbook Showcase application

This recipe is available in the PrimeFaces Cookbook Showcase application on GitHub at `https://github.com/ova2/primefaces-cookbook`. You can find the details there for running the project. When the server is running, the showcase for the recipe is available at `http://localhost:8080/primefaces-cookbook/views/chapter9/dynaImage.jsf`

Mapping with Google Maps

The `gmap` component provides ways to integrate Google Maps into JSF applications. It is built upon Google Maps API V3.

How to do it...

In order to use the component, the Google Maps API script should be referenced from the page, ideally in the header section.

```
<script src="http://maps.google.com/maps/api/js?sensor=true"
type="text/javascript"></script>
```

The `sensor` parameter in the URL is mandatory and it specifies whether the application requires a sensor, such as a GPS locator.

A simple definition for a placing a map canvas on the page will be as follows:

```
<p:gmap center="41.106261, 29.057465" zoom="10" type="hybrid"
style="width:600px;height:400px" />
```

This output will be rendered as follows:

How it works...

The gmap component depicts the four attributes that should be set, as shown in the previous example, in order to use the map canvas properly. The center attribute defines the center of the map in [latitude, longitude] format. The zoom attribute defines the zoom level of the map. Zoom levels between 0 (the lowest zoom level, in which the entire world can be seen on one map) and 21+ (down to individual buildings) are possible. The type attribute defines the type of the map: roadmap (the default value), satellite, hybrid, or terrain. The style attribute could be used to define the dimensions of the map canvas.

There's more...

It is also possible to bind the component to a model with an instance of org.primefaces.model.map.MapModel. PrimeFaces provides org.primefaces.model.map.DefaultMapModel as the default model implementation. DefaultMapModel is a wrapper class for markers, polylines, polygons, circles, and rectangles.

```
<p:gmap center="41.106261, 29.057465" zoom="10" type="roadmap" style="
width:600px;height:400px" model="#{mapController.markerModel}" />
```

Placing markers

It is possible to add markers onto the map via the data model. The marker should be an instance of org.primefaces.model.map.Marker. Markers can be easily constructed by providing an instance of org.primefaces.model.map.LatLng to define their position. The latitude and longitude values could be provided to the LatLng class as constructor parameters. Markers will be added to the data model via the addOverlay method.

```
MapModel markerModel = new DefaultMapModel();

markerModel.addOverlay(new Marker(new LatLng(41.073399,
  29.051971), "Bosphorus"));
markerModel.addOverlay(new Marker(new LatLng(41.118418,
  29.134026), "Bosphorus"));
```

This output will be rendered as follows:

The attributes of `org.primefaces.model.map.Marker` are listed in the following table:

Property	Default	Type	Description
`title`	`null`	`String`	Text to display on rollover
`latlng`	`null`	`LatLng`	Location of the marker
`icon`	`null`	`String`	Foreground image of the marker
`shadow`	`null`	`String`	Shadow image of the marker
`cursor`	`pointer`	`String`	Cursor to display on rollover
`draggable`	`False`	`Boolean`	Defines if the marker can be dragged
`clickable`	`True`	`Boolean`	Defines if the marker can be clicked
`flat`	`False`	`Boolean`	Shadow image not displayed when set to `true`
`visible`	`True`	`Boolean`	Defines the visibility of the marker

Drawing polylines

It is possible to draw polylines on maps by providing a data model. The polyline should be an instance of `org.primefaces.model.map.Polyline`. Polylines can be easily constructed by adding instances of `org.primefaces.model.map.LatLng` to their path definition to define the point elements of the polyline.

```
MapModel polylineModel = new DefaultMapModel();

Polyline polyline = new Polyline();
polyline.getPaths().add(new LatLng(41.073399, 29.051971));
polyline.getPaths().add(new LatLng(41.118418, 29.134026));
polyline.getPaths().add(new LatLng(41.027807, 29.049973));

polylineModel.addOverlay(polyline);
```

The attributes of `org.primefaces.model.map.Polyline` are listed in the following table:

Property	Default	Type	Description
`paths`	`null`	`List<LatLng>`	List of polyline elements
`strokeColor`	`null`	`String`	Color of the line
`strokeOpacity`	`1`	`Double`	Opacity of the line
`strokeWeight`	`1`	`Integer`	Width of the line

Drawing polygons

It is possible to draw polygons on maps by providing a data model. The polygon should be an instance of `org.primefaces.model.map.Polygon`. Polygons can be easily constructed by adding instances of `org.primefaces.model.map.LatLng` to their path definition to define the point elements of the polygon.

```
MapModel polygonModel = new DefaultMapModel();

Polygon polygon = new Polygon();
polygon.getPaths().add(new LatLng(41.073399, 29.051971));
polygon.getPaths().add(new LatLng(41.118418, 29.134026));
polygon.getPaths().add(new LatLng(41.027807, 29.049973));

polygonModel.addOverlay(polygon);
```

The attributes of `org.primefaces.model.map.Polygon` are listed in the following table:

Property	**Default**	**Type**	**Description**
`paths`	`null`	`List<LatLng>`	List of polygon elements
`strokeColor`	`null`	`String`	Color of the polygon line
`strokeOpacity`	`1`	`Double`	Opacity of the polygon line
`strokeWeight`	`1`	`Integer`	Width of the polygon line
`fillColor`	`null`	`String`	Background color of the polygon
`fillOpacity`	`1`	`Double`	Opacity of the polygon

Drawing circles

It is possible to draw circles on maps by providing a data model. The circle should be an instance of `org.primefaces.model.map.Circle`. Circles can be easily constructed by providing an instance of `org.primefaces.model.map.LatLng` and `radius` as the constructor parameters.

```
MapModel circleModel = new DefaultMapModel();
Circle circle = new Circle(new LatLng(41.073399, 29.051971), 50000);
circleModel.addOverlay(circle);
```

The attributes of `org.primefaces.model.map.Circle` are listed in the following table:

Property	**Default**	**Type**	**Description**
`center`	`null`	`LatLng`	Center of the circle
`radius`	`null`	`Double`	Radius of the circle in meters
`strokeColor`	`null`	`String`	Stroke color of the circle
`strokeOpacity`	`1`	`Double`	Stroke opacity of the circle
`strokeWeight`	`1`	`Integer`	Stroke weight of the circle
`fillColor`	`null`	`String`	Background color of the circle
`fillOpacity`	`1`	`Double`	Opacity of the circle

Handling events

It is also possible to invoke a server-side method instantly with the interactions on the map. The `gmap` component provides AJAX behavior events to handle these interactions.

Event	Listener parameter	When fired
`overlaySelect`	`org.primefaces.event.map.OverlaySelectEvent`	When an overlay is selected
`stateChange`	`org.primefaces.event.map.StateChangeEvent`	When the map's state changes
`pointSelect`	`org.primefaces.event.map.PointSelectEvent`	When an empty point is selected
`markerDrag`	`org.primefaces.event.map.MarkerDragEvent`	When a marker is dragged

The overlay selection example, given next, will output the selected `title` and the `[latitude, longitude]` attribute of the selected marker with a Faces message.

```
<p:gmap id="withAJAX" center="41.106261, 29.057465"
zoom="10" type="roadmap" style="width:600px;height:400px"
model="#{mapController.markerModel}">
  <p:ajax event="overlaySelect" listener="#{mapController.
onMarkerSelect}" update="growl" />
</p:gmap>

public void onMarkerSelect(OverlaySelectEvent event) {
  Marker selectedMarker = (Marker) event.getOverlay();
  MessageUtil.addInfoMessageWithoutKey(selectedMarker.getTitle(),
selectedMarker.getLatlng().toString());
}
```

Placing the information window

The `gmap` component uses the `gmapInfoWindow` helper component to display an information window, that is, when a marker is selected. The following is the definition of a map component that renders two markers with an information window attached.

```
<p:gmap id="withInformation" center="41.106261, 29.057465"
zoom="10" type="roadmap" style="width:600px;height:400px"
model="#{mapController.markerModel}">
  <p:ajax event="overlaySelect" listener="#{mapController.
selectMarker}" />
```

```
    <p:gmapInfoWindow id="infoWindow">
      <p:graphicImage value="/resources/images/map/#{mapController.
  selectedMarker.data}" />
    </p:gmapInfoWindow>
  </p:gmap>
```

The chart will be rendered as shown in the following screenshot:

Controlling the map

The `gmap` component provides two attributes: `navigationControl` and `mapTypeControl`, to set the visibility of the map controls. The `mapTypeControl` attribute enables/disables the map type control that lets the user toggle between map types (such as Map and Satellite). By default, this control is visible and appears on the top right-hand side corner of the map. The visibility of the navigation controls can be set with the `navigationControl` attribute. Alternatively, the `gmap` component provides the `disableDefaultUI` attribute. By setting it to `true`, controls will be removed regardless of the status of other attributes. The `disabledDoubleClickZoom` attribute disables the zooming on a double-click. The `draggable` attribute defines the "draggability" of the map; it could be used to define static maps.

Enabling the street view

It is possible to enable the street view by setting the `streetView` attribute to `true`. Then, the user will be able to drag the human icon onto the blue lines on the map, which depict the viewable streets/roads.

Then the map will transit into street view and allow the user to navigate in a 360-degree view.

PrimeFaces Cookbook Showcase application

This recipe is available in the PrimeFaces Cookbook Showcase application on GitHub at `https://github.com/ova2/primefaces-cookbook`. You can find the details there for running the project. When the server is running, the showcase for the recipe is available at `http://localhost:8080/primefaces-cookbook/views/chapter9/map.jsf`.

See also

For details about the `MessageUtil` class, see the *Internationalization (i18n) and Localization (L10n)* section in *Chapter 1, Getting Started with PrimeFaces*

10
Miscellaneous, Advanced Use Cases

In this chapter we will cover:

- The power of the PrimeFaces selectors
- Programmatic updating and scrolling with RequestContext
- Two ways to trigger JavaScript execution
- Adding AJAX callback parameters – validation within a dialog
- Navigating to another page in AJAX calls
- Polling – sending periodical AJAX requests
- Blocking page pieces during long-running AJAX calls
- Remembering the current menu selection
- Controlling form submission by DefaultCommand
- Clever focus management in forms
- Layout pitfalls with menus and dialogs
- Targetable messages with severity levels
- Leveraging Schedule's lazy loading feature

Introduction

PrimeFaces has an impressive number of components that are usually suitable for all common and advanced use cases. It is almost impossible to cover all scenarios in just one book and discuss all solutions for this case or that. The key aspect of this chapter consists in giving users tips that can be applied quickly for often-raised questions.

In this chapter, we will go beyond the basics and introduce more interesting features of the PrimeFaces library. We will learn about `RequestContext`—a helpful utility that allows marking components as updatable targets at runtime, adding AJAX callback parameters, and more. We will also develop a couple of real-world samples such as, for example, blocking UI during AJAX calls, periodic polling, focus handling, controlling form submission, and targetable messages. Furthermore, after reading this chapter you should be aware of some pitfalls of menus within the layout units and nested panels.

The power of the PrimeFaces selectors

PrimeFaces integrates jQuery Selector API (`http://api.jquery.com/category/selectors`) with the JSF component referencing model. Partial processing and updating of the JSF components can be done by using the jQuery Selector API instead of a regular server-side approach with `findComponent()`. This feature is called **PFS** (**PrimeFaces Selector API**). PFS provides an alternative, flexible approach to reference components to be processed or updated partially. In comparison to regular referencing, there is less CPU server load because the JSF component tree is not traversed on the server side in order to find client IDs. PFS is implemented on the client side by looking at the DOM tree. Another advantage is avoiding naming container limitations and thus the `cannot find component` exception, since the component we were looking for was in a different naming container.

The essential advantage of this feature, however, is speed. If we reference a component by an ID, jQuery uses a native browser call `document.getElementById()` behind the scene. This is a very fast call, much faster than that on the server side with `findComponent()`. The second use case where selectors are faster is if we have a lot of components with the `rendered` attributes set to `true` or `false`. The JSF component tree is very big in this case and the `findComponent()` call is time-consuming. On the client side, only the visible part of the component tree is rendered as markup. The DOM is smaller than the component tree and selectors work faster.

In this recipe, we will learn PFS in detail. PFS is recognized when we use `@(...)` in the `process` or `update` attribute of ajaxified components. We will use this syntax in four command buttons to reference the parts of the page we are interested in.

How to do it...

The following code snippet contains two `p:panel` tags with `input`, `select`, and `checkbox` components respectively. The first `p:commandButton` processes/updates all components in the form(s). The second one processes/updates all panels. The third one processes `input`, but not `select` components, and updates all panels. The last button only processes the `checkbox` components in the second panel and updates the entire panel.

> In terms of jQuery selectors, regular input field, select, and checkbox controls are all inputs. They can be selected by the `:input` selector.

```
<p:messages id="messages" autoUpdate="true"/>

<p:panel id="panel1" header="First panel" style="margin-bottom:10px;">
  <h:panelGrid columns="2">
    <p:outputLabel for="name" value="Name"/>
    <p:inputText id="name" required="true"/>

    <p:outputLabel for="food" value="Favorite food"/>
    <h:selectOneMenu id="food" required="true"
    style="padding:3px;">
      <f:selectItem itemLabel="" itemValue=""/>
      <f:selectItem itemLabel="Pizza" itemValue="Pizza"/>
      <f:selectItem itemLabel="Pasta" itemValue="Pasta"/>
    </h:selectOneMenu>

    <p:outputLabel for="married" value="Married?"/>
    <p:selectBooleanCheckbox id="married" required="true"
    label="Married?">
      <f:validator validatorId="org.primefaces.
      cookbook.validator.
      RequiredCheckboxValidator"/>
    </p:selectBooleanCheckbox>
  </h:panelGrid>
</p:panel>

<p:panel id="panel2" header="Second panel">
  <h:panelGrid columns="2">
    <p:outputLabel for="address" value="Address"/>
    <p:inputText id="address" required="true"/>
```

```
      <p:outputLabel for="pet" value="Favorite pet"/>
      <h:selectOneMenu id="pet" required="true"
      style="padding:3px;">
        <f:selectItem itemLabel="" itemValue=""/>
        <f:selectItem itemLabel="Cat" itemValue="Cat"/>
        <f:selectItem itemLabel="Dog" itemValue="Dog"/>
      </h:selectOneMenu>

      <p:outputLabel for="gender" value="Male?"/>
      <p:selectBooleanCheckbox id="gender" required="true"
      label="Male?">
        <f:validator validatorId="org.primefaces.cookbook.validator.
        RequiredCheckboxValidator"/>
      </p:selectBooleanCheckbox>
    </h:panelGrid>
  </p:panel>

  <h:panelGrid columns="5" style="margin-top:20px;">
    <p:commandButton process="@(form)" update="@(form)"
      value="Process and update all in form"/>

    <p:commandButton process="@(.ui-panel)" update="@(.ui-panel)"
      value="Process and update all panels"/>

    <p:commandButton process="@(.ui-panel :input:not(select))"
      update="@(.ui-panel)"
      value="Process inputs except selects in all panels"/>

    <p:commandButton process="@(#panel2 :checkbox)"
      update="@(#panel2)"
      value="Process checkboxes in second panel"/>
  </h:panelGrid>
```

The following screenshot shows what happens when the third button is pushed. The `p:inputText` and `p:selectBooleanCheckbox` components are marked as invalid. The `h:selectOneMenu` component is not marked as invalid although no value was selected by the user.

Name: Validation Error: Value is required.
Married?: Validation error: Value is required.
Address: Validation Error: Value is required.
Male?: Validation error: Value is required.

First panel

Name *

Favorite food *

Married? *

Second panel

Address *

Favorite pet *

Male? *

Process and update all in form | Process and update all panels | Process inputs except selects in all panels | Process checkboxes in second panel

How it works...

The first selector from the first button `@(form)` selects all forms on the page. The second selector `@(.ui-panel)` selects all panels on the page as every main container of PrimeFaces' `p:panel` component has this style class. Component style classes are usually documented in the *Skinning* section in the *PrimeFaces User's Guide* (`http://www.primefaces.org/documentation.html`). The third selector, `@(.ui-panel :input:not(select))`, only selects `p:inputText` and `p:selectBooleanCheckbox` within `p:panel`. This is why `h:selectOneMenu` was not marked as invalid in the preceding screenshot. The validation of this component was skipped because it renders itself as an HTML `select` element. The last selector variant, `@(#panel2 :checkbox)`, intends to select `p:selectBooleanCheckbox` in the second panel only. In general, it is recommended to use Firebug (`http://http://getfirebug.com`) or a similar browser add-on to explore the generated HTML structure when using jQuery selectors.

> A common use case is skipping validation for the hidden fields. Developers often hide some form components dynamically with JavaScript. Hidden components get validated anyway, and the form validation can fail if the fields are required or have other validation constraints. The first solution would be to make the components disabled (in addition to hidden). Values of disabled fields are not sent to the server. The second solution would be to use jQuery's `:visible` selector in the `process` attribute of a command component that submits the form.

There's more...

PFS can be combined with regular component referencing as well, for example, `update="compId1 :form:compId2 @(.ui-tabs :input)"`.

PrimeFaces Cookbook Showcase application

This recipe is available in the demo web application on GitHub (`https://github.com/ova2/primefaces-cookbook`). Clone the project if you have not done it yet, explore the project structure, and execute the built-in Jetty Maven plugin to see this recipe in action. Follow the instructions in the `README` file if you do not know how to run Jetty.

When the server is running, the showcase for the recipe is available under `http://localhost:8080/primefaces-cookbook/views/chapter10/pfs.jsf`.

Programmatic updating and scrolling with RequestContext

`RequestContext` is an easy-to-use utility class that provides useful goodies. `RequestContext` is available for AJAX as well as non-AJAX calls. The most important goodies will be revealed in this book.

In this recipe, we will see how to specify components to be updated at runtime rather than specifying update targets at compile time declaratively. We will also see how to scroll to any component after the current AJAX request completes. Scrolling to the given component with AJAX updates is very handy in long pages and can increase the website's usability.

How to do it...

In the first example, we will develop a counter that will be incremented in an action listener. The current counter value will be displayed in two output components `h:outputText`. A decision what `h:outputText` is responsible for the output is provided by a checkbox `p:selectBooleanCheckbox`. The user can decide at runtime if he/she would like to update the first or the second output component.

```
<p:selectBooleanCheckbox id="checkbox" itemLabel="Update first output"
  value="#{requestContextController.firstOutput}"/>

<h:panelGrid columns="2" style="margin-top:10px;">
  <h:outputText value="First Output"/>
  <h:outputText id="firstOutput"
  value="#{requestContextController.counter}"/>
```

```
    <h:outputText value="Second Output"/>
    <h:outputText id="secondOutput"
    value="#{requestContextController.counter}"/>

    <f:facet name="footer">
      <p:commandButton value="Increment counter"
      actionListener="#{requestContextController.incrementWithUpdate}"
      process="@form" style="margin:10px 0 10px 0;"/>
    </f:facet>
  </h:panelGrid>
```

In the next example, we will take the same counter, which is displayed by `h:outputText`, and a very long text output, so that the browser's scrollbars appear. At the end of the text output, we will place a command button that increments the counter and scrolls to the counter's output when the AJAX response comes back. The logic for scrolling is implemented inside the button's action listener.

```
<h:panelGrid id="counter" columns="2" style="font-weight:bold;">
  <h:outputText value="Counter"/>
  <h:outputText value="#{requestContextController.counter}"/>
</h:panelGrid>

<p>Some text</p>
...
<p>Some text</p>

<p:commandButton value="Increment counter"
  style="margin:10px; "process="@form" update="counter"
  actionListener="#{requestContextController.incrementWithScroll}"
```

The managed bean with the action listeners `incrementWithUpdate()` and `incrementWithScroll()`, mentioned in the preceding code snippets, looks as follows:

```
@ManagedBean
@ViewScoped
public class RequestContextController implements Serializable {

  private boolean firstOutput = true;
  private int counter = 0;
```

```
    public void incrementWithUpdate(ActionEvent ae) {
      counter++;

      RequestContext requestContext =
      RequestContext.getCurrentInstance();

      if (firstOutput) {
        requestContext.update("firstOutput");
      } else {
        requestContext.update("secondOutput");
     }
    }

    public void incrementWithScroll(ActionEvent ae) {
      counter++;

      RequestContext requestContext =
      RequestContext.getCurrentInstance();
      requestContext.scrollTo("counter");
    }

    public boolean isFirstOutput() {
      return firstOutput;
    }

    public void setFirstOutput(boolean firstOutput) {
      this.firstOutput = firstOutput;
    }

    public int getCounter() {
      return counter;
    }
  }
```

The following screenshot shows a snapshot result of the first example:

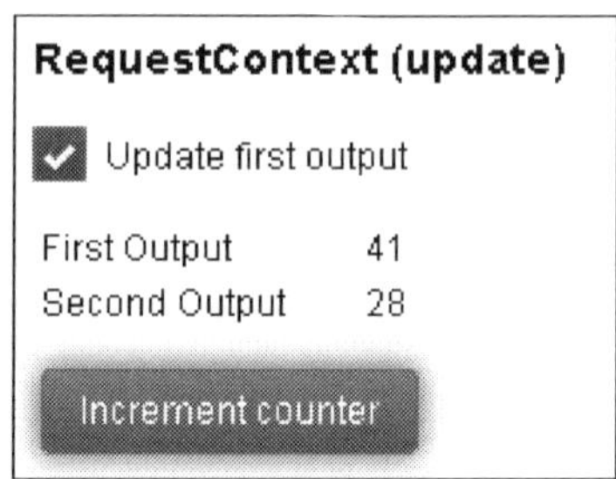

How it works...

The `RequestContext` instance can be obtained, similar to `FacesContext`, as `RequestContext.getCurrentInstance()`. The `update()` method of the `RequestContext` instance expects the client IDs of the components to be updated. These components are `firstOutput` and `secondOutput`. Depending on the user's checkbox selection (boolean variable `firstOutput`), either the first or the second `h:outputText` will be updated.

The scrolling to a given component is done by the `scrollTo()` method. This method expects a client ID of the component that we want to scroll to. The call `requestContext.scrollTo("counter")` ensures that the user will see the counter value after a click on the **Increment counter** button.

There's more...

The client-side API for scrolling is also available to use directly as follows:

```
PrimeFaces.scrollTo("clientId")
```

PrimeFaces Cookbook Showcase application

This recipe is also available in the demo web application on GitHub (`https://github.com/ova2/primefaces-cookbook`). Clone the project if you have not done it yet, explore the project structure, and execute the built-in Jetty Maven plugin to see this recipe in action. Follow the instructions in the `README` file if you do not know how to run Jetty.

When the server is running, the showcase for the recipe is available under `http://localhost:8080/primefaces-cookbook/views/chapter10/requestContext.jsf`.

Two ways to trigger JavaScript execution

The `RequestContext` utility class provides an easy way to execute any JavaScript code after the current AJAX request completes. The JavaScript block has to be coded in Java and can be executed by passing it to the `execute()` method. An alternative approach would be to update a script block on a page and trigger the script execution manually. In this case, the JavaScript block is coded directly into a page.

In this recipe, we will see both solutions for JavaScript execution. For this purpose, we will develop a `Menu` component and toggle enabling/disabling of menu items with two command buttons. The first command button should toggle enabling/disabling with the server-side approach and the second one with the client-side approach.

How to do it...

Let's write a `p:menu` tag with three menu items. We also need two `p:commandButton` tags with appropriate action listeners.

```
<h:outputText id="indicator" value="Enabled? -
   #{javaScriptExecController.enabled}"/>

<p:menu id="menu" style="margin:20px 0 10px 0;">
  <p:submenu label="JavaScript Libraries">
    <p:menuitem value="jQuery" url="http://jquery.com"/>
    <p:menuitem value="Yahoo UI" url="http://yuilibrary.com"/>
    <p:menuitem value="Prototype" url="http://prototypejs.org"/>
  </p:submenu>
</p:menu>

<p:commandButton id="toggle1" value="Toggle Menuitems (server-side)"
    process="@this" update="indicator"
    actionListener="#{javaScriptExecController.toogleMenuitems}"/>

<p:commandButton id="toggle2" value="Toggle Menuitems (client-side)"
    process="@this" update="indicator toggleScriptWrapper"
    actionListener="#{javaScriptExecController.toogleEnabled}"/>

<h:panelGroup id="toggleScriptWrapper">
  <script type="text/javascript">
    /* <![CDATA[ */
    if (#{facesContext.partialViewContext.ajaxRequest}) {
      $('#menu a').each(function() {
        if ($(this).attr('href')) {
          // disable item
          $(this).attr('data-oldhref', $(this).attr('href'))
          .removeAttr('href').addClass('ui-state-disabled');
        } else {
        // enable item
          $(this).attr('href', $(this).attr('data-oldhref'))
          .removeAttr('data-oldhref').removeClass
          ('ui-state-disabled');
        }
      });
    }
```

```
  /* ]]> */
  </script>
</h:panelGroup>
```

The `PanelGroup` with the ID `toggleScriptWrapper` contains the script logic that gets executed after each update on this `PanelGroup`. The managed bean packs the same logic in a `String` variable `script` and executes it with `requestContext.execute(script)`.

```
@ManagedBean
@ViewScoped
public class JavaScriptExecController implements Serializable {

  private boolean enabled = true;

  public void toogleMenuitems(ActionEvent ae) {
    RequestContext requestContext =
    RequestContext.getCurrentInstance();

    String script;
    if (enabled) {
      script = "$('#menu a').each(function() {"
        + "$(this).attr('data-oldhref', $(this).attr('href'))"
        + ".removeAttr('href').addClass('ui-state-disabled');"
        + "});";
    } else {
    script = "$('#menu a').each(function() {"
        + "$(this).attr('href', $(this).attr('data-oldhref'))"
        + ".removeAttr('data-oldhref').removeClass('ui-state-
        disabled');"
        + "});";
    }

    requestContext.execute(script);

    enabled = !enabled;
  }

  public void toogleEnabled(ActionEvent ae) {
    enabled = !enabled;
  }
```

```
    public boolean isEnabled() {
      return enabled;
    }
  }
```

The following screenshot shows what disabled menu items look like:

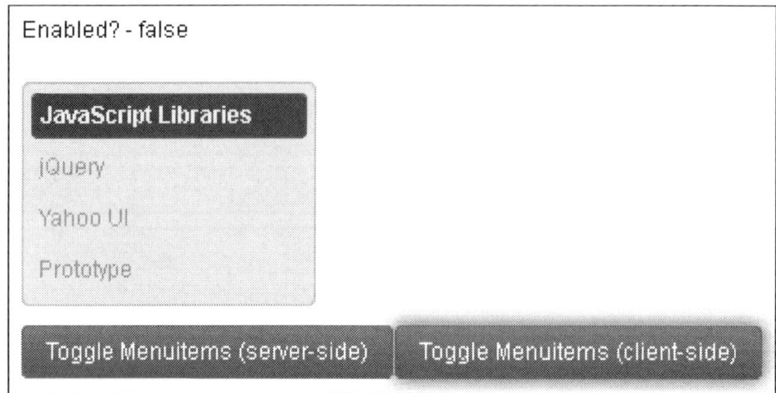

How it works...

Both client-side and server-side scripts implement the same logic. To disable a menu item, its URL has to be copied from the anchor's `href` attribute to a `data-oldhref` attribute. The `href` attribute should be removed then and the link should be styled with a proper jQuery ThemeRoller class such as `ui-state-disabled`. This style class makes elements appear disabled. To enable a menu item, its URL has to be restored from the `data-oldhref` attribute and assigned to `href`. The style class `ui-state-disabled` should be removed. Also consider the `if` statement with the EL expression `#{facesContext.partialViewContext.ajaxRequest}`. This statement prevents an initial script execution on page load (`GET` request).

PrimeFaces Cookbook Showcase application

This recipe is also available in the demo web application on GitHub (`https://github.com/ova2/primefaces-cookbook`). Clone the project if you have not done it yet, explore the project structure, and execute the built-in Jetty Maven plugin to see this recipe in action. Follow the instructions in the `README` file if you do not know how to run Jetty.

When the server is running, the showcase for the recipe is available under `http://localhost:8080/primefaces-cookbook/views/chapter10/javaScriptExec.jsf`.

Adding AJAX callback parameters – validation within a dialog

This recipe will continue with the discussion on `RequestContext` that we began in the previous recipes. There may be cases where we need values from backing beans in AJAX callbacks. Suppose we have a form in a dialog; when the user submits the form, the dialog should stay open to display any validation errors and it should be closed otherwise.

In this recipe, we will learn how the described task can be done with AJAX callback parameters. We will develop an `oncomplete` callback for a command button within `p:dialog`.

How to do it...

The developed page contains a `Dialog` component with an input field. The dialog will be visible when the page is loaded. There is only one valid input value—`PrimeFaces Cookbook`. When the user inputs this value and clicks on the **Save** button, the dialog should be closed. In any other case, it should stay open. The button `p:commandButton` defines an `oncomplete` callback `handleComplete(xhr, status, args)`. It gets processed when the AJAX request completes. There, we check `args.validName` and close the dialog if this value is `true`.

```
<p:growl id="growl" autoUpdate="true"/>

<p:dialog header="What is the name of this book?" visible="true"
    widgetVar="dlgWidget">
  <h:inputText id="name" value="#{ajaxCallbackParamController.name}"/>

  <p:commandButton id="save" value="Save" style="margin:10px;"
    process="@this name" update="name"
    actionListener="#{ajaxCallbackParamController.save}"
    oncomplete="handleComplete(xhr, status, args)"/>
</p:dialog>

<h:outputScript id="handleCompleteScript" target="body">
/* <![CDATA[ */
  function handleComplete(xhr, status, args) {
    if(args && args.validName) {
      dlgWidget.hide();
    }
  }
/* ]]> */
</h:outputScript>
```

The corresponding managed bean compares the input value with the valid one and creates either an info or an error message for the `Growl` component. Furthermore, it adds a callback parameter `validName` with the value `true` for a valid input, and `false` otherwise.

```
@ManagedBean
@ViewScoped
public class AjaxCallbackParamController implements Serializable {
  private String name;

  public void save(ActionEvent ae) {
    RequestContext requestContext =
    RequestContext.getCurrentInstance();

    String message;
    FacesMessage.Severity severity;

    if ("PrimeFaces Cookbook".equals(name)) {
      message = "All right!";
      severity = FacesMessage.SEVERITY_INFO;

      requestContext.addCallbackParam("validName", true);
    } else {
      message = "Name is wrong, try again";
      severity = FacesMessage.SEVERITY_ERROR;

      requestContext.addCallbackParam("validName", false);
    }

    FacesMessage msg = new FacesMessage(severity, message, null);
    FacesContext.getCurrentInstance().addMessage(null, msg);
  }

  public String getName() {
    return name;
  }

  public void setName(String name) {
    this.name = name;
  }
}
```

How it works...

The `oncomplete` callback function takes three arguments: `XMLHttpRequest`, status string, and optional parameters provided by the `RequestContext` API. Parameters can be added by the method `addCallbackParam(key, value)`. They are serialized to **JavaScript Object Notation** (**JSON**) and can be accessed in AJAX callbacks by the `args` argument. In the example, we accessed the value of the callback parameter `validName` by `args.validName`. We can add as many callback parameters as we want. Not only primitive values, but also **POJOs** (**Plain Old Java Objects**) are supported. POJOs are serialized to JSON as well.

By default, the `validationFailed` callback parameter is added implicitly if JSF validation fails, so that it is possible to check the failed validation with an `if` statement, `args.validationFailed == true`.

PrimeFaces Cookbook Showcase application

This recipe is available in the demo web application on GitHub (`https://github.com/ova2/primefaces-cookbook`). Clone the project if you have not done it yet, explore the project structure, and execute the built-in Jetty Maven plugin to see this recipe in action. Follow the instructions in the `README` file if you do not know how to run Jetty.

When the server is running, the showcase for the recipe is available under `http://localhost:8080/primefaces-cookbook/views/chapter10/ajaxCallbacks.jsf`.

Navigating to another page in AJAX calls

PrimeFaces' users often ask "Why don't navigations work with PrimeFaces `CommandButton` and `CommandLink`?", "How can we navigate to any page on a node click in a `Tree`?", or "How can we change the view when a row in a `DataTable` is double-clicked?". These are questions that are mainly related to JSF rather than PrimeFaces, but we will give answers to these questions in this book due to their importance.

In this recipe, we will show a programmatic navigation with JSF `NavigationHandler` as well as a declarative way to do a cross-page navigation in AJAX calls.

How to do it...

All three questions mentioned above have the same nature. JSF and PrimeFaces do not support a forward-based navigation within an AJAX request. We need to do a redirect instead or set the `ajax` attribute in the command components to `false`.

The showcase application of this book has a `Tree` component with nodes representing the recipes. A click on a node redirects the user to a well-defined page (view). This task was achieved programmatically with JSF `NavigationHandler` as follows:

```
public void onNodeSelect(NodeSelectEvent event) {
    ...

  String view = ((BookTreeNode)
  event.getTreeNode().getData()).getView();
  FacesContext fc = FacesContext.getCurrentInstance();
  fc.getApplication().getNavigationHandler()
    .handleNavigation(fc, "null", "/views/" + view +
    "?faces-redirect=true");
}
```

The `onNodeSelect()` method is an AJAX listener that is invoked by `p:ajax` placed directly under `p:tree`.

```
<p:ajax event="select" listener="#{bookController.onNodeSelect}"/>
```

The second way to do a navigation in AJAX calls consists of appending `?faces-redirect=true` to an action outcome. This can be done in Java code or directly in Facelets (the so-called declarative approach).

```
<p:commandButton action="home.xhtml?faces-redirect=true"
value="Go Home"/>
```

How it works...

Command components such as `CommandButton` or `CommandLink` are ajaxified by default. That means, they send AJAX requests instead of full-page requests. Also, events on components such as a click on a tree node or a table row can only send AJAX requests. To do a navigation in AJAX calls, we need to force a redirect.

A **redirect** is a response, with a status code beginning with `3`, that causes a browser to display a different page. The different codes describe the reason for the redirect. The URL of the redirect target is given in the `Location` header of the HTTP response.

The redirect response caused by the HTTP `POST` request is also known in web development as a **Post/Redirect/Get** (**PRG**) design pattern. In JSF 2, this pattern is accomplished by setting `faces-redirect` to `true` in the logical outcome. Such logical outcomes can be either passed to `handleNavigation()` or specified as an action outcome.

Polling – sending periodical AJAX requests

Polling is a way to poll a server periodically in order to trigger some server-side changes or update parts of a web page. The polling technology in PrimeFaces is represented by the Poll component. It is an AJAX component that has an ability to send periodical AJAX requests.

In this recipe, we will update a feed reader periodically to show current sports news. A Growl component will be updated with the same interval too, in order to show the time of the last feed update.

How to do it...

The p:poll component in the following code snippet invokes the listener method showMessage() every 10 seconds and updates a feed reader and growl. The listener method generates the current time. Furthermore, we will define a widget variable in order to stop or start polling, using the client-side API. This occurs via command buttons.

```
<p:growl id="growl"/>

<p:poll id="poll" listener="#{pollingController.showMessage}"
  update="sportFeed growl" interval="10" widgetVar="pollWidget"/>

<p:commandButton type="button" value="Stop Polling"
  style="margin:15px 5px 15px 0;" onclick="pollWidget.stop();"/>
<p:commandButton type="button" value="Start Polling"
  style="margin:15px 0 15px 0;" onclick="pollWidget.start();"/>

<h:panelGroup id="sportFeed" layout="block">
  <p:feedReader value="http://rss.news.yahoo.com/rss/sports"
    var="feed" size="10">
    <h:outputText value="#{feed.title}"
    style="font-weight: bold"/>
    <br/>
    <h:outputText value=
    "#{feed.description.value}" escape="false"/>
    <p:separator/>
  </p:feedReader>
</h:panelGroup>
```

The corresponding screenshot illustrates an update with `p:poll`.

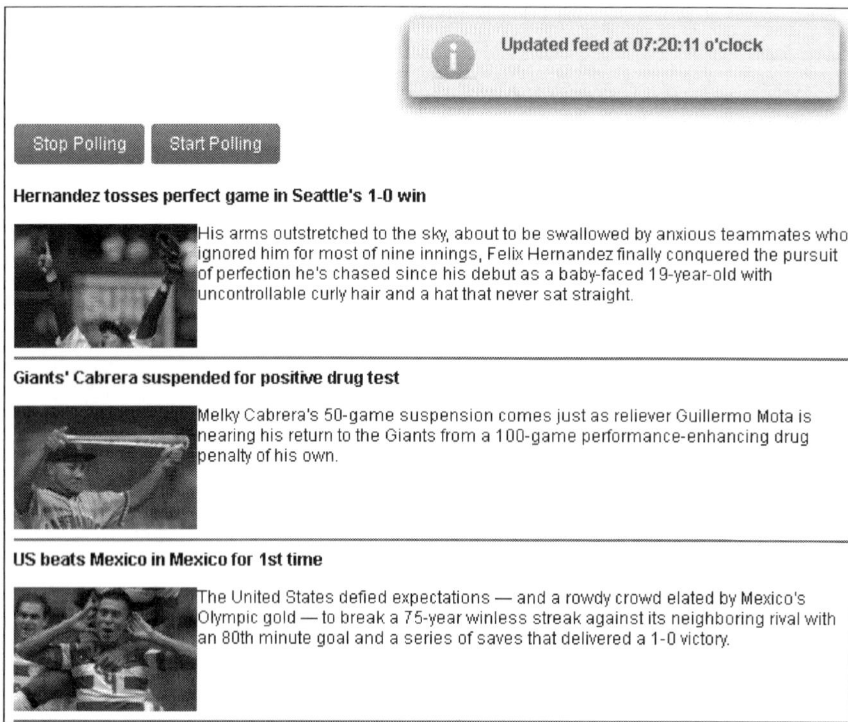

How it works...

The `interval` attribute of `p:poll` defines the time interval, in seconds, at which to execute periodic AJAX requests. The default value is 2 seconds. In the example, we set it to `10`. Similar to any other ajaxified components, we can specify components to be updated or processed partially with the `update` or `process` attribute. The `update` attribute in the example contains IDs of `p:feedReader` and `p:growl`.

Polling can be stopped and be started by using the widget methods `stop()` and `start()` respectively. We defined two push buttons to execute `pollWidget.stop()` and `pollWidget.start()` on a click event. There is also an attribute `stop`. It accepts boolean values that can be bound to it at any arbitrary time. When the value is `true`, polling will be stopped.

There's more...

`Poll` also supports the `autoStart` mode. By default, polling starts automatically on page load. To prevent this behavior, set the `autoStart` attribute to `false`.

PrimeFaces Cookbook Showcase application

This recipe is available in the demo web application on GitHub (`https://github.com/ova2/primefaces-cookbook`). Clone the project if you have not done it yet, explore the project structure, and execute the built-in Jetty Maven plugin to see this recipe in action. Follow the instructions in the `README` file if you do not know how to run Jetty.

When the server is running, the showcase for the recipe is available under `http://localhost:8080/primefaces-cookbook/views/chapter10/polling.jsf`.

Blocking page pieces during long-running AJAX calls

The `BlockUI` component allows us to block any piece(s) of a page during AJAX calls. Blocking is initiated by one or more trigger components. `BlockUI` adds a layer and any custom content over the target elements to be blocked and gives the appearance and behavior of blocking user interaction. It's very handy if you have, for example, a large data table, and sorting, filtering, pagination takes much time. You can block almost everything, even the entire page.

In this recipe, we will implement blockable `p:panel` and `p:dataTable` in order to learn all the features of `p:blockUI`.

How to do it...

The `panel` component in the following code snippet gets blocked when the command button is clicked and unblocked when the AJAX response is received. We will see a semi-transparent layer over the panel, which blocks user interactions within it. The action listener on the command button simulates a long-running task.

```
<p:panel id="panel" header="Blockable Panel" style="height:90px;">

  <h:outputText value="Click on Save to block me."/>

  <p:commandButton id="saveBtn" value="Save" style="margin:10px;"
  actionListener="#{blockUIController.doSomething}"/>
</p:panel>

<p:blockUI block="panel" trigger="saveBtn"/>
```

The following example demonstrates a `DataTable` component that gets blocked on pagination and sorting. The `BlockUI` component displays custom content with an animated image and the text `Please wait, data is being processed....`

```
<p:dataTable id="dataTable" var="message"
  value="#{blockUIController.messages}"
  paginator="true" ...>
  <p:ajax event="page" listener="#{blockUIController.doSomething}"/>
  <p:ajax event="sort" listener="#{blockUIController.doSomething}"/>
  <p:column sortBy="#{message.subject}">
    <f:facet name="header"> <h:outputText value="Subject"/>
    </f:facet>
    <h:outputText value="#{message.subject}"/>
  </p:column>
  <p:column sortBy="#{message.text}">
    <f:facet name="header">
      <h:outputText value="Text"/>
    </f:facet>
    <h:outputText value="#{message.text}"/>
  </p:column>
</p:dataTable>

<p:blockUI block="dataTable" trigger="dataTable">
  <h:panelGrid id="blockContent" columns="2">
    <h:graphicImage library="images" name="ajax-loader.gif"
    style="margin-right:12px; vertical-align:middle;"/>
    <h:outputText value="Please wait, data is being processed..."
    style="white-space:nowrap;"/>
  </h:panelGrid>
</p:blockUI>
```

The following screenshot shows the blocked `DataTable` component, when the user has clicked on the page 2 button:

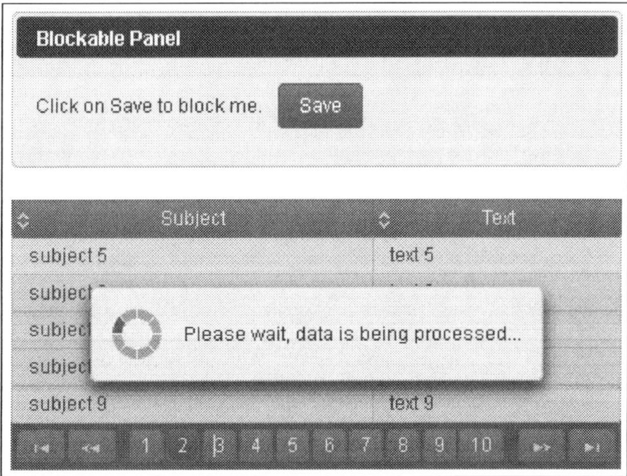

How it works...

`BlockUI` requires the `trigger` and `block` attributes to be defined. The `trigger` attribute defines the ID of the component (in terms of `findComponent`) that sends an AJAX request and triggers blocking. It is also possible to define multiple triggers as a comma-separated list. The `block` attribute defines the ID of the component (in terms of `findComponent`) to be blocked.

[`BlockUI` does not support absolute or fixed-positioned components, for example, `Dialog`.]

In the first code snippet, we pointed the `trigger` attribute to the button's ID, `saveBtn`, and in the second one to the table's ID, `dataTable`. The `block` attribute points to the panel's ID, `panel`, and to the table's ID, `dataTable`, respectively. In the case of `DataTable` blocking, we placed custom content inside the `p:blockUI` tag. In this way we can display any content we want.

There's more...

There are two widget methods to be used on the client side. The `show()` method blocks the specified component and the `hide()` method unblocks it. They can be used in the `onstart` and `oncomplete` callbacks respectively.

PrimeFaces Cookbook Showcase application

This recipe is available in the demo web application on GitHub (`https://github.com/ova2/primefaces-cookbook`). Clone the project if you have not done it yet, explore the project structure, and execute the built-in Jetty Maven plugin to see this recipe in action. Follow the instructions in the `README` file if you do not know how to run Jetty.

When the server is running, the showcase for the recipe is available under `http://localhost:8080/primefaces-cookbook/views/chapter10/blockUI.jsf`.

Remembering current menu selection

PrimeFaces' `Menu` component is often used for navigation. The current menu selection helps to identify the current navigation target, which is most likely to be a web page. `Menu` in PrimeFaces does not remember the selected menu item in terms of visual selection. One of the requirements for the `Menu` component, therefore, is to display the currently clicked menu item as selected.

In this recipe, we will implement a solution for remembering the current menu selection. This will improve the menu's usability during navigation between pages.

How to do it...

Assume we have a menu with three menu items. Each menu item has URL-based navigation to a specific page. To mark a menu item as selected, we need a client-side callback bound to `onclick` and a `styleClass` with server-side binding.

```
<p:menu id="viewList">
  <p:menuitem value="View 1"
  styleClass="#{naviController.getMenuitemStyleClass('page1')}"
    onclick="selectMenuitemLink(this)" ajax="false"
    url="/views/chapter10/page1.jsf"/>
  <p:menuitem value="View 2"
  styleClass="#{naviController.getMenuitemStyleClass('page2')}"
    onclick="selectMenuitemLink(this)" ajax="false"
    url="/views/chapter10/page2.jsf"/>
  <p:menuitem value="View 3"
  styleClass="#{naviController.getMenuitemStyleClass('page3')}"
    onclick="selectMenuitemLink(this)" ajax="false"
    url="/views/chapter10/page3.jsf"/>
</p:menu>
```

The `onclick` callback is a JavaScript function `selectMenuitemLink`.

```
function selectMenuitemLink(link) {
```

```
        $("#viewList").find(".ui-state-active").
        removeClass("ui-state-active");
        $(link).addClass("ui-state-active");
    }
```

Server-side binding in `styleClass` is applied to the managed bean's method `getMenuitemStyleClass`.

```
@ManagedBean
@SessionScoped
public class NaviController implements Serializable {

  public String getMenuitemStyleClass(String page) {
    String viewId = getViewId();
    if (viewId != null && viewId.equals(page)) {
      return "ui-state-active";
    }

    return "";
  }

  private String getViewId() {
    FacesContext fc = FacesContext.getCurrentInstance();
    String viewId = fc.getViewRoot().getViewId();
    String selectedComponent;
    if (viewId != null) {
      selectedComponent =
      viewId.substring(viewId.lastIndexOf("/") + 1,
      viewId.lastIndexOf("."));
    } else {
      selectedComponent = null;
    }

    return selectedComponent;
  }
}
```

Every click on any menu item shows a corresponding page with the visible menu selection.

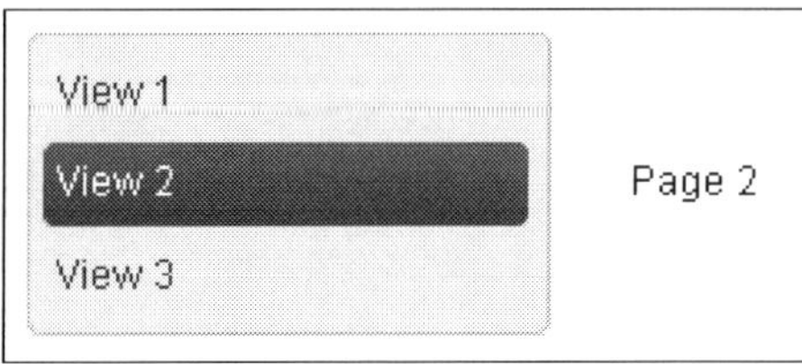

How it works...

The JavaScript function `selectMenuitemLink` removes the jQuery ThemeRoller class `ui-state-active` from all menu items and adds this class to the clicked item only. In this way we can mark the clicked item as selected. This is necessary because of long-running requests. The user should immediately get a visual feedback.

The JavaScript solution is not enough because such a selection is not persistent—it does not survive navigation between pages. As soon as a new page is shown, the current item selection is cleared away. We need server-side logic to restore the proper style class. This is why we bound EL expressions such as `#{naviController.getMenuitemStyleClass('page1')}` to the `styleClass` attributes of `p:menuitem`. The `getMenuitemStyleClass` method expects a `viewId` of the page to be navigated to. We can now compare the passed `viewId` with the `viewId` extracted from the view root. If they are identical, the method returns `ui-state-active` as a `String`, otherwise an empty `String`.

See also

- The `ui-state-active` style class is described in the *Understanding the structural and skinning CSS* recipe in *Chapter 2, Theming Concept*.

PrimeFaces Cookbook Showcase application

This recipe is available in the demo web application on GitHub (`https://github.com/ova2/primefaces-cookbook`). Clone the project if you have not done it yet, explore the project structure, and execute the built-in Jetty Maven plugin to see this recipe in action. Follow the instructions in the `README` file if you do not know how to run Jetty.

When the server is running, the showcase for the recipe is available under `http://localhost:8080/primefaces-cookbook/views/chapter10/rememberMenu.jsf`.

Controlling form submission by DefaultCommand

The *Enter* key makes form submission so easy that users always tend to use it. The most intuitive way is that the user can enter some text or make some changes to the existing text and then hit the *Enter* key to submit the form. But what for command component will submit the form if we have more than one of them? Browsers, especially IE, behave differently here. The `DefaultCommand` component solves this problem by normalizing the command (for example, `button` or `link`) that submits the form when the *Enter* key is hit.

In this recipe, we will discuss `p:defaultCommand` in detail. We will implement a `p:selectOneMenu` for dynamic selection of the command button used for form submission when the *Enter* key is hit.

How to do it...

We intend to save the chosen command button used for form submission in a backing bean. To achieve this, we need a `p:selectOneMenu` with listed command buttons (their IDs) and an attached `p:ajax`. Such an ajaxified `p:selectOneMenu` component should update `p:defaultCommand` on a change event automatically, so that the chosen command button will be used in `p:defaultCommand`. A `p:inputText` should take inputs and a corresponding `h:outputText` should display the same inputs when the *Enter* key is hit. Furthermore, we want to display the pressed button as a growl notification.

```
<p:growl id="growl" autoUpdate="true"/>

<h:panelGrid columns="2" cellpadding="5">
  <h:outputLabel for="btnSelect" value="Select default button:"/>
  <p:selectOneMenu id="btnSelect"
  value="#{defaultCommandController.btn}">
    <p:ajax update="@form"/>
    <f:selectItem itemValue="btn1" itemLabel="Button 1"/>
    <f:selectItem itemValue="btn2" itemLabel="Button 2"/>
    <f:selectItem itemValue="btn3" itemLabel="Button 3"/>
  </p:selectOneMenu>
</h:panelGrid>

<h:panelGrid columns="3" cellpadding="5"
  style="margin:15px 0 15px 0;">
  <h:outputLabel for="text" value="Text:"/>
  <p:inputText id="text"
  value="#{defaultCommandController.text}"/>
  <h:outputText id="display"
  value="#{defaultCommandController.text}"/>
</h:panelGrid>

<p:commandButton id="btn1" value="Button1"
  actionListener=
  "#{defaultCommandController.showMessage('Button1')}"
  update="display"/>
```

```
<p:commandButton id="btn2" value="Button2"
  actionListener=
  "#{defaultCommandController.showMessage('Button2')}"
  update="display"/>
<h:commandButton id="btn3" value="Button3"
  actionListener=
  "#{defaultCommandController.showMessage('Button3')}"
  update="display"/>

<p:defaultCommand id="defCommand"
target="#{defaultCommandController.btn}"/>
```

The following screenshot shows what will happen when the second button is chosen as default, the user enters `sometext`, and hits the *Enter* key:

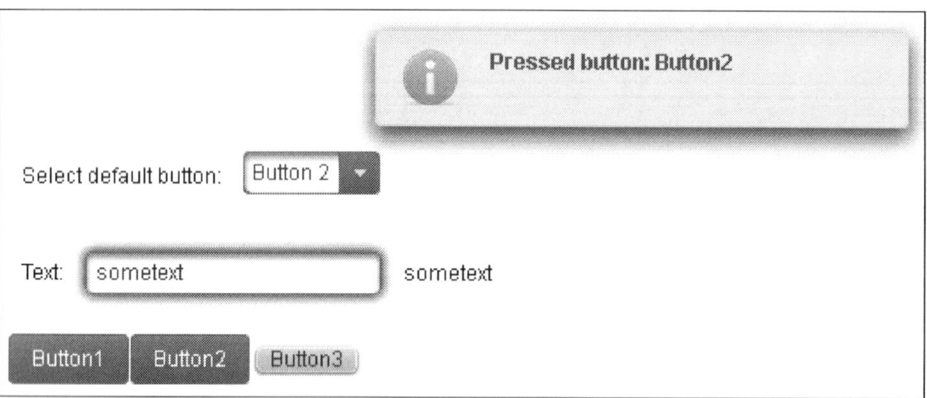

How it works...

`DefaultCommand` must be in a form in order to work and the `target` attribute is required to refer to an identifier of a clickable command component. The `target` in the developed example references such an identifier via the EL expression `#{defaultCommandController.btn}`. Possible identifiers are `btn1`, `btn2`, and `btn3`. The button with the identifier in the `target` attribute is used as default. That means it gets clicked and submits the form when the user enters something into the input field and presses the *Enter* key. In addition, the action listener `showMessage` generates a message text for `p:growl`.

To perform the form submission on a key press, an input field must be focused due to the browser's nature.

There's more...

Besides `target` there is also the `scope` attribute, which is needed for multiple default commands on the same page. The `scope` attribute restricts the area for the *Enter* key handling. It refers to the ancestor component of input field(s) considered by this `p:defaultCommand`.

PrimeFaces Cookbook Showcase application

This recipe is available in the demo web application on GitHub (`https://github.com/ova2/primefaces-cookbook`). Clone the project if you have not done it yet, explore the project structure, and execute the built-in Jetty Maven plugin to see this recipe in action. Follow the instructions in the `README` file if you do not know how to run Jetty.

When the server is running, the showcase for the recipe is available under `http://localhost:8080/primefaces-cookbook/views/chapter10/defaultCommand.jsf`.

Clever focus management in forms

`Focus` is a component that makes it easy to manage the focus setting on a JSF page. By default, the `Focus` component finds the first enabled (editable) and visible input component on the page and applies focus. Typically, input components are associated with HTML elements such as `input`, `textarea`, and `select`.

In this recipe, we will learn about the default and advanced behaviors of the `Focus` component. We will develop two `h:panelGrid` with several input components in order to demonstrate behavior of `p:focus` in detail.

How to do it...

The default behavior of the `Focus` component can be restricted by the `context` attribute. Although we have two `h:panelGrid` components, only the second will be considered for `p:focus`.

```
<p:messages/>

<p:focus context="secondGrid"/>

<h:panelGrid columns="2" style="margin-bottom:10px;">
  <h:outputLabel value="Dummy"/>
  <p:inputText/>
</h:panelGrid>
```

```
<h:panelGrid id="secondGrid" columns="2">
  <h:outputLabel for="firstname" value="Firstname *"/>
  <p:inputText id="firstname" required="true" label="Firstname"/>

  <h:outputLabel for="surname" value="Surname *"/>
  <p:inputText id="surname" required="true" label="Surname"/>
</h:panelGrid>

<br/>

<p:commandButton value="Submit" update="@form"/>
```

The following screenshot shows a focus set for the **Surname** field after a form is submitted. We entered something into the **Firstname** field, but left the **Surname** field empty.

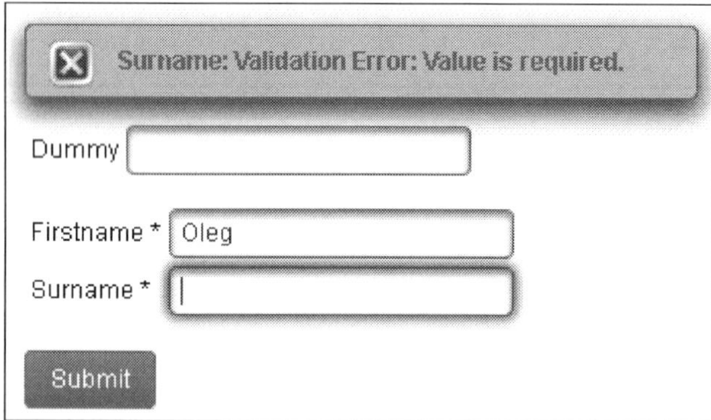

How it works...

The `context` attribute points to the identifier (in terms of `findComponent`) of the `root` component from which the `Focus` component starts to search for input components. The first `h:panelGrid`, thus, gets ignored. If there are no validation errors, the focus is set implicitly on the first editable and visible input field within the second `h:panelGrid`. This is the **Firstname** field. In case of any validation errors, the first invalid input component will receive the focus. This is the **Surname** field in the preceding screenshot.

To get this feature working on AJAX requests, you need to update the `p:focus` component as well.

There's more...

If we need to set focus explicitly on an input component, we can use a `for` attribute that points to the identifier of this input component.

Another feature is the `minSeverity` attribute. It specifies the message's minimum severity level to be used when finding the first invalid component. The default value is `error`. If you set it, for example, to `info`, the focus will not be normally set on the first invalid component due to higher severity level of created validation message(s) matching this threshold. In this case, the default behavior is used—the focus setting on the first enabled and visible input component.

PrimeFaces Cookbook Showcase application

This recipe is available in the demo web application on GitHub (`https://github.com/ova2/primefaces-cookbook`). Clone the project if you have not done it yet, explore the project structure, and execute the built-in Jetty Maven plugin to see this recipe in action. Follow the instructions in the `README` file if you do not know how to run Jetty.

When the server is running, the showcase for the recipe is available under `http://localhost:8080/primefaces-cookbook/views/chapter10/focusManagement.jsf`.

Layout pitfalls with menus and dialogs

When working with the `Layout` component, we should be aware of pitfalls with menus and dialogs inside layout units. Beginners often face *overlap* issues and try to find several workarounds. In fact, there are easy solutions available.

In this recipe, we will show how to overcome these issues. We will integrate `p:menubar` and `p:dialog` into layout units.

How to do it...

Assume we have a full page layout with two layout units, `center` and `north`. The `north` unit contains a `Menubar` component with quite normal options.

```
<p:layout fullPage="true">
    <p:layoutUnit position="center">
        Center
    </p:layoutUnit>
    <p:layoutUnit position="north" size="80" resizable="false">
        <h:form>
            <p:menubar>
```

```
                <p:submenu label="JavaScript Libraries">
                    <p:menuitem value="jQuery" url="#"/>
                    <p:menuitem value="Yahoo UI" url="#"/>
                    <p:menuitem value="Prototype" url="#"/>
                </p:submenu>
                <p:menuitem value="Go Back" url="#"/>
            </p:menubar>
        </h:form>
    </p:layoutUnit>
</p:layout>
```

If we try to open the menu, it gets partially hidden by the layout unit as shown in the following screenshot. We can see scrollbars on the right side as well.

To overcome this wrong appearance, we will set `overflow` to `visible` for the content container (`div` element) of the `north` layout unit. This CSS setting can be placed within `h:head`.

```
<h:head>
    <f:facet name="first">
        <meta http-equiv="Content-Type" content="text/html;
        charset=UTF-8"/>
        <meta http-equiv="pragma" content="no-cache"/>
        <meta http-equiv="cache-control" content="no-cache"/>
        <meta http-equiv="expires" content="0"/>
    </f:facet>
    <f:facet name="last">
        <style type="text/css">
            .ui-layout-pane-north .ui-layout-unit-content {
                overflow: visible;
            }
        </style>
    </f:facet>
</h:head>
```

The menu now appears correctly. It overlaps the layout unit when opening.

The second potential problem is modal dialog inside a layout unit. Assume we place such a dialog with default options inside the `center` layout unit. The semi-transparent layer of the modal dialog overlaps the dialog itself and prevents any interactions with it. This is shown in the following screenshot:

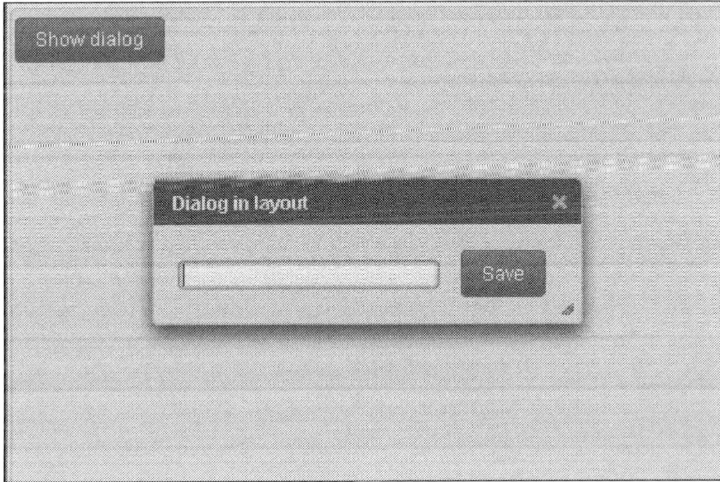

To overcome this issue, we need to set the `appendToBody` attribute to `true`.

```
<p:layoutUnit position="center">

    <p:dialog header="Dialog in layout" modal="true"
        widgetVar="dlgWidget" appendToBody="true">
        <h:form>
            <h:inputText/>
            <p:commandButton value="Save" action="..."/>
        </h:form>
    </p:dialog>
```

```
        <p:commandButton value="Show dialog" type="button"
        onclick="dlgWidget.show()"/>
    </p:layoutUnit>
```

The semi-transparent layer is placed behind the dialog now.

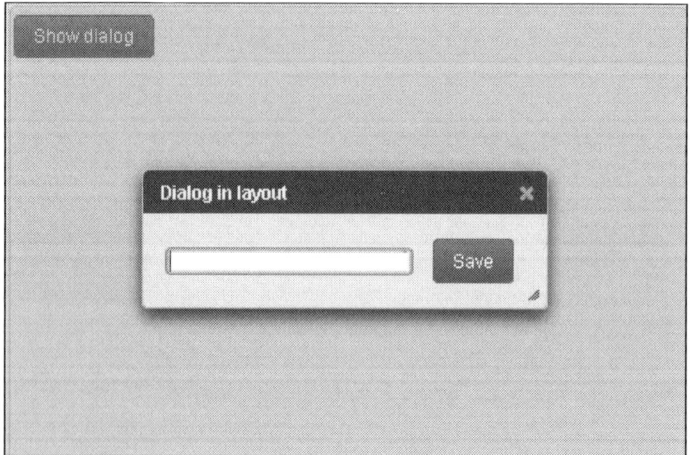

How it works...

Drop-down and pop-up menus often need to overlap adjacent layout units (panes). An ideal solution would be to append the menu elements to the body tag. In this case, no additional effort is needed to use PrimeFaces menus with `Layout`. When this is not possible for some reason, there is an option for handling the menus. If the menu appears in a non-scrolling layout unit, we should give the unit's content container the CSS property `overflow: visible` and ensure it is the last unit in the HTML markup. By making it last, it has a naturally higher stack-order.

Setting `appendToBody` to `true` appends the dialog as a child of the document body. The same is valid for the PrimeFaces overlay panel in a modal dialog. Enable `appendToBody` when `OverlayPanel` is in another panel component such as `Layout` and/or `Dialog`.

It is also important to say that components with `appendToBody` set to `true` need a `h:form` tag inside. But avoid nested `h:form` tags. Nested forms bring an unexpected behavior and JavaScript errors, even if you set `appendToBody` to `true`.

PrimeFaces Cookbook Showcase application

This recipe is available in the demo web application on GitHub (`https://github.com/ova2/primefaces-cookbook`). Clone the project if you have not done it yet, explore the project structure, and execute the built-in Jetty Maven plugin to see this recipe in action.

Follow the instructions in the `README` file if you do not know how to run Jetty.

When the server is running, the showcase for the recipe is available under `http://localhost:8080/primefaces-cookbook/views/chapter10/layoutPitfalls.jsf`.

See also

- The `Layout` component is discussed extensively in the *Creating complex layouts* recipe in *Chapter 4, Grouping Content with Panels*.

Targetable messages with severity levels

We sometimes need to target a `FacesMessage` instance to a specific component. For example, suppose we have `p:growl` and `p:messages/p:message` tags on the same page, and need to display some messages as `p:growl` and some as `p:messages/p:message`. PrimeFaces has a grouping feature for messages to associate a notification component to specific command components, so that messages created as a result of an action will be displayed in the associated message(s) or the growl tags.

In this recipe, we will develop samples for targetable messages. Furthermore, we will discuss the `severity` attribute. By means of `severity`, we can display messages depending on their severities.

How to do it...

Let us use one `p:messages` and two `p:growl` tags, as shown in the following code snippet:

```
<p:messages for="save" showDetail="true"/>
<p:growl for="change" showDetail="true"/>
<p:growl globalOnly="true" showDetail="true"/>

<p:commandButton value="Save" update="@form"
  action="#{targetableMessagesController.addSaveMessage}"/>
<p:commandButton value="Change" update="@form"
  action="#{targetableMessagesController.addChangeMessage}"/>
<p:commandButton value="Delete" update="@form"
  action="#{targetableMessagesController.addDeleteMessage}"/>
```

Three command buttons create `FacesMessage` instances. The first button creates two messages that are displayed only by the `p:messages` tag. The second command button creates one message that is displayed only by the first `p:growl` tag with the `for` attribute set to `change`. The message created by the third command button is displayed only by the second `p:growl` tag with `globalOnly` set to `true`. The action methods look as follows:

```
public String addSaveMessage() {
  addMessage("save", FacesMessage.SEVERITY_INFO,
  "Sample info message", "First data was successfully saved");
  addMessage("save", FacesMessage.SEVERITY_INFO,
  "Sample info message", "Second data was successfully saved");

  return null;
}

public String addChangeMessage() {
  addMessage("change", FacesMessage.SEVERITY_INFO,
  "Sample info message", "Data was successfully changed");

  return null;
}

public String addDeleteMessage() {
  addMessage(null, FacesMessage.SEVERITY_INFO,
  "Sample info message", "Data was successfully deleted");

  return null;
}

private void addMessage(String key, FacesMessage.Severity severity,
String message, String detail) {
  FacesMessage msg = new FacesMessage(severity, message, detail);
  FacesContext.getCurrentInstance().addMessage(key, msg);
}
```

Let us now use the `p:messages` and `p:growl` tags without the `for` attribute but with a `severity` attribute.

```
<p:messages severity="error" showDetail="true"/>
<p:growl severity="info, warn" showDetail="true"/>
<p:growl showDetail="true"/>

<p:commandButton value="Generate error message" update="@form"
        action="#{targetableMessagesController.addErrorMessage}"/>
```

The command button should create an error message with the `error` severity.

```
public String addErrorMessage() {
    addMessage(null, FacesMessage.SEVERITY_ERROR,
    "Sample error message", "Operation failed");

    return null;
}
```

The created message is only displayed by the `p:messages` tag with `severity` set to `error` and the second `p:growl` tag without a `severity` attribute.

How it works...

The key of an added `FacesMessage` instance should match the `for` attribute of the `p:growl`, `p:messages`, or `p:message` components to be displayed. If the `for` attribute is missing, all added `FacesMessage` instances will be accepted. If a notification component has set the `globalOnly` flag (`globalOnly="true"`), only the `FacesMessage` instances without a defined key (key is `null`) will be displayed.

PrimeFaces utilizes the component's `clientId` parameter as key.

The `severity` attribute of a notification component defines exactly which severities can be displayed by this component. It accepts a space-separated list. Possible values are `info`, `warn`, `error`, and `fatal`. They match Java constants `FacesMessage.SEVERITY_INFO`, `FacesMessage.SEVERITY_WARN`, `FacesMessage.SEVERITY_ERROR`, and `FacesMessage.SEVERITY_FATAL` respectively. If the `severity` attribute is missing, messages with any severity will be displayed.

PrimeFaces Cookbook Showcase application

This recipe is available in the demo web application on GitHub (`https://github.com/ova2/primefaces-cookbook`). Clone the project if you have not done it yet, explore the project structure, and execute the built-in Jetty Maven plugin to see this recipe in action. Follow the instructions in the `README` file if you do not know how to run Jetty.

When the server is running, the showcase for the recipe is available under `http://localhost:8080/primefaces-cookbook/views/chapter10/targetableMessages.jsf`.

Leveraging Schedule's lazy loading feature

The `Schedule` component provides a calendar to manage events, such as Outlook Calendar or iCal. By default, a whole set of events is eagerly provided via `ScheduleModel`. That means all events are loaded at once on page load. Lazy loading feature helps to improve performance if we have a huge dataset of events or events take much time to load. In the lazy loading mode, only events that belong to the displayed time frame are fetched.

In this recipe, we will implement a small example for the `Schedule` component's lazy loading feature.

How to do it...

By default, the view `month` is displayed, so the user sees a whole month and can switch between months. Assume we have to load events for 12 months and every month needs, on average, 1.5 seconds for event loading. The default eager mode would take 18 seconds (12 x 1.5) to load all events. This is too long, so using the lazy loading feature is recommended to increase performance. The piece of the XHTML page with `p:schedule` looks easy.

```
<p:schedule id="lazySchedule"
value="#{scheduleController.lazyScheduleModel}"/>
```

We reference a `LazyScheduleModel` in the managed bean `ScheduleController`. This model implements lazy loading for only one month. In the example, the loading time is simulated with `Thread.sleep(1500)`.

```
@ManagedBean
@ViewScoped
public class ScheduleController implements Serializable {

  private ScheduleModel lazyEventModel;

  @PostConstruct
  public void initialize() {
    lazyEventModel = new LazyScheduleModel() {

      @Override
      public void loadEvents(Date start, Date end) {
        try {
          // simulate a long running task
          Thread.sleep(1500);
        } catch (Exception e) {
          // ignore
        }
```

```
        clear();

        Date random = getRandomDate(start);
        addEvent(new DefaultScheduleEvent
            ("Lazy Event 1", random, random));

        random = getRandomDate(start);
        addEvent(new DefaultScheduleEvent
            ("Lazy Event 2", random, random));
      }
    };
  }

  public Date getRandomDate(Date base) {
    Calendar date = Calendar.getInstance();
    date.setTime(base);
    date.add(Calendar.DATE, ((int) (Math.random() * 30)) + 1);

    return date.getTime();
  }

  public ScheduleModel getLazyScheduleModel() {
    return lazyEventModel;
  }
}
```

The following screenshot shows the mentioned `month` view and two lazy-loaded events:

How it works...

To enable lazy loading of the `Schedule` component's events, we need to provide an instance of `org.primefaces.model.LazyScheduleModel` and implement the `loadEvents` method. This method is called with new date boundaries every time the displayed time frame is changed. Events are now loaded on demand on the initial page load or during switching between months. That means the maximal delay for the event's loading is not longer than 1.5 seconds.

PrimeFaces Cookbook Showcase application

This recipe is available in the demo web application on GitHub (`https://github.com/ova2/primefaces-cookbook`). Clone the project if you have not done it yet, explore the project structure, and execute the built-in Jetty Maven plugin to see this recipe in action. Follow the instructions in the `README` file if you do not know how to run Jetty.

When the server is running, the showcase for the recipe is available under `http://localhost:8080/primefaces-cookbook/views/chapter10/scheduleLazyLoad.jsf`.

Index

Symbols

A

D

E

F

G

N

O

P

Q

R

T

Thank you for buying
PrimeFaces Cookbook

About Packt Publishing

Packt, pronounced 'packed', published its first book "*Mastering phpMyAdmin for Effective MySQL Management*" in April 2004 and subsequently continued to specialize in publishing highly focused books on specific technologies and solutions.

Our books and publications share the experiences of your fellow IT professionals in adapting and customizing today's systems, applications, and frameworks. Our solution based books give you the knowledge and power to customize the software and technologies you're using to get the job done. Packt books are more specific and less general than the IT books you have seen in the past. Our unique business model allows us to bring you more focused information, giving you more of what you need to know, and less of what you don't.

Packt is a modern, yet unique publishing company, which focuses on producing quality, cutting-edge books for communities of developers, administrators, and newbies alike. For more information, please visit our website: `www.packtpub.com`.

About Packt Open Source

In 2010, Packt launched two new brands, Packt Open Source and Packt Enterprise, in order to continue its focus on specialization. This book is part of the Packt Open Source brand, home to books published on software built around Open Source licenses, and offering information to anybody from advanced developers to budding web designers. The Open Source brand also runs Packt's Open Source Royalty Scheme, by which Packt gives a royalty to each Open Source project about whose software a book is sold.

Writing for Packt

We welcome all inquiries from people who are interested in authoring. Book proposals should be sent to author@packtpub.com. If your book idea is still at an early stage and you would like to discuss it first before writing a formal book proposal, contact us; one of our commissioning editors will get in touch with you.

We're not just looking for published authors; if you have strong technical skills but no writing experience, our experienced editors can help you develop a writing career, or simply get some additional reward for your expertise.

32835572R00185

Made in the USA
Lexington, KY
03 June 2014